The Pacific Theater

Mr. Michel's War

From Manila to Mukden:
An American Navy Officer's
War With the Japanese,
1941–1945

By John J. A. Michel

★
PRESIDIO

Copyright © 1998 by John J. A. Michel

Published by Presidio Press
505 B San Marin Drive, Suite 300
Novato, CA 94945-1340

Library of Congress Cataloging-in-Publication Data

Michel. John J. A.
    Mr. Michel's War : from Manila to Mukden, an American Navy officer's war with the Japanese, 1941–1945 / by John J. A. Michel.
        p.   cm.
    ISBN 0-89141-643-9 (hardcover)
    1. Michel, John J. A. 2. World War, 1939–1945—Naval operations, American. 3. World War, 1939–1945—Campaigns—Pacific Area. 4. World War, 1039–1945—Personal narratives, American. 5. Sailors—United States—Biography. 6. United States. Navy—Biography.
    I. Title. II Title: Mister Michel's war.
    D767.M45   1998
    940.54'5973—DC21   97-28805
                                        CIP

My account of Lieutenant Commander Donovan's "marooning" on Christmas Island was first published in SHIPMATE (USNA Alumni Magazine) some years ago and is included here with permission.

Photos from the author's collection unless otherwise noted.
Printed in the United States of America

To the memory of shipmates who did not come home.

Forsan et haec olim meminisse juvabit.

—Vergil

(Perhaps some day it will be pleasant to remember these things.)

Preface

The Philippine Islands were not the worst place to be in the spring of 1941. As a young naval officer assigned to an old four-piper destroyer of the U.S. Asiatic Fleet, I found Manila interesting and enjoyable (between periods of boredom spent training in the southern islands).

Preparations for the inevitable war with Japan were underway. Disposition of fleet units well to the south of Luzon reflected the realization that there would be inadequate air cover in the event of enemy attack. The bombing of Pearl Harbor came as a surprise because the conventional wisdom expected the Philippines to be the initial target. But hostilities were not long in coming. On 10 December 1941, Cavite Navyyard was destroyed in a massive raid by Japanese bombers that attacked almost completely unopposed.

From there on it was a delaying action for the US Asiatic Fleet—a retreat. It has been said that a retreat is the most difficult operation to accomplish successfully. It calls for aggressive counter attacks in disadvantaged circumstances.

The old four-pipers made those attacks, surprising a better equipped and organized enemy. They hit the Japanese forces in night actions at Balikpapan and near Bali, and finally in the Java Sea.

For me "going to the well" for a third time was unlucky. My ship, USS *Pope* (DD225), was sunk on 1 March 1942, (in company with HMS *Exeter* and *Encounter*). After two and a half days in the (fortunately warm) water of the Java Sea the *Pope* survivors were picked up by a Japanese destroyer. Thus began a captivity that lasted three and a half years.

I was initially taken to camp in Makassar, Celebes. Six months later I was transferred in a group of 1000 POWs to a camp near Nagasaki,

Kyushu, to work in a shipyard. In April 1945, (with Okinawa under attack) the Japanese transferred large groups of POW officers to Korea and Manchuria. I ended my Japanese sponsored travels in Mukden, Manchuria, where I stayed until war's end.

The war seemed to have ended with the same kind of suddenness with which it began.

An OSS team from the China-Burma Theater parachuted into a field outside Mukden and was brought into the Hoten POW camp. The camp commandant was informed that the team had come to pick up General Wainwright (who was not held in this camp) and that the war was over, which was news to the commandant. A few days later the Russians arrived in Mukden and officially liberated the camp.

A short while later a repatriation team arrived in camp to begin the ex-POWs on their long way home. While awaiting transportation they were briefed on the various campaigns of the war and given information about the unbelievably powerful atomic bomb.

On the way home I was reunited on Okinawa with friends and shipmates I had left at Camp Fukuoka #2, Nagasaki. There had been no casualties in the camp. Later during a stopover at the fleet hospital on Guam I was informed by a friend who had been planning hospital construction for the scheduled invasion of Kyushu that one million American casualties had been projected.

As I progressed on my travel homeward I found the three and one-half years of captivity becoming a detached memory unrelated to what had gone before and the events after liberation. I decided to put the memory of that period in writing while it was still fresh.

This book was written about fifty years ago. It is being published now without any material changes to the original manuscript.

Acknowledgments

A special debt of gratitude is owed my wife Kathy who with infinite patience transcribed my pencil manuscript into a usable copy those many years ago.

I wish to express thanks to all those friends who offered advice and encouragement along the way. It would be remiss of me, however, not to make particular mention of Nancy Maury whose suggestions and gentle (but persistent) prodding put me on the path to Presidio Press.

1

When I first received orders assigning me to duty in the U.S. Asiatic Fleet, I was more than a little despondent. The thought of spending two and a half years so far from home was not a pleasant prospect. I had just spent more than a year in the Hawaiian Detachment aboard the USS *Salt Lake City*. Although the duty had not been without its pleasant aspects, I felt a strong desire to return to the States. I had some leave while the "Swayback Maru" was in Mare Island, California, for overhaul, and I lost no time in getting home to New York, but its pleasures made my orders to the Asiatic Fleet hard to swallow.

Time, and a few days' leave in San Francisco, where I was awaiting the sailing of the SS *President Grant*, soon put me in a more cheerful frame of mind. Before long I was looking forward to the trip out. Thirty days on a commercial steamship would leave me with nothing to do but eat, sleep, and drink. There would be no midwatch and no gun drills. I'd see Honolulu, Kobe, Shanghai, and Hong Kong en route to my final destination—Manila. The lure of the Orient was beginning to cast its spell, and the tales of the old "China hands" came readily to mind. *Yes,* I thought, *this will be all right.*

My roommate for the trip, as I learned from the steamship office in San Francisco, was to be Cass Mayo, a reserve ensign who had just finished his training course. It so happened that he was staying at the same hotel I was, and together we whiled away the days before we sailed. That was not hard to do in San Francisco.

Finally the day of departure arrived. We piled our luggage into a cab—my trunk had been left at the pier a week before and was already aboard—and we were soon on board too.

Our first view of the SS *President Grant* was not encouraging; she looked a bit the worse for wear—definitely not a luxury liner. But across the pier was the USS *Henderson,* an even less appealing naval transport we knew would also be going to the Orient, and our *President Grant* began to look more promising.

Once past the Golden Gate, the ship began rolling and pitching in the moderate seas. A cold, brisk wind drove most of the passengers below, and the few hardy souls who remained topside made the rounds of the deck with a steady, if not hurried, gait.

The first few days on board were spent getting used to the ship and the new faces. Our stateroom was diminutive, and the prospect of spending thirty days in what amounted to an oversized telephone booth filled with suitcases prompted me to ask the purser if there were any other available staterooms. Happily there were several that would not be needed until we reached Kobe. I soon found myself in a stateroom twice the size of the previous one.

Our fellow voyagers proved to be a heterogeneous group: British families returning to the colonies after leave in England, engineers going out to oil fields at Bahrein, naval officers going to join the Asiatic Fleet, a consul returning to Swatow, a German-Jewish refugee hoping to find freedom in Palestine, a cowboy—still wearing his high-heeled boots—seeking a change of occupation (carpentry) in Hawaii, and a prostitute seeking greener pastures in Honolulu (her morals on the trip out were without flaw).

In spite of the usual catty remarks and backbiting by both sexes and all nationalities, our mixed group got along fairly well. An ocean voyage seems to produce a feeling of camaraderie and friendliness.

As one who could hardly be described as an Anglophile, I was surprised to find myself enjoying the company of several Britishers aboard. I admired the confidence they displayed: England would win somehow. This—in the days when things were blackest for England—from people who had returned to England on leave during the blitz because England was home, Luftwaffe or no Luftwaffe.

My attitude toward the conflict was that it's anybody's war and they can have it. But the fact that we would be in it eventually was inescapable: Our press had been conducting a campaign against Hitler almost from the beginning of his rise to power, our industry had received a shot in the arm from orders placed by Allied purchasing commissions, and American and German ideologies were in opposition. More and more we were committing ourselves.

As a naval officer, though a raw one, I could not help but think that too much emphasis was being placed on Germany and not enough on Japan. Japan had a powerful navy as well as an army, and the country had been on the march a long time, pressing every opportunity in the Orient.

Before leaving the USS *Salt Lake City*, I had asked my commanding officer, Captain Zacharias, what he thought of the situation in Asia. I knew that he had been a Japanese language student in Japan and also that he had called on Admiral Nomura when the admiral stopped in San Francisco en route to Washington. The captain's reply was not reassuring, despite the quiet smile that accompanied it. He said that the war was coming but not immediately; there would be a few months before the hostilities began.

Of course Japan had not been left without a watchful eye (the eye was to relax its vigilance on a future tragic day). A new Hawaiian Detachment had been formed in September 1939, basing carriers, heavy cruisers, and additional destroyers and submarines at Pearl Harbor. In April 1940 the Pacific Fleet was based in Hawaii more or less permanently. Army garrisons on the islands had been steadily reinforced. Nevertheless, the feeling prevailed that Germany was the inevitable foe. Japan, though watched, was regarded with contempt—a fifth-rate power masquerading as first rate.

I didn't spend much time worrying about the coming war. Young people tend to live in the present, and I was no exception. Life aboard the *President Grant* was much to my liking. The food was good, liquor was plentiful, deck sports and flirtations were available, and leisure time seemed endless.

After five days of rough weather, often with a biting wind, I awoke one morning to find the sea calm and the air balmy. We were close enough to the Hawaiian Islands to enjoy its famous weather ("the climate California brags about"). Early Sunday morning we passed Molokai and by afternoon we were tied up in the shadow of Aloha Tower. There was no Royal Hawaiian Band to greet us—that was reserved for Matson Liners, whose tourists got the full Chamber of

Commerce treatment. I was not disappointed, however; on the pier someone was waiting for me with a lei and a smile. The only disappointment was the fact that all passengers were required to be back aboard by midnight because the ship would sail shortly thereafter.

Honolulu had changed little in the few months I had been back in the States. A new nightclub had opened, and more uniforms were in evidence; otherwise, life seemed much as before. After dinner in a Waikiki restaurant, Nancy (with the lei and the smile) and I decided to see the new nightclub. The place was decorated in the beach-comber style popular at the time: oddities that had washed up on a beach and lots of bamboo. Because of the Sunday "blue laws" there was no dancing, but an orchestra was playing Hawaiian music. Although the nightclub was crowded, few women were present. Most of the men were young officers on shore leave, and their desire to take my place as Nancy's escort was obvious. I was glad not to be staying in Hawaii to meet the stiffening competition. I don't know why I thought the situation would be better in Manila.

Midnight rolled around all too quickly and I had to return to the ship. Bidding good-bye to Nancy was not easy, for I was saying good-bye to America at the same time. I would be a stranger when I returned after my two and a half years of Asiatic duty.

Back aboard ship I began to take a dismal view of my orders to the Asiatic Fleet. I was leaving home and friends for duty in a place completely unfamiliar to me. I had had just enough to drink during the evening to think there was some truth to the saying that if you threw your lei overboard as your ship was leaving Hawaii, you would return to the islands. I threw my lei overboard. With the ship slowly steaming out of the harbor, I turned in to let sleep dispel my depression.

The first couple of days out of Honolulu were pleasant, but as the ship left the lee of the Hawaiian Islands heading for Kobe, cold weather was upon us again. For about a week we bucked a stiff wind and heavy seas. The automobiles and trucks loaded on the after well deck received a generous dousing whenever the ship yawed and waves hit the starboard quarter. I could imagine the saltwater corroding the chassis of those cars, and I made a mental note that if I ever shipped a car of my own I would avoid sending it as deck cargo.

The steady head wind and buffeting sea slowed the ship considerably, and the estimated fourteen days between Honolulu and Kobe began to look optimistic. After the ship took on water through the forward well deck hatch, the rumor was that a return to Honolulu would be necessary. However, the ship plugged along and finally hit better weather.

Meanwhile there was ample opportunity to get to know the other passengers. A British vice-consul named Bumstead and his wife were going back to North China after several months' leave in England. He was typically British in his quiet reserve, devotion to his pipe, and love for cricket.

Another passenger was a member of the Shanghai harbor police returning from a sojourn in California. He was accompanied by his bulldog, which for all its hereditary ugliness was a mild-tempered animal. The dog's master took great pride in the fact that the dog was within ounces of the optimum weight at which dogs of this breed had fought with bulls.

A British woman was on her way to join her army officer husband in Karachi, India. Her two-and-a-half-year-old son, Peter, wandered the decks at will, and the fact that he never fell overboard was due only to Providence and the watchful eyes of the other passengers. The woman's chief topics of conversation were the poorness of the service and the rudeness of the servants. Despite her physical attractiveness, she was not one of my favorite passengers.

When an aircraft assembly engineer, on his way to Singapore, was not drinking, he was seeking the affection of a heavyset mulatto from Trinidad who was on her way to South Africa to join her husband. What success he had was never publicly known, but after a jaunt ashore at Kobe, he announced brightly to all and sundry: "I went up to see the whores and they liked me swell."

Routine aboard ship was enjoyable—especially the meal schedule. After breakfast I would walk on deck to get a bit of air and sunshine. About eleven o'clock a steward would appear with bouillon and crackers. This brief repast would bring warmth and stay the pangs of hunger until luncheon. After lunch, which was usually a hearty meal, I would sit on deck and read. I must have done more sleeping than reading because it took me nearly the entire voyage to finish the book, but I always managed to be awake when tea was served.

After tea it was time for a shower. Because my room had no attached bath, I had to shower across the corridor. At the beginning of the trip the bath steward inquired whether passengers preferred a shower or tub and the preferred time of bathing. Because the tub meant a saltwater soak with a freshwater rinse, I chose the fresh water shower.

Because the *President Grant* was not a luxury liner, dressing for dinner entailed merely wearing a coat and tie. Dressing was not time-consuming; therefore, little time elapsed between shower and cocktails. I was not surprised after a couple of weeks aboard ship to find that my weight was increasing steadily.

Days were much the same on board ship, and monotony threatened to become tedious. Our arrival at Kobe was now being viewed as a relief from shipboard life and a chance to see new faces. Most of us had not been to Japan before, and we were excited to see this picturesque country with its strange customs.

A little more than two weeks out of Honolulu, the mainland of Japan was sighted—but just barely because of the rain and mist. We also saw a Japanese submarine. The *President Grant*'s thirteen knots was no speed for overtaking it, however, and all I could see was that it was large.

The breakwater of Kobe harbor finally came into view. Among the many ships anchored there was the German liner *Gneisenau*. One of the Britishers mentioned that she had probably been fitted out as a commerce raider and was most likely waiting for an opportune time to leave port. Also in the harbor were tramp steamers, rusty and dirty, being loaded and unloaded, one with a heavy deck load of grain listing dangerously. Coolies were working aboard without concern, apparently used to such precarious conditions.

After we anchored, the Japanese quarantine and immigration officials arrived, and all passengers were requested to report to the lounge for passport inspection. When my turn came I presented my passport and waited for the official questions, which were not long in coming. You are a naval officer? Where are you going? Why? What ship are you reporting to? Why do you want to go ashore in Kobe? My answers, which gave little more information than my passport, were apparently satisfactory, and my visa was stamped for Japan.

Our inspection went fairly rapidly, considering the almost insatiable curiosity of the Japanese officials. The ship moved alongside the dock, and I went ashore with a young American who was returning to his job in China with the British American Tobacco (BAT) Company. Because he had been in Kobe before, he knew the city well and we had no trouble finding our way.

One of our fellow passengers, Dr. Hogshire, a naval officer also on his way to Manila, had had the forethought to buy yen before leaving San Francisco and was kind enough to sell us some at half the rate prevailing in Japan. (The official rate was about four yen per U.S. dollar. In the United States at the Yokohama Specie Bank, a semiofficial government agency, the rate was eight to twelve yen per U.S. dollar. In Shanghai the so-called "black market" rate was more than twenty yen per U.S. dollar.)

At a customs barrier we had to pass before leaving the dock area, the chief interest of the customs inspector seemed to be American cigarettes. He placed his chop (official stamp) on each of the ten cigarettes apiece we were allowed to take ashore; all others had to be surrendered.

Kobe's harbor area and downtown were built in Western-style architecture with numerous large, imposing buildings. The streets were dirty and smelled of sewage and fish, and most natives seemed unclean and shabbily dressed. Buses with attachments for using charcoal instead of gasoline indicated the prevailing austerity. As we headed toward our hotel, we passed "doctors'" offices advertising quick cures for all types of venereal disease.

At the Oriental Hotel we were told that rationing hours prevented us from getting a glass of beer or sake, so we strolled the streets. At a modern and clean-looking department store we noticed that the goods offered for sale were expensive considering their quality. In the Mikimoto store along the famous Moto Machi, a seaside boardwalk with stores on both sides, we saw cultured pearls for sale; they were beautiful, and the prices were high. Students—wearing visored caps, kimonos, and geta (wooden clogs)—seemed to find us as interesting and amusing as we found them. One of the passengers from our ship attracted a good deal of attention; he was six feet six inches tall, a giant among the Japanese.

We passed young women with elaborate coiffures and excessively powdered and rouged faces (we assumed they were geisha). Weather-beaten coolies were pulling a heavily loaded cart. They were wearing straw sandals and rough smocks; some wore rubber-soled canvas shoes with a split for the big toe (the foot counterpart of a mitten).

In the course of our wanderings we came across the Kobe Sex Store, which displayed all manner of devices for enhancing erotic pleasures. The catalog explained various items at length in the malaprop style of English peculiar to the Orient.

We entered several bars in search of a drink, but the soiled labels of the liquor bottles on display made us suspect that the bottles had been used over and over to purvey who knows what brew. In a bar that finally passed muster, the drinks were not bad; the whiskey may have been cut, but only with water.

By this time we were hungry, and my companion suggested sukiyaki. We hailed a cab—or rather a cab hailed us, the driver squeezing his air horn to attract our attention—and we were soon before the door of a sukiyaki house, a wooden structure in typical Japanese style, with a pagoda-style curved roof. We had to leave our shoes at the door. Because the slippers available were much too small, we entered in our stocking feet.

In the hallway were suits of samurai armor, some of the finest in Japan we were told. Our guide, a Japanese woman who spoke some English, took us to a large room whose walls were lined with lifelike masks used in the No drama, classic Japanese dance-drama with highly stylized action, costumes, and scenery. The room was simple with occasional bright decorations in red and gold lacquer, which relieved the austere lines. Our tour concluded in the exquisite garden in which Japanese patience had reproduced in miniature a wooded park with a tiny lake and a delicately arched bridge. Just off the garden was a shrine with statues, some of which were contemplative Buddhas.

The floor of the private room in which our meal would be served was covered with thick straw mats; in the center was a brazier with a charcoal fire for cooking. The walls of the room—bamboo frames with thin paper stretched over them—could apparently be slid back to make adjoining rooms into one large room.

The girl assigned to cook and serve our meal could speak no English, but by sign language we made known our desires. We selected a dish that combined eggs, vegetables, and meat; it tasted much better than it looked. We tried to order sake but had to be content with tea. Although the meal was an interesting experience, I didn't think I would relish a steady Japanese diet—even of sukiyaki, which is not everyday Japanese food.

We headed back to the ship. Our desire for something picturesque and unusual had not been left completely unsatisfied, but Japan was a disappointment. I could not help recalling that when I was about twelve years old I had submitted an essay in a contest to win a free trip to Japan. After collecting stacks of literature from travel agencies, I wrote about how much I wanted to see the beauties of the Land of the Rising Sun. What beauty I had seen in Kobe was too overshadowed by the general drabness and sordidness of the place. Granted I had not seen any of the famous beauty spots, such as Kyoto, nor was late winter the best time to see the country. And a total of six hours in a strange land is not enough time for a fair evaluation. For Japan six years is not too much.

Judging entirely by my first impression of just a small part of Japan, I considered the country poor in a material sense. A decent standard of living could probably have been achieved by forgoing a large army and navy and not pursuing armed aggression in Asia. Japan's lack of materials would probably prevent waging a major war. The "China Incident" had already caused shortages and increased taxes; a major war would seriously disrupt Japan's economy. I decided that Japan would press every advantage, bluffing where necessary but stopping short of actual war with the United States.

Looking back on my opinions in these days in March 1941, I have no difficulty in tearing them apart. Youth sees too many things as clear-cut issues—everything is black and white with no intermediate shades. I had not considered that Japan's standard of living might have been improved by her having developed a strong armed force, thus preventing domination by a foreign power and at the same time allowing her industrial development to proceed unhampered. Japan's later use of her army and navy as an offensive weapon to further her commercial enterprises was inevitable, and she proceeded to improve her position at the expense of others. Unfortunately for Japan, the world of that period (or of this period for that matter) was not one in which an advantage, once gained, remained uncontested. Each gain required still another to give security to the previous one.

Whether Japan would have developed as much as she had without a strong army and navy is debatable. Militarily weak nations maintain their freedom and prosper only when there are enough strong nations opposing each other to prevent their seizure.

During our absence from the ship, many new passengers embarked. By some good fortune I was still permitted to use the stateroom I had acquired in San Francisco; however, at Shanghai I would have to rejoin Cass Mayo in our tiny quarters. Among the new passengers were a number of American missionaries who had been warned by our government to leave Japan. Until now it had been sufficient to have the Father, Son, and Holy Ghost in the Trinity; now one more had to be added—the Emperor.

Also in the group of new arrivals were young British Indians. They seemed shy among the Europeans and stayed to themselves. There was also a Britisher who had worked for the *Japan Times and Advertiser;* his services were no longer required because the paper was being taken over by Japanese interests (and the name changed to *Nippon Times*). He spoke bitterly about the Japanese.

The arrival of new passengers resulted in more formal general conduct. It may have been the number of missionaries aboard, or simply the fact that there were more strangers. There was little mingling between cliques of old passengers and the new arrivals.

The day after leaving Kobe, we came upon Japanese cruisers holding target practice. Our proximity (and the fact that we were probably fouling the range) caused them to check their fire for a while. I recalled short-range practices on midshipmen cruises when a Japanese freighter or tanker would invariably steam right into the line of fire. Just as we used to think the Japanese were spying on our practice, so must they have thought the *President Grant* was spying on them.

Later in the day we passed a couple of modern-looking Japanese cruisers fairly close aboard. As they headed toward the shore, they laid a smoke screen from smoke-making apparatus on their sterns. This maneuver was obviously intended to impress us, but the smoke was patchy and the cruisers were in evidence the entire time. I could visualize an officer being reprimanded by his captain for causing the Japanese Imperial Navy to "lose face" before an American ship.

We were sailing in muddy water—something one does not generally expect to encounter at sea. The Yangtze, which has much in common with the Mississippi River, discharges its mud for miles along the coast as it empties into the sea.

Hours later we picked up our pilot from the pilot ship anchored in the mouth of the Whangpoo. On the way up the river, we passed several outbound Japanese transports. Their gray color, landing boats, and numerous troops on deck were an abrupt reminder that we were approaching a country at war and a city, except for the International Settlement, completely occupied by Japanese troops. On the other hand, Chinese junks sailing up the river looked so old and weather-beaten that I felt that Marco Polo himself might have seen these very craft.

We could discern the tall buildings of Shanghai in the haze ahead. On either side of the river, the country was flat and treeless; here and there were mounds, obviously manmade—mounds to the dead, explained one of the passengers. On our right were the battered Woosung forts that had given the Japanese navy such a battle a few years back. The scars were visible along the shore for a good distance. Closer to the harbor, numerous ships were moored in the stream or along the banks. A Japanese freighter was unloading at an apparent supply depot; in the background were rows of shiny, new trucks.

Many passengers familiar with Shanghai were able to point out landmarks as we approached our moorings: the power plant; the Union Beer (UB) Brewery, which sponsored the news programs of Carroll Olcott (whose constant heckling of the Japanese had caused more than one attempt on his life); the *Idzumo,* flagship of the Japanese naval forces in Shanghai; and the *Conte Verde,* an Italian liner that had been taking refuge in Shanghai since Italy's entry into the European war.

Tiny sampans that dotted the water moved with startling speed for their single sculling oar propulsion. Larger sampans and barges served as living quarters and as a livelihood. In one of the barges I saw a woman preparing a meal: she dipped a pan of water out of the river and set it over a small brazier to boil some cabbagelike greens. It seemed that mere boiling would not render the water safe for drinking or cooking, but the fact that occupants of the boat were in apparent vigorous health indicated that they were either immune to the germs in the water or were made of sterner stuff than we.

Just before reaching our moorings we passed close aboard a new Japanese light cruiser. She was well gunned and looked efficient. In no time we would be checking firsthand the fighting efficiency of these Japanese men-of-war.

We finally moored in midstream, and before long a lighter was alongside to take passengers and baggage ashore. Dr. Hogshire, Cass Mayo, the British Tobacco man, and I boarded the lighter as soon as we could, eager to see Shanghai. However, the lighter remained alongside. The cause for the delay turned out to be Mr. Bumstead, who had thoughtfully provided himself with tons of canned goods for his stay in China. The crates were being loaded on the lighter as we grew more impatient by the minute.

On the way in we passed an Italian gunboat and a British gunboat moored not far apart. Because Shanghai was a neutral port, they maintained a truce—and fought their battles ashore in the local bars. An American gunboat, the USS *Wake*, was moored too far upstream for us to get a good look at her.

After the familiar calm aboard ship, we were unnerved by the activity ashore. Rickshas, cars, ox-drawn carts, and pedestrians passed along the Bund in seemingly endless streams. Automobile horns and Chinese voices filled the air with constant noise. We made our way to the Palace Hotel, which lacked the glitter (and high prices) of the newer hotels but seemed clean and pleasant enough. The price of the room, twenty-seven dollars, seemed steep until I realized that the room clerk meant Chinese dollars, not U.S. dollars. At the exchange rate of twenty Chinese dollars to one U.S. dollar, the room rate was reasonable. A collection box and a poster urging contributions to a "Spitfire Fund" at the desk were reminders of the European war and indicated the sympathy of this part of Shanghai.

After quickly washing up, we all gathered for drinks in the room of the British Tobacco man, who had graciously consented to be our guide in Shanghai. He introduced us to the intricacies of ordering drinks. One could not request five scotch and sodas. One had to ask for a five piece whiskey-soda. The price per drink came to something less than fifteen cents in U.S. money; at that rate everyone was only too happy to buy the next round.

The little party went on until one of the clearer heads in the group suggested that we go out for dinner while we could still stand up. A friend who had come to greet the British Tobacco man had made a reservation for ten people at one of the Chinese restaurants. We went to the restaurant aboard a double-decker bus similar to those on New York City's Fifth Avenue.

The streets were crowded, and the reckless driving of the ricksha coolies made me happy to be aboard motorized transport. In food shops the display windows were filled with hams and gleaming "shellacked" ducks. The profusion of billboards and electric signs left no doubt that Western civilization had reached Shanghai.

Our restaurant, Sun Ya, was reputed to have the best Chinese food in the city. Our guide and his friend ordered the meal, saving us from such gaucheries as asking for chop suey or chow mein. The meal that was served included a delicious duck soup, spring rolls (a kind of egg roll with bean sprouts) cooked to a golden brown, sweet and sour pork, beef and greens, chicken and almonds, and copious bottles of beer. A bowl of steaming hand towels was within easy reach and proved of great value before the meal was finished. I had never held finger bowls in high esteem; I was now convinced that they were completely inadequate compared to this "quaint Chinese custom."

With a fine meal under our belts, we decided to go out on the town. Our first stop was Ciro's, a large dance hall cum bar and restaurant of a type that seems to flourish in the Far East. We bought drinks for our dancing partners—Austrian refugees who were taxi dancing here. They invariably ordered a nonalcoholic drink that looked like cherry brandy. With the drinks they received chits that they apparently cashed in at the end of the evening. The girls seemed pleasant; I wondered what the status of their families had been in Europe before the Anschluss had caused them to flee Austria.

We left Ciro's, promising the girls that we would be back later, and made our way to another dance hall. Here we ran into some of our fellow passengers from the *President Grant*. Although the place was lively, there were so few taxi dancers and such poor-quality liquor that we left. Our next stop, the Majestic, was not crowded; a gangster bombing a couple weeks before was keeping away most of the regular customers. Our British Tobacco man soon had a beautiful Korean girl (one of the hostesses) at our table. Her height and her fine figure surprised me; I was under the impression that all Asian women were short and flat-chested. A few young stewards from the *President Grant* joined us for a drink. One of them had been haggling, without success, with one of the Russian "princesses." In what was definitely a buyer's market, her price seemed steep.

The Majestic was dull, so we left for the Little Club. It had its own currency, a practice popular with Shanghai bistros. I was surprised to see a young Chinese couple in Western-style dress and jitterbugging. American culture à la Hollywood was obviously having an effect in the Orient. The Little Club was quiet, so we wandered on to the Casanova, where the hostesses and barmaids were supposedly Russian. The girl I spoke to turned out to be an Estonian, but who was I to quibble? Moreover she made no claims to noble lineage, so I missed hearing any reminiscences of Czarist splendors.

The next morning, Cass Mayo looked much too fresh for someone who had been up all night. We went to breakfast, although I had no desire to eat. Because I had gotten into the habit, at an early age, of doing things not because I wanted to but because they were good for me, I managed to finish a moderate meal.

Cass had neglected to get his passport visa for Hong Kong while he was still in San Francisco, so he decided he had better get it here in Shanghai or be content to remain aboard ship in Hong Kong. The British consulate was located in a parklike compound that felt far away from the rush and noise of Shanghai traffic. I accompanied him there and was fully appreciative of its tranquillity.

On our way back to the ship we were accosted by Chinese urchins begging for pennies. They swarmed around us, noisily crying, "*Cumshaw,* master" (they pronounced master with a broad "a," probably picked up from the British). After little success with us, they ran off to another westerner. (Americans and Europeans were apparently considered immensely wealthy and were expected to spread bounty in their wake.) At the landing we learned that the *President*

Grant would remain in port until midnight. Cass decided to stay ashore and shop; I went aboard to bed.

All was quiet until the rest of the passengers returned in bumboats and launches, making the ship just in time. From the shouts and laughter, they sounded as though missing the ship would have been a good excuse to go back ashore and continue where they had left off.

The passenger list was augmented during our stay in Shanghai. There were many Chinese men and women aboard, most of them wearing native dress. In the club room loud, animated mah-jongg games had supplanted the earlier quiet bridge games. An old Chinese gentleman, who spent most of his time at the game, wore a black skullcap, a long black mandarin coat, and black slippers; he lacked only a drooping black mustache. He seemed cheerful, but his habitual cough and consequent expectoration (a sequence of sounds I later learned is known as "the call of the East") was nerve-racking. Another of the mah-jongg enthusiasts was an attractive Chinese woman who showed a strong interest in the game and received obvious enjoyment from it. She spoke English, and it was not long before she was teaching the game to a group of Americans and Britishers.

Most of the Chinese were going to Chungking via Hong Kong—some for business reasons, some to rejoin their families, and others for safety from the Japanese. Many of them realized that eventually the Japanese would move into the International Settlement, eliminating that important "unoccupied" pocket.

That night, we passed through a large concentration of Japanese transports. We assumed that these ships were either on their way to a South China port or to French Indochina. The rugged terrain of the China coast near Hong Kong with its many coves brought to mind stories of China Sea pirates, and I wondered how many of the apparently peaceful junks heading into Hong Kong harbor actually engaged in piracy or trafficked with the pirates. Later I learned that most junks carried antiquated brass cannon to ward off pirate attacks. I also heard some bloodcurdling tales of the torture meted out to those who attempted to resist the pirate attacks.

Oil tanks and gun emplacements on the shore were camouflaged to blend in with the background, but across the entrance to Hong

Kong harbor was stretched a net supported at regular intervals by large buoys. The entire area except for prescribed channels was heavily mined. The European war, which seemed so far away, was brought closer on seeing these defenses in an outpost of the British Empire.

The *President Grant* tied up on the Kowloon side, a peninsula of the China mainland. (Victoria, the principal city, is across the bay on the island of Hong Kong.) Although it was still early in the evening, it was dark before we were permitted to go ashore. Cass Mayo, Dr. Hogshire, and I decided to go to Victoria, because Kowloon did not appear to have promising diversions. On our way to the ferry we walked through the slum area surrounding the docks. The buildings looked crowded and drab. On one corner we noticed a money changer's shop and stopped to convert some of our money to Hong Kong currency. The rate was four Hong Kong dollars to one U. S. dollar, which made it easy to determine prices. Before reaching the ferry we passed several large air raid shelters— more indications that the British considered war with Japan only a matter of time.

We were soon among the bright lights of Victoria. We saw numerous British soldiers, mostly Scottish, but no British women. Later we learned that all British women, except those needed for essential jobs, had been evacuated from Hong Kong because of the growing international tension. Meanwhile the British men were having to make do with non-British talent. The city was consequently quiet. We visited a nightclub, but it turned out to be a dance hall serving only soft drinks. We learned that Hong Kong dance halls were not issued liquor licenses. Regular habitués of these establishments had working agreements with the management that enabled them to be served liquor in teapots—à la prohibition-era speakeasies.

A few hours of Hong Kong night life was about all we could stand. From the ferry landing in Kowloon we took rickshas back to the ship. My ricksha "boy" (in the Far East all male service people are "boys" regardless of age) wanted to take me to see the "sing a song" girls; with some difficulty, for he was a persistent old devil, I managed to convince him that I just wanted to get back to the ship.

The next day we went ashore to see the "sights." In true tourist style we went up "the Peak" in the cable car. The view was magnificent, although a good part of the Peak was devoted to army barracks and restricted areas. We did see Indian troops bivouacked around antiaircraft-gun emplacements. Down the road from the military reservation was an area of pleasant-looking private residences, which I gathered was one of the exclusive sections of Hong Kong. Because the weather was cool, we decided not to visit Repulse Bay, the beach resort of Hong Kong.

It was probably the altitude that sharpened our appetites, so we returned to Victoria for lunch. We finally found the Red Dragon restaurant, which had been recommended by a gentleman whose appearance indicated a liking for good food. The restaurant consisted of seven or eight stories, all devoted to serving meals. On some floors were special banquet rooms and private rooms; on others were regular dining rooms. Our luncheon, or tiffin, was served by Chinese girls assigned to wait on each individual of the party. Their duties consisted of serving the food, handing the diner his implements, and making comments—in Chinese—about his appearance. Blue eyes, light-colored or curly hair, and long noses were particularly amusing features. The girls were pretty, but their clothes were soiled. The food was good, though not as good as our meal at Sun Ya in Shanghai, and the girls kept us laughing most of the time (merely by laughing at us).

Our visit in Hong Kong would not have been complete without buying souvenirs, so we stopped at some shops and haggled awhile, usually buying nothing. I finally bought a wicker picnic basket (for my dirty laundry) and a bottle of scotch (at $1.50 U.S., I should have bought more).

On our way back to the ship we were introduced to a Chinese funeral. It consists of an interminable procession of hired coolies bearing pictures of the deceased, slogans, musical instruments, and anything else that's deemed appropriate. The main purpose of the procession is to give an impression of wealth and grief (measured in direct proportion to the length and noise). It was an effort to draw ourselves away from this spectacle.

Back aboard ship we amused ourselves until sailing time by tossing coins to a Chinese man who was diving from a sampan alongside the ship. Although the water was cold, the diver acted as though it did not bother him. Surely there must have been an easier way to make a living.

Leaving Hong Kong meant that Manila was the next stop, and Manila meant back to work. When we had crossed the 180th meridian we had to send radiograms reporting our presence aboard the *President Grant* with orders to report to the Asiatic Fleet. Our ship assignments were received by radio shortly after leaving Shanghai. My assignment was to the USS *Pope,* which I knew was an old four-stacker. Cass Mayo drew the USS *Houston.* Having a preference for cruisers, I had hoped to get the USS *Houston* or the USS *Marblehead.* Now I could look forward to a tropical duty tour in a hot "tin can."

The weather after our departure from Hong Kong was warm, and we spent most of the daylight hours either playing deck tennis or swimming. The pool was about fifteen feet by thirty feet, just long enough to swim a few strokes and then turn around. The deck tennis proved too tame for some of the athletes. This was remedied by improvising a volleyball game using a medicine ball. The trick was to try to send the ball crashing down on someone's head across the net. This game fell out of favor when a large number of sprained thumbs reduced the pool of available players.

2

On the morning of April 1, 1941, we awoke aboard the *President Grant* to find the green mountains of Luzon on our port side. An army bomber skimming the water as it circled the ship created a stir among the passengers, for not a single airplane had been sighted during the entire trip.

Because we were scheduled to arrive in Manila that afternoon, we naval officers arranged a cocktail party before lunch to bid farewell to our friends who were continuing on their voyage. By lunchtime we were passing Corregidor, a rugged-looking island with steep sides and heavy vegetation. We knew it was a fortress, and the fact that no guns were visible made it seem more formidable.

In landlocked Manila Bay we began to feel the tropical heat. Last-minute packing in our tiny stateroom proved to be a sweltering operation, and the thought that my room aboard the USS *Pope* might be even smaller was painful to contemplate.

Before going alongside the dock, the ship was inspected by the port medical and immigration officials, and we went through our passport inspection routine once again. In the couple of hours' delay that ensued we tried to pick out our prospective ships in the naval anchorage off Manila. The cruisers and other large ships were easily distinguished, but the destroyers could be identified only by the numbers on their bows. One keen-eyed individual finally picked out the *Pope*'s "225."

As the *President Grant* was being moored, I noticed a familiar face on the dock. Herb Kriloff, a classmate of mine from the naval academy, had apparently come down to greet me. When the gangplank was put over, Herb and another naval officer, Kenny Wheeler, came aboard. Wheeler's friend aboard the *Pope*, Jack Fisher, had told him to meet me when the *President Grant* docked. The *Pope,* according to Kenny, had come off patrol to pick me up and would be going out again immediately. With the help of Kenny and Herb, I tried to get through customs as quickly as possible, but it turned out that each item of luggage had to be inspected thoroughly. Kenny left to take care of other business, and Herb finally got me down to the Army-Navy Club, landing in time to find that the *Pope* had already gotten under way again.

We left the luggage at the club and went out to dinner. Herb proceeded to fill me in on Manila. The navy families had already been evacuated, the army families would soon follow suit, and the families of American civilians were being urged to return to the States. Bachelors seeking feminine companionship would meet stiff competition in the limited field remaining. Most of the time, finding a date in Manila would be irrelevant, because the ships spent much time operating in the southern islands (Sulu Archipelago) and were in Manila only occasionally.

We went out to Herb's ship, the *William B. Preston,* to spend the night. The *Preston* had been a four-stacker; conversion to a seaplane tender had left her a two-stacker with considerable improvements over the usual destroyer of that type. The wardroom had been enlarged to permit a mess hall for aviators. What had been the forward fire room was now a bunk room. Gasoline stowage was built below. The ship had been converted in Brooklyn, where Herb had joined her. (Herb had started out on the *Salt Lake City* with me and had gotten his orders in 1940 when that ship was in Pearl Harbor.)

Herb seemed happy in his billet. The only thing about the *Preston* that caused him anxiety was the gasoline tank: "If anything ever hits that . . ." His view of the international situation was not optimistic. All indications added up to eventual war. If Japan was only bluffing, all well and good, but if she was not, this little part of the navy would really catch hell.

We turned in early because I had to report aboard the *Houston* in the morning. The *Pope* was not in port, so I had to report to the senior officer present, who was commander of the Asiatic Fleet (Admiral Hart) on the USS *Houston.* Actually I would report to a member of his staff.

Aboard the *Houston* I met a couple of classmates from the naval academy and other friends whom I had known as midshipmen. I was offered a suit of white service by C. D. Smith so I could report in uniform. As midshipmen C. D. and I had been about the same size, but I had trouble getting into his uniform now—due to the ten to fifteen pounds I had gained on board the *President Grant*. As it turned out, the reporting was just a formality, and I was told that the *Pope* would return that afternoon.

After lunch I went back to the Army-Navy Club and awaited the arrival of the *Pope*. The club's landing was the official landing for officers' boats. This was a convenient arrangement from all points of view, for if an officer wanted to go ashore for a game of tennis, a swim, a drink, or a meal, the landing was as far as he had to go. It was also an ideal place for meeting friends from other ships.

Late afternoon found me and my luggage in the *Pope's* motorboat heading out to the ship. Bill Spears greeted me at the gangway and warned me to walk only on the raised planks (the well deck had just been painted and was still wet). I soon came to learn that the well deck had to be painted so often that this "boardwalk" of planks was the usual condition of the well deck.

Bill showed me to my stateroom. It was small (as were all staterooms in four-stackers), but I would have it to myself. Its chief disadvantages were its proximity to the forward fire room and its nonfunctioning ventilator.

After seeing that my luggage was aboard, I went to the wardroom to meet the rest of the ship's officers. The executive officer was Lieutenant Antrim, who was acting as commanding officer during the captain's illness. (Lieutenant Commander Wray never resumed his command; he was transferred back to the States for further hospitalization.) "Red" Bassett, a big, easygoing fellow, was the engineering officer. Bill Lowndes, whom I remembered as a midshipman, was the gunnery officer. The disbursing officer of the 59th Destroyer Division was also aboard; he was Jack Fisher, a "native son" and ardent fan of California.

The next day Antrim informed me that my jobs would be communications and commissary. Because I knew little about either job, I would be a busy ensign for the next few weeks. In addition to these tasks I would stand the usual deck watches. I was happy to learn that I would have time off for meals and sleep—if I did not have the midwatch.

I worked hard at my new jobs, but my efforts were not always to the executive officer's complete satisfaction. As time went on I became more accustomed to my work and accomplished more than I had at the beginning. Whenever the *Pope* anchored off Manila I was usually caught up with my work, so I could spend time in port at whatever amusements the city had to offer.

Called "the Pearl of the Orient," Manila was a beautiful city. On Dewey Boulevard, which skirted the bay, were many attractive homes and apartment houses. Throughout the city were countless churches, some of which had been built in the early days of Spanish colonization. The government buildings, which had been constructed on a grand scale, lent dignity to the surroundings.

The original Spanish city had been surrounded by massive stone walls and a moat. Over the years Manila had grown to such an extent that this section formed only a minor part of the modern city. The moat had been filled in and converted to a golf course. The walls remained as a monument to Spanish colonization. Intramuros, as this area was now called, was a picturesque, crowded place filled with churches and curio shops.

On the north bank of the Pasig River was the bustling business district. Most of the movie theaters were located here; in general their architecture and decoration showed better taste and more restraint than their American counterparts. Most of the shops, department stores, and good restaurants were located in this district, so its streets were usually crowded until late evening.

The main evening attraction was jai alai. The game was played in a large modern building (named Jai-Alai) that housed several bars, a restaurant, and a nightclub—all air-conditioned. The betting on the matches was conducted on a pari-mutuel basis, with the house taking about 12 percent. The playing court ran the length of the building; the grandstand was on one side of the court with a large net in front of it to prevent the ball from leaving the court.

The betting booths were located behind the top tier of the grandstand, and a bar on the same level provided liquid refreshment.

Above the grandstand was a mezzanine with tiers of seats; above that was the nightclub. Some tables on the nightclub level were placed so that the game could be watched from there, although most of the tables were located in the ballroom. There was also a modern circular bar next to the ballroom. On the street level at the front of the building was a large attractive restaurant and bar.

The followers of jai alai were many. The regular betters nearly all followed "infallible" systems. One officer from the *Pope* bet regularly and showed a substantial gain in six months. But for every winner there are several losers, and not a few people found themselves in difficulty from betting too heavily.

There were numerous nightclubs in Manila. Most had private rooms where patrons could gamble at cards and dice, the "house" in many cases using methods to improve its already favorable odds.

Santa Ana, a ballroom near Cavite, called itself the largest dance hall in the world. The taxi dancers (or ballerinas, as they referred to themselves) were Filipinas who usually claimed to be Spanish. Often each girl's mother would accompany her to the dance hall and wait for her until the end of the evening, so there was little chance of the girls' virtue being compromised, or at least not without sufficient compensation. The girls were usually excellent dancers and liked to include jitterbugging with their congas and rumbas. (The girls met their match at jitterbugging when the mess attendants from a cruiser not attached to the Asiatic Fleet joined them on the dance floor and left them gasping for breath.)

There were several excellent hotels in Manila, the Manila Hotel being the largest and most elaborate. Occasionally, Antrim, Bassett, Fisher, and I and perhaps another officer from the *Pope* would go to the hotel for mint juleps served on the lawn. Antrim was the instigator of these parties, usually giving for a reason the beauty of the sunset over Manila Bay. In reality the mint juleps were almost always more inspiring than the sunset.

It had been customary in the past for the Asiatic Fleet to visit China during the summer months to avoid the humid summer heat of the Philippines. Because of the tense international situation, it was considered unwise to send U.S. ships to Shanghai and Tsingtao, where they would be trapped in case of hostilities between the United States and Japan. To keep the ships concentrated in Manila Bay was equally inadvisable. At frequent intervals the ships were ordered to operate in the southern islands of the Philippines. Aside from security from enemy attack, the Sulu Archipelago offered excellent operating conditions especially during the typhoon season (late summer and early autumn). The disadvantage of the islands was the lack of ports with suitable recreation.

Shortly after I joined the *Pope* we were ordered along with the rest of the 59th Destroyer Division to operate in the southern islands. We had a new captain aboard, Lieutenant Commander Blinn. When I expressed enthusiasm about going south, the other officers looked at me with pity. I would soon find out why.

As we approached the anchorage at Jolo Island we passed a number of Moro praus. These outrigger canoes carried a surprising amount of sail and made good speed in a light wind. I could not decide whether their colorful sails were designed with an eye to beauty or made up from whatever bits of cloth were available.

A large bay on the south side of Jolo Island provided an excellent anchorage that was to be our operating base for the next couple of weeks. Each morning we would get under way, and after clearing the bay we would commence exercises. Sometimes we would have gunnery drills and make runs all morning and afternoon to drill the pointers and trainers of the guns—no ammunition would be used. It was dull but necessary. On other days we would have ship maneuvering and practice forming lines of bearing.

After a few days of this sort of practice, it was difficult to tell one day from the next. Each evening we would anchor in the bay to view the evening's entertainment. There was always a motion picture (more often than not a grade B). It did not take me long to realize why a southern cruise was viewed with disdain.

The monotony of our operations in the southern islands was at last broken by shore leave and liberty in Jolo, the principal town on the island of Jolo. As soon as we anchored offshore, praus surrounded the ship. Some had come out of curiosity, others for business. Vendors displayed their wares (usually fruits) and shouted to attract attention. Women in some of the boats offered to wash clothes; several sailors took advantage of this opportunity to escape the chore of doing their own laundry, and the women were soon doing a thriving business. A small boy had paddled out to the ship in a tiny peanut shell of a canoe. It was hollowed out from a single log and was barely large enough to hold him. The canoe was tippy, but the boy was dressed for such eventualities, wearing nothing but what he was born in.

After lunch Fisher and I went ashore to see the town. The landing was a short walk from the town proper, and on the way we passed two sentry posts, one on each side of the road. The posts, sturdily built of stone and concrete, had iron bars on the windows and a door of similar construction. At first I thought these were just detention cells, but Fisher explained that the Moros occasionally went "juramentado" and the constabulary used these posts as protection. (A "juramentado" is a Moro who takes an oath to die while killing Christians. The Moros are Muhammadans and take religious differences seriously.)

In the middle of the town was a large open-air market covered by a corrugated tin roof. Inside were all kinds of commodities, from hardware to foodstuffs. Fish seemed to be a favorite food, and the stench of old fish assailed one's nostrils at every turn.

As we approached what looked like a temple, we heard a voice chanting in a language unknown to us. A closer inspection revealed a man with a shaved head chanting alone in a monotone inside the temple. Having heard many stories of juramentados, we immediately concluded that he was a Moro going through the "purification" ceremony before running amuck; we did not linger to find out if our conclusions were correct.

Along the waterfront reaching out over the water on pilings was a motley collection of rickety shacks, houses, and stores. This was the local Chinatown. From the odor it was obvious that refuse was dumped into the water. Fishermen were repairing nets at one end of the main plank walkway, and in sunny spots fish were laid out to dry. Children were everywhere, the smaller ones running about naked. A number of children had dry, scaly skin, perhaps from unsanitary living conditions. As we walked along we had to watch our step; many of the planks of the boardwalks were either missing or worm-eaten.

It was not long before we had our fill of this exotic community, and we wandered back into the main part of town searching for a cold beer. We found a store in which a number of American sailors were quenching their thirst. The proprietor assured us that he had plenty of cold beer and led us to a private "room" in which to drink it.

While we were there, a couple of our men came in to tell us that there had been a riot in a barrio outside the town. A group of Moros had attempted to attack a constabulary station about five miles away. The Moros, armed with daggers called krises, rushed across an open field almost up to the barbed-wire-enclosed constabulary post. The constabulary (mostly Filipinos from the northern islands such as Luzon) had held their fire until the Moros were very close and then opened up with shotguns and rifles.

Fisher and I decided to take a taxi to the scene of the attack. Our driver, a Filipino, had a healthy respect for the Moros and did not want to go all the way out, but we bullied him into driving us onto the field. We passed a number of Moros carrying off their dead and wounded on blood-soaked litters, and we stopped to take pictures. The Moros did not seem to mind our taking photographs, but they looked sullen, and the women we saw were weeping.

Twenty-three Moros had been killed in this mad attack. We never learned its immediate cause. There was a traditional hatred between Moros and Filipinos, and an occasional bloodletting seemed to be the only release valve.

When we returned to town we noticed a general tension, and constabulary and armed deputies were patrolling the streets in pairs. It was now late afternoon, so we went back to the ship for dinner. Men who returned later reported that our sailors were being urged back aboard their ships because more violence was expected—possibly an attack on the town.

The next morning the 59th Destroyer Division left Jolo as scheduled. We were preparing for our "full power run," and we started building up to our required speed. The well-protected Sulu Sea was completely calm; the only waves were those created by the ships of our division. The fact that we were eventually steaming at high speeds created enough breeze to make the ship pleasantly cool. At low speeds the relentless sun and no wind would have stewed us.

Late that afternoon we passed the British cruiser HMS *Liverpool*, which had had part of her bows blown off in the Mediterranean and was on her way back to the States for repairs. She had apparently put into Manila for temporary repairs, but the damage was still evident. A few days later HMS *Warspite* came into Manila Bay and anchored off Cavite for repairs. She had also been damaged in the Mediterranean and had half her antiaircraft battery knocked out by a German bomb. It was expected that the *Warspite* would also go to the States. As a neutral nation the United States seemed to be doing a terrific partisan repair business.

Manila had many interesting and beautiful churches, and whenever possible I heard Sunday Mass ashore in preference to hearing it aboard one of the naval vessels. Some churches dated from the time of the Spanish settlement, and the bones of many dons had been entombed beneath the stones of the church floors.

The congregations were interesting because of the variety of costumes. The Spanish women and mestizas wore black lace mantillas and black or dark-colored dresses. The older Filipina women wore colorful starched piña dresses. Women in modern styles looked prosaic in these gatherings. The men, regardless of nationality, generally wore suits made of linen or a similar lightweight fabric. (Filipino men as a rule take great pride in their clothes, but their styles are inclined to be extreme. Regardless of style, however, they look neat and well groomed.)

The sermons in many of the churches were given in Spanish, for nearly all Filipinos speak that language better than English. (In the Philippines there are many native dialects, Tagalog being the official one. Most Filipinos speak several dialects. Spanish is slowly giving way to English as a second language, but a habit of three hundred years' standing is not easily changed.) Occasionally announcements were made in English for the benefit of the few American servicemen and civilians in the church.

One Sunday morning I met Herb Kriloff at the Army-Navy Club to make a trip we had been talking about for some time: a visit to Pagsanjan Falls. Jerry Greenspahn, an army doctor whom Herb had known as a boy in Chicago, and another army officer were making the trip with us. We hired a taxi to take us to Pagsanjan, the small town below the falls. The ride through the Luzon countryside past Laguna de Bai, a large lake southeast of Manila, took several hours.

At Pagsanjan we made arrangements for canoes to take us upstream to the falls; we changed into our swimming trunks while we were waiting. The first part of the voyage was on a quiet stream, but as we approached the falls the stream narrowed and the water became turbulent. At times we passed through narrow shaded gorges, a welcome relief from the hot sun.

Several times before we reached the falls it was necessary to leave the canoes and clamber past rapids while the boatmen pulled and paddled the canoes upstream. Near the falls we overtook several other parties of servicemen. Most were in uniform and wet to the knees from the rapids they had to climb past.

The falls were not large or particularly high, but the crashing water filled the canyon with a constant rumble. Herb and I took a swim in the pool below the falls, but the water was too cold to enjoy it. The steep cliffs alongside the stream shut out the sun, and the air cooled by the falls had a damp chill.

The return trip in the canoe was more enjoyable than the upstream leg. It was not necessary to get out of the canoes, and shooting the rapids was fun, although the boatmen made it look a good deal simpler than it was.

While I was getting acquainted with life in the Philippines and my jobs aboard ship, important events were taking place elsewhere. Hitler launched his attack against Russia in June 1941. This action reduced the probability of a Russian attack on the Manchurian border against Japan. This in turn gave Japan the opportunity to broaden its occupation of French Indochina.

Increased apprehension as to what other plans Japan might have for Southeast Asia showed itself in activities that we could observe in the Philippines. The buildup of American and Filipino armed forces was readily apparent. National Guard units were arriving from the States. A navy oiler with a deck load of motor torpedo boats arrived in Manila Bay accompanied by the heavy cruiser *Louisville*. The oiler and cruiser did not become part of the Asiatic Fleet, but some newly arrived fleet type of submarines did, augmenting the six old S-boats.

Aboard the *Pope* there were personnel changes. We received Lt. Ike Wilson, whose tour of duty as a Japanese language student in Tokyo had ended abruptly. We also received a "fresh-caught" reserve ensign, Donald Austin. Our mess attendants were replaced by retired personnel recalled to active duty. Bill Spears took over my communications job and I took over his first lieutenant slot. The *Pope* itself had a change when we painted her haze gray and obliterated the traditional destroyer large bow numbers.

It was not a great surprise to learn that the entrances to Manila Bay were to be mined and that the 59th Destroyer Division would be assigned minefield patrol duty. The laying of the minefields was conducted by army minelayers. We were disturbed to see how many mines exploded prematurely.

The *Pope* and the *Ford* were scheduled for navy yard overhaul, which meant that we would have more time ashore and might be able to take leave to visit the mountain resort at Baguio or Lake Taal. But it was not to be. The other two ships of our division, the *Pillsbury* and the *Peary*, had been conducting training exercises south of Luzon. During simulated night attacks there was a collision. The battered ships limped back to Manila and were assigned the *Pope* and *Ford* overhaul slots at Cavite.

We continued our minefield patrolling, which was usually uneventful. One day, however, a merchant ship that had not heard about the mined entrance attempted to enter Manila Bay. When she did not respond to our signals, our gunnery officer, Ike Wilson, put a couple of shots across her bow. We then got her complete attention and were able to guide her through the prescribed channel.

We alternated our patrol assignments with the *Ford* (week in, week out) to permit liberty for the crews in Manila. During these periods in port it seemed that the captain was making more frequent visits to fleet headquarters, accompanied by a growing sense of urgency. One day he asked me for my requisition to bring our commissary stores up to full allowance for 120 days. (We had been avoiding this because of our expected yard overhaul; now it seemed that there were other plans afoot.) The next day a lighter pulled alongside, and we had an "all hands" working party bringing the stores aboard.

A few days later, back on patrol duty, we anchored for the night off Mariveles, across the channel from Corregidor. In the darkness an S-39, one of our older submarines, came alongside to top off her freshwater supply. Her commissary officer (Monk Hendrix, a classmate from the naval academy) came aboard to get any luncheon meat we could spare. He explained that the submarines issued rations for midwatch standers, usually sandwiches. We let him have as much as he could use. As he left he mentioned that the S-39 was headed for an assigned "war patrol" station.

3

On Sunday night, December 7, 1941, I caught the last boat back to the ship. I had spent most of the evening at the club getting my fill of San Miguel beer, for I expected that we would be on minefield patrol for another week starting Monday. It was a sticky, breathless night typical of Manila Bay, and I had finally dropped off to sleep when Bill Spears awakened me.

"I don't suppose you're particularly interested right now, but Pearl Harbor was bombed and we're at war with Japan."

"The bastards," I said and went back to sleep.

The next morning I was up early, wondering what we were going to do now that the war had finally begun. On shore, church bells were ringing continuously to rouse the inhabitants. Sailors were returning to the ship in whatever transportation was available, and excited groups gathered to discuss the turn of events. Meanwhile the *Pope* was made ready to get under way at a moment's notice. On the forecastle, my station for getting under way, I listened to my chief boatswain's mate, Sperandio, deliver his opinion of the Japanese.

"I've been waiting three years to take a crack at those slant-eyed sons of bitches and now I'm going to have my chance." With occasional glances skyward, he related incidents in Tsingtao and Chefoo by which the Japanese had won his disfavor. Despite his high time ashore in Manila the previous night followed by little sleep, he was ready for action.

While we were standing by, we proceeded with our "strip ship bill"—removing everything from the ship that was nonessential and a possible fire hazard. A motor launch from the *Holland* had been sent over to take these articles ashore. The captain and the executive officer hurried everyone lest we be required to get under way

31

immediately, but gradually most of the officers and crew settled into a less frantic pace. The captain was summoned to a conference ashore and returned with orders to get under way in the evening. We were to escort a convoy out of Manila.

We left at dusk and headed toward the entrance to Manila Bay. The *Pope* and the *Ford* were to escort a naval tanker and two tenders. On the afternoon of the ninth we contacted the ships that were to take over our convoy. As soon as we were relieved we headed back for Manila and during the night passed several of our submarines heading south. We arrived off Corregidor before daybreak on the tenth and had to wait until dawn before entering Manila Bay. Several merchantmen were also waiting to get into port. The situation was tense that morning because we had no idea of what to expect in the way of Japanese men-of-war. There was the possibility of submarines and even surface vessels being in the vicinity.

We proceeded to the navy yard at Cavite to fuel. We had received word over the radio that there had been a bombing attack on Manila during the night. The marine sentry on the fuel dock became our source of firsthand information: Japanese planes had attacked Nichols Field in Manila guided by flares set by fifth columnists. The damage was negligible but it had been an exciting night.

When fueling was completed we left the dock and anchored in the bay midway between Manila and Cavite. It was a clear, bright day; the fact that a war was going on seemed incongruous. More merchantmen than I had ever seen there before were anchored in the bay; few ships were behind the breakwater because another bombing attack was expected. We had our antiaircraft defense standing by, but we knew that our 3-inch .25-caliber popgun and our .50-caliber machine guns would be effective only against aircraft flying close to our ship.

Just as we were finishing our noon meal, the air raid sirens on shore sounded. Nearly everyone on the ship rushed topside to see what was happening. After a short wait we heard the drone of airplane motors; high above us the silver wings of Japanese bombers glistened in the sunlight. It was a flight of twenty-seven planes; at such an altitude the planes looked tiny and almost harmless. Japanese fighters at a lower altitude were coming in to strafe Nichols Field.

They apparently carried bombs, for a series of explosions erupted from the field and clouds of smoke indicated large fires. The heavy bombers began their runs. Following down the line, they made a run on the dock area and the ships in the bay. Geysers leaped upward as bombs exploded in the water. Smoke rose from several ships, although no serious damage was apparent from our angle.

The *Pope*, which had gotten under way at the first warning, kept circling to make sure that we presented a poor target. Meanwhile Antrim had his hands full trying to keep the crew under cover. Only the gun crews were supposed to be topside, but everyone wanted to see the show and would rather suffer a casualty than miss his first air raid.

The bombers headed toward Corregidor, but a heavy antiaircraft barrage caused a change of plan: Cavite seemed to be next on the list. We cheered as the first bombs landed in the water short of the navy yard, but as the splashes moved into the base our cheers turned to groans. Fires broke out immediately, and the volume of smoke indicated widespread damage. Ships in the yard put up a determined but ineffectual barrage. The *Otus* backed out and got clear, but some of the small ships appeared damaged. Fighter planes swooped over the *Pope*, and we fired a few salvos at them. Some planes crashed near Cavite, but we could not determine their country of origin. During the attack, motor torpedo boats scooted at high speed, firing their machine guns at strafing planes. Submarines tried in vain to submerge in shallow Manila Bay.

After the raid, boats began bringing wounded from Cavite to Manila. Later, when a boat from the *Otus* came alongside us to deliver mail, we learned that the *Peary* and the *Pillsbury* had been damaged and that one of the submarines had been sunk. For once we were glad that our navy yard overhaul had been postponed, for both the *Pope* and the *Ford* would have been occupying the berths where the *Peary* and the *Pillsbury* had been damaged. The Army-Navy Club was being used as a first aid station. There had apparently been attempts at sabotage in Cavite, and the marines had shot down some fifth columnists.

That evening we received orders to take another convoy out of Manila. With the smoke from Cavite still visible against the setting sun, we escorted the remaining large naval vessels out of Manila. This time we knew we would not be coming back. Our base had been badly damaged, and with the constant expectation of air raids it was practically useless.

The next day the *Ford* provided excitement for the convoy by firing one of her torpedoes. It had started to run in the tube and was fired to prevent any damage to the ship. In the afternoon a plane was reported and a silvery object was spotted high in the sky. The gun crews loaded and waited. Various people reported a plane diving and changing course, but there was something strange about the plane.

I suggested over the phone to the gunnery officer, Bill Lowndes, that the object might not be a plane but the planet Venus. He replied that it might also be the moon. When I started up to the bridge to check on the approximate position of Venus, I found that the same conclusion had been reached there, and a check had been made bearing out that view. I did not fail to inform Lowndes as soon as I could, but I didn't get much satisfaction from him.

Later we joined up with more of our destroyers and headed for Balikpapan, in Borneo. We patrolled the entrance to the harbor while the larger ships went through the minefield, then we followed them in. Most of the surface ships of the Asiatic Fleet were inside the harbor.

Balikpapan seemed to be a mass of oil derricks and refining plants. It could be an object of Japanese attention before long.

We were not surprised to see the *Langley* at anchor and undamaged. (Radio Tokyo had reported the *Langley* sunk. In the first week of the war, every ship in the Asiatic Fleet was "sunk" at least once with "complete loss" of personnel.) We anchored until the tanker USS *Trinity* was ready to take us alongside for fueling.

While we were taking on oil, the *Preston* tied up to the opposite side of the *Trinity*. This gave me an opportunity to speak to Herb Kriloff again. The *Preston* had been at Davao, in Mindanao, when the war started and was the object of an air raid on Monday, December 8, from Japanese aircraft-carrier planes. They had caught some of our PBY seaplanes on the water and destroyed them, killing several crew members. One of the officers from the *Preston* had been ashore, and while crossing an open field he received personal attention from a Japanese fighter. The fact that he had tripped and fallen to one side was the only reason he escaped uninjured.

We remained moored to the *Trinity* after fueling. That evening, just as I was about to turn in, I was told to go over to the *Holland* with Strouse, my shipfitter, for a rush job on a section of pipe. I cannot recall a darker night. The sky was overcast, and not a light was showing either ashore or on the ships. We set out in the whaleboat in the general direction of the *Holland,* and by inquiring from each ship as we passed we finally found her. When the job was finished we learned that the ship would soon be getting under way to leave Balikpapan, and we headed back to the *Pope* as fast as we could. In the darkness ahead of us we saw a destroyer under way, and before long Antrim's voice hailed us and told us to hook on for hoisting aboard.

The ship was at general quarters and had orders to patrol outside the minefield with other destroyers until the main units of our force sortied. By the time we secured from general quarters and set condition watches, it was my turn for the officer of the deck watch—the four to eight. It was this watch that caused me to lose my faith in coffee as a sleep preventative. Despite innumerable cups, I found myself beginning to doze standing up. The coffee had its effect in a different way, however, and at last I asked Captain Blinn to relieve me while I went below for a few minutes. The exercise of climbing back up to the bridge seemed to wake me completely, and I got through the rest of the watch without sleeping.

Our destination, we soon learned, was Makassar, on Celebes. No one on board ship knew of the place, but we found it mentioned in *Sailing Directions,* and a Java-China-Japan Line chart in the wardroom gave us its location. All day we passed logs and clumps of vegetation floating in the water. Some of the logs were large enough to damage our thin hull if we hit them.

At Makassar we had the boring duty of maintaining at anchor a sound watch against submarines. It was a Sunday, and several men asked about going ashore to church. Antrim was favorably disposed, but the probability of our getting under way at any moment made church unfeasible. The fact that so many of the men were interested in going to church seemed surprising, until I realized that many of them felt that they might be going into action at any time and wanted to make their peace while they had the opportunity.

Finally, Austin was sent ashore for necessary supplies. He returned with them, and a Dutch dictionary. Because he did not drink, we didn't have a chance to taste any good Dutch beer, but he did have a weakness for chocolate, and he brought back some excellent samples.

After a couple of days in Makassar, the *Pope* and the *Ford* were ordered back to Balikpapan to escort the *Marechal Joffre* to Surabaja, in Java. The ship, a French liner that had been operating from French Indochina, was taken over by the United States at the start of the war with Japan. In Balikpapan we refueled while the *Marechal Joffre*, with a change of plan, proceeded alone. We joined up with the *Boise* and headed for Surabaja.

We arrived off Surabaja the afternoon of December 24. After a short submarine scare during which Dutch ships dropped depth charges, we followed the *Boise* through the minefield. The trip in was tricky, for all we had to guide us (aside from following in the wake of the ship ahead) was an eight-inch by ten-inch photostatic chart of the minefield. It was night before we anchored a few miles from the main harbor area. This was the most un-Christmaslike Christmas I had ever spent. But at least we were not at sea.

The next morning we went alongside the dock to fuel. After a short conference with Chief Commissary Steward Wadley regarding a suitable Christmas dinner, I decided we had better see what we could get from our tender, USS *Black Hawk*, which was moored in the channel not far from us. The best we were offered were chickens and enough bread to give each man one slice (we had been out of bread for a week and had been using biscuits and hardtack as a substitute). Still, with a war going on we would have to expect a few inconveniences.

We had made a change in our system of serving food shortly after the war started. Previously, meals had been served in the crew's compartments, but the heat there and the practicality of keeping the men close to their stations brought about a change to a cafeteria style of serving. Most of the men ate topside, and the meals had the air of a picnic. I noticed that the men enjoyed their food more and that there was less waste. Breakage of china (an item hard to replace) was also reduced.

After fueling we tied up alongside the *Black Hawk* to commence a six-day overhaul. It was much needed, although it would be a poor stopgap for the navy yard overhaul we had missed. The *Black Hawk* personnel were not feeling friendly toward destroyers. None had been available to escort her when the war started, so the *Black Hawk* had had to rely on her own inadequate protection and maximum speed of ten knots in making her way through Makassar Straits. The lack of destroyer escort was considered an unfilial act toward a devoted mother.

Regarding the attitude that a mother ship often takes toward its ward, the avowed purpose of a tender is to take care of the ships assigned to it—this is its only excuse for being. The attitude some tenders eventually take is that these ships are a bother and must be given only the services and supplies that will not inconvenience the tender. As a result the tender tries to have as many jobs as possible done by the ships themselves, and supplies are provided only after much haggling.

Toward evening we learned that shore leave would be permitted with certain restrictions. Fisher and I were in the section allowed shore leave and lost no time in leaving. We hailed a cab and after some effort made our driver understand that our destination was the Orange Hotel; from *Black Hawk* sources we learned that this hotel was centrally located and was being used as U.S. Navy headquarters.

Between the port area and the main part of town was a section that seemed to consist mainly of bamboo huts. Along the roads were sheds—the local version of supermarkets. Scattered about were large earthen air raid shelters reinforced with bamboo; they were apparently designed to stop only splinters and fragments. Soldiers of the Netherlands East Indies (NEI) Army, with their tropical green uniforms, were stationed at points along the road. Their large numbers and smart dress seemed to indicate that the Japanese would find Java a hard nut to crack.

In town we saw Dutch and American uniforms; in fact, almost every Dutchman seemed to be in uniform. Most of the natives seemed involved in their normal occupations. The combination of war and Christmas produced a feeling that was not quite like the spirit of either.

The Orange Hotel proved to be substantial and comfortable looking—the same impression most Dutchmen give. Its European architecture had been modified to meet tropical conditions, and despite the outside heat, it was cool within.

We soon learned the rate of exchange and the best beer. The Dutch like good beer and plenty of it; as a result they do not bother with twelve-ounce bottles but use full-liter bottles. I had tasted Heineken beer a few years before and was not impressed, but now with a more mature taste and an ample supply I found myself raving about it. Woe to the *djongos* who tried to give me Anker Pils instead.

After we had been in the hotel awhile, Herb Kriloff joined us. With a careful look around for a possible eavesdropper, he proceeded to give us his latest estimate of the situation. Events in the Philippines were not favorable: Manila would probably fall soon. We had lost a lot more planes there than were indicated by news reports. Reinforcing the islands was out of the question. Pearl Harbor had apparently been a successful raid for the Japanese in spite of our own reports. We would have to fight a delaying battle, trying to hold what little we could until an offensive could be launched.

Because Herb had always approached problems realistically, I agreed with his opinions. But there was little we could do but await the course of events—which meant having another beer to help time fly. Later we went into the dining room for a meal that was remarkable only in the number of turbaned Javanese serving it.

At Chez Willi, a small nightclub, I learned after trying to order beer in German that German was banned in Java. (Because Dutch and German are related languages, most Dutchmen speak German; but when Germany invaded the Netherlands, the language naturally became unpopular.) I was angered by the way in which the local ban was brought to my attention. The mentality behind such a ban is similar to the one that banned the teaching of German in American schools in 1917 (and changed the word *sauerkraut* to *liberty cabbage*).

I thought bitterly of the fact that the Dutch in Holland had played with the Germans until the last minute, and the invasion had come before British and French troops were allowed to take proper positions in Holland. The Dutch resistance had been seriously weakened by Dutch fifth columnists aiding German agents, and the ensuing German march through the lowlands came close to ending the war then and there.

I returned to the ship that night with a feeling that the U.S. Navy was not particularly welcome in Java. Incidents related to me by enlisted men the following morning strengthened my belief. Several men had been asked why they had come to Java, the inference being that the war was going on in the Philippines and the U.S. Navy should have remained there. When some Dutchmen went so far as to suggest that our ships had withdrawn out of cowardice, our men answered with swinging fists.

On other occasions our enlisted men supplied the provocation. One American seaman walked into a bar and proclaimed to the assemblage in general: "You Dutchmen can relax now—the American navy is here to protect you." On the other hand, I attended a pleasant dinner party at the Simpang Club, a private club in Surabaja, with an attractive Dutch girl who spoke English well (as did most of the educated Dutch). Because of the war in Holland she had been unable to complete her university training there and was now teaching high school science in Surabaja.

Our week alongside the tender went quickly. At the end of our overhaul we were supposedly ready to give battle with maximum efficiency. When we got under way to leave Surabaja, we were informed that our destination was Darwin, Australia.

We learned upon arriving at Darwin that several Japanese submarines had been sunk off the entrance to the harbor. The news was a definite boost to morale. Most of the reports up to this time had been depressing, so it was good to know that the Japanese had at last suffered losses.

Never before had Darwin harbor seen so many ships at anchor at one time. The tiny pier near the cluster of houses that made up the town seemed inadequate for the transport unloading there. The flat terrain surrounding the harbor was depressing, or perhaps it was just the heat off the semidesert hinterland that made it seem that way. Obviously all Darwin could offer was a relatively safe anchorage. The question of a suitable operating base for the Asiatic Fleet remained unsettled.

While we were anchored, the minesweeper *Heron* stood in. En route from Manila she had been under attack for several hours by Japanese bombers and torpedo planes, which she repelled after damaging and possibly shooting down several Japanese planes. But about half of the *Heron*'s crew had been killed or wounded. As the *Heron* passed the stern of the *Houston,* cheers went up from the cruiser saluting the courage of the crew of that tiny minesweeper. The other ships in the harbor joined in as the *Heron* continued to her anchorage.

Later we fueled from a British tanker in the harbor. The *Houston* was fueling from the same tanker, and C. D. Smith invited me aboard for lunch. The fare aboard the *Houston* was decidedly superior to the *Pope*'s; a destroyer does not have food storage and preparation facilities comparable to those of a large ship. Aside from the food, I was envious of the new quadruple mounts of 1.1-inch antiaircraft guns that the *Houston* had received in Cavite a few weeks before the war. One such mount was about the equal of all our antiaircraft defense. (We had a 3-inch .25-caliber gun on our fantail, but anyone familiar with the gun and its position can attest to its general ineffectiveness.)

The next morning we left Darwin with the *Marblehead* and some destroyers escorting the *Bloemfontein,* a Dutch ship being used to transport U.S. troops. We expected to go all the way to Java with the *Bloemfontein,* but after a few hours the *Pope* and most of the other destroyers received a change of orders from the *Marblehead.* The *Bloemfontein* continued on to Java escorted by a couple of destroyers. Sending American troops into Java seemed to indicate an attempt to strengthen the Netherlands East Indies (Indonesia) because it was now impossible to reinforce the Philippines.

Our destination turned out to be Kupang, on Timor. This island not far from Australia is owned partly by the Dutch and partly by the Portuguese. Just before the beginning of the war, Japan had made arrangements with Portugal to establish a commercial airfield on the island. The actual activities of the Japanese went farther than the airdrome, and there was evidence that a large submarine base was being prepared. With the outbreak of the war, the Dutch took over the entire island despite Portuguese protests. The Australians sent in troops to defend the island against possible Japanese attack; it would be an ideal jumping-off place for an invasion of Australia.

Our stay at Kupang was brief. A submarine alert livened things up a bit, and the strong possibility that the presence of our force had been reported caused us to get under way before dawn the next day.

For about a week we dodged in and out of the islands, hoping to avoid detection by Japanese reconnaissance planes. The scenery was incomparable, the weather was clear, and the sea was a deep blue. In passing through one of the straits among the islands we found ourselves surrounded by an enormous school of porpoises; the sea seemed to be packed with them. At night we occasionally saw the glow of volcanoes.

Meanwhile we had joined up with the *Boise* and her destroyers. We were now a fair-sized striking force of two light cruisers and about seven destroyers. One evening when we went alongside the *Boise* to refuel, we heard the rumor that we would set out the next day to attack a Japanese force coming from the north.

The *Boise* was known to the crew as the "Reluctant Dragon" because her skipper had objected to remaining with the Asiatic Fleet when the war started. Supposedly Admiral Hart requested that more cruisers be assigned his command. This request was not granted, so the admiral refused to detach the *Boise,* which had come to Manila as a convoy escort before the start of the war. Though she was on her way back to Pearl Harbor when the war broke out, she was still technically under Admiral Hart's command. The captain of the *Boise* tried vigorously to have his ship detached but received a firm no.

The next day we were steaming north in a cruising formation. Antrim, our executive officer, called the crew together and gave them a brief description of our plan of attack and what to expect. We were heading for Kema, a town on Celebes near Menado. A Japanese landing force had arrived in that vicinity, and we were going in to knock off as many transports as possible. The *Boise* and *Marblehead* would take care of any heavy opposition. It would be a night attack, and we would have a fair chance of getting out safely. Just in case, however, we were urged to prepare personal abandon-ship kits (matches, medicine, money, and so forth) to be used if the ship was sunk and we were able to get ashore. Apparently it would be a long swim or walk back to Allied territory.

This information was not exactly cheering. Not a man on the ship had been in battle before. There were many thoughtful countenances about the ship, and more than a couple of Bibles were dug up from the bottoms of seabags.

After nearly twenty-four hours steaming toward our objective, we received a signal to reverse course and increase speed. This seemed to be a strange order; then we learned that the Japanese force had already left Kema and was now southwest of us at Kendari, on Celebes. Having a superior force in a position to cut us off from our base was not a pleasant state of affairs. Broad daylight eliminated our advantage of surprise, and if sighted we would have to fight a difficult withdrawal.

Scouting planes launched by the *Boise* to warn of a Japanese force served to relieve our anxiety. Later as we passed through a string of islands, a scouting plane dived toward the water directly ahead of the cruiser. Then the *Boise* stopped in the water. By the time she was moving again, we had the story: the *Boise* had grazed an uncharted coral head in the straits and sustained extensive damage. The pilot of the plane had attempted to warn his ship of the coral head by diving toward it, but the ship did not respond quickly enough.

The force proceeded to a landlocked bay in one of the smaller islands of the archipelago and anchored. The captains of all ships were called to a conference, and as soon as our captain returned we got under way with the destroyers *Ford, Parrott,* and *Paul Jones.* The *Boise* would have to be repaired before she could go into action, which meant she would have to leave the NEI, there being no base here with facilities to handle her. Everyone on board the *Pope* was glum. Without a battle, our force had lost the use of its most powerful unit. We felt let down from being ready to go into action and having the attack called off. Our new assignment was to proceed to the Postillion Islands and patrol in that vicinity until further notice.

On the morning of January 21 the four destroyers of our group were patrolling when an interisland steamer was sighted. We challenged the ship and were surprised to receive snappy signals in return. In the semaphore exchange that followed we learned that the crew of one of our submarines was aboard the steamer. The submarine had gone aground near Makassar, on Celebes, and after several unsuccessful attempts to float her she had been blown up to prevent possible capture by the Japanese. We escorted the steamer for a couple of hours.

Visibility this morning was poor, and the frequent rain squalls gave way to steady wind and rain. The gun crews on deck were drenched and looked miserable. In the forenoon we received a radio message, and just as we finished decoding it, a signal from the *Ford* formed the destroyers into a column. The message reported a heavy concentration of Japanese ships at Balikpapan. The *Pope, Ford, Parrott,* and *Paul Jones* were ordered to attack the force at night and withdraw to Surabaja. The *Marblehead* and two destroyers would support our group, and we were to rendezvous with them after the attack. Our orders were to save our torpedoes for the larger ships and, after expending torpedoes, attack with gunfire.

When this news got around the ship, excitement ran high. There was a different feeling from the time we set out for Kema. Now everyone felt that at last we were going to get into action, and that the battle itself would probably be a lot easier than waiting for something to happen.

Our column headed north, making twenty-five knots into stiff winds and rough seas. Spray swept over the *Pope* constantly, and now and then a wall of water would crash down on the forecastle. A sheet of water hit the bridge structure, knocking out all the windows and drenching everything not under cover.

The rain continued most of the day. Although we had cursed it earlier, we were now praying that it would continue. As long as the weather remained inhospitable, Japanese planes would not be out to spot us. Our only chance for success in this attack was to arrive at Balikpapan unheralded.

Toward evening the rain stopped and the sea grew calmer as we advanced farther into Makassar Straits. This change was to my personal advantage: I had the deck for the first dog watch and managed to stay dry throughout it.

A message sent by a navy patrol plane reported four Japanese cruisers of a class similar to the *Marblehead* headed north. It did not take us long to figure out who the four "cruisers" were. The plane had apparently taken our four destroyers for cruisers and, knowing that there was only one cruiser of the *Marblehead* type in these waters, assumed we were Japanese. (At a distance the old flush-deck destroyer with its four stacks looked much like a cruiser of the *Marblehead* type, which also had stacks and a flush deck.) The fact that one of our planes was out on patrol meant that Japanese planes might also be out. We were happy to see night approaching,

After the evening meal I tried to get some rest; our plans called for general quarters at eleven, and there would be little sleep the remainder of the night. For several hours I rolled and tossed on the transom in the darkened wardroom but did not sleep. The rush of the water against the ship's hull was background music for my random thoughts—every possible calamity that could befall the ship, how I would react under fire, and what our chances would be of survival. By the time the general alarm sounded, I was more than ready to go to my station and get the whole thing over with, come what may.

On deck the men were hurrying to their stations. The traffic was not heavy because most of the men stayed close to their stations even off watch. I made my way to the bridge, climbed to the fire control platform over the bridge, and waited for the lookout to come down from the crow's nest so I could take my station.

In the crow's nest I tried to make myself as comfortable as possible, but the bulky kapok life jacket did not permit much freedom of movement. My job was to spot our shell fire and give corrections to range and deflection as necessary. Because I would not be needed for this task until late in the engagement, after all torpedoes had been expended, my immediate job was battle lookout: I was to report the sighting of ships, lights, land, and so forth.

Our speed was back up to twenty-five knots again, and as we steamed along in column astern of the *Ford,* with the *Parrott* and the *Paul Jones* astern of us, our wakes were startlingly bright. The ships appeared as dark masses—hard to see at any distance over a few thousand yards. The sky was still overcast, and visibility in general was poor.

I reported a glow on the horizon ahead of us to the bridge and was informed that it was probably one of the ships bombed by Allied planes earlier in the day. The radio had reported air raids on Japanese ship concentrations near Balikpapan.

We altered course to the left, putting us on the last leg of our journey. Ahead of us the air became increasingly hazy, and the sky overhead grew darker. When we saw flames in the distance we realized that the oil installations and wells at Balikpapan had been set afire. The haze had been caused by the smoke from the fires. A tremendous amount of oil must have been burning, for the clouds of smoke filled the sky for miles around. As we advanced toward Balikpapan the visibility improved, but the canopy of smoke hung over us, lending a sinister touch to the proceedings. We seemed cut off from the rest of the world as we approached a misplaced corner of Hell.

Suddenly, ships loomed ahead of us, and before long we were among them. We passed close aboard an escort type of vessel that was either lying to or at anchor. As one of the crew aptly put it, we could have hit the ship by throwing spuds at her. She was too small for us to waste a torpedo; besides, we did not want to reveal our presence until we'd had a chance at some of the larger ships.

None of the ships challenged us. Either the watch on board were asleep or they mistook us for Japanese destroyers patrolling the area. We continued deeper into the Japanese anchorage. I kept peering into the night for large ships. Not sighting any, I began to wonder if we had been wise in passing up the smaller vessels.

It seemed like hours since we had entered the area. At this rate, I thought, it will be dawn before we get anything done, and then we'll never get away from here. Just at that moment there was a flash ahead of us, and a great mushroom of flame leaped hundreds of feet into the air. My first reaction was to curse the Dutch for picking this moment to blow up more oil wells, but the light from the fire revealed the outlines of a ship, and I realized that our force had scored its first hit. I later learned from someone who had been stationed on the bridge that the *Ford* had reported over the TBS (voice radio) the sighting of the ship, and Commander Talbot on the *Ford* had given orders to commence firing with torpedoes.

The explosion caused a stir among the Japanese. Recognition lights were turned on aboard all the Japanese ships. In rapid succession our destroyers fired broadsides of torpedoes where the concentration of lights seemed heaviest. This point was a fair distance off, and we never knew exactly what the result was.

The attack had reached the point when our identity would soon be apparent to the Japanese, and we fired our remaining torpedoes at the nearest targets regardless of size. One of them appeared to be a destroyer, and it was sinking.

With the *Pope*'s torpedoes expended, Captain Blinn gave the order to stand by to commence firing with our 4-inch battery. Wilson, our gunnery officer, told me to pick out a target for the guns, and I chose a small ship on our starboard bow. The range was about two thousand yards and closing rapidly. The guns were trained on the target, and the captain gave the gunnery officer the order to commence firing.

At this moment the *Ford* stopped suddenly. To avoid ramming her, the *Pope* swung out of the column to port, which placed the *Ford* squarely in front of our guns trained on the starboard bow. I frantically yelled into my phones to prevent our firing on the *Ford*. Wilson came back with the reassuring answer that although he had received the order to commence firing, he had not yet passed the word to the guns.

Just before all this had happened, the *Ford* was heading a little to the right of what appeared to be the bow of a large ship sticking out of the water. The ship we had picked for a target was heading toward this wreckage, which we assumed was the result of one of the torpedo salvos from our force. The *Ford* was rapidly approaching a cul-de-sac, for other Japanese ships were crossing ahead of her. This we later decided was the reason for the *Ford*'s unexpected maneuvers.

Meanwhile the *Pope* swung around to the left and, picking up another target, commenced firing. We got two salvos into the ship when the combination of high speed and short range made it impossible for the guns to bear on the target. Our first salvo hit the after part of the ship, and I spotted in deflection to bring the bridge structure of the ship under fire. (Our point of aim was actually the bridge structure, but either our guns could not keep up with the rapid change of bearing or our primitive fire control instruments were not designed to cope with unusual situations such as this.) Our second salvo was better placed but still needed a deflection spot. The results of our firing were not spectacular, but we knew we had hit and done damage.

Until now the Japanese had not opened fire. The flashes from our guns gave them their first indication of our position, but the fact that we were in the midst of their ships gave them a poor target. There was some gunfire from the Japanese ships, but nothing landed near the *Pope*. Looking back toward the *Ford* we saw her mixing it up with some Japanese ships. Because it would have been impossible to rejoin the *Ford* without getting into her line of fire, the *Pope* continued operating alone. The *Parrott* and the *Paul Jones*, when I had a chance to look astern, had disappeared in the gloom. We had probably lost them when we swung out of line to avoid the *Ford*. We picked up another target and managed to get off two salvos.

We were finally getting the knack of training our guns on a target almost directly ahead of us to give us time to get off as many salvos as possible before the target dropped astern of us. Just as we were getting used to this, the *Pope* altered course to seaward, and word came over the phones that we were withdrawing. The gun crews remained ready at the guns, and all hands not otherwise occupied were told to keep a sharp lookout in all directions.

The familiar outline of one of our destroyers was sighted ahead of us, and we joined up with the *Parrott*. A little later the *Paul Jones* overtook us and fell in column. At least three of the four destroyers were still afloat. We wondered what had happened to the *Ford*. Fires were still burning behind us, but there were no flashes of gunfire. Then the *Ford* came steaming up on our starboard hand. We'd had phenomenal luck: the *Ford* had received slight damage from a 3-inch shell, and the *Pope, Parrott,* and *Paul Jones* escaped without a scratch.

The sky was growing light, and we suddenly realized we had been up all night and were tired. The important thing at the moment was to leave the area before any Japanese ships came out to pursue us. In full daylight the battle might be less one sided. As the force was building up speed, the engineering plant of the *Pope* suffered a casualty, limiting our speed to twelve knots. The rest of the force slowed to stay with us, and our engineers worked feverishly to make repairs.

We received orders to secure from general quarters and set condition watches. As I came down from my station, I noticed how drawn and tense the men looked. Most of the gun crews were covered with soot from the guns, and the ship looked as if it had not been cleaned in months. Word soon came from the engineers that the casualty had been repaired and high speed could be resumed.

At about 0700 we sighted the *Marblehead* and her two escorting destroyers. It was a relief to have their company for the voyage back to Surabaja. With four destroyers without torpedoes and the ships' crews greatly fatigued, we would have been easy pickings for a Japanese naval force. But with the *Marblehead* and two "fresh" destroyers accompanying us, our chances of survival would be greatly improved. Our vulnerability to air attack was still to be considered, however, and our only defense would be to get back to Java as quickly as possible. But there was another difficulty: our fuel supply was low, precluding the maintenance of high speed for the entire run. The engineering officer had all fuel tanks sounded, and he computed the best speed we could make for the amount of fuel on hand—about seventeen knots.

After joining up with the *Marblehead,* all hands except the anti-aircraft defense crews (machine-gun crews and the crew for the 3-inch .25-caliber gun) and those people actually on watch were secured. Breakfast was served, and the ship began to take on a more normal aspect. After breakfast most of the ship's complement turned in for a much-needed sleep. As luck would have it, it was my turn for the forenoon watch (eight to twelve). I spent most of the watch looking for aircraft. Keeping station in the formation was done loosely—a smart appearance was not a major consideration right now.

The division commander asked for a report from each of the four destroyers regarding the number of enemy ships sunk or damaged. The final composite report indicated that from six to eight enemy ships had been sunk and a large number damaged. The task of determining damage inflicted in a night action is always difficult. In our case the enemy losses may well have been greater—or fewer. (Subsequent information revealed that our estimates were conservative, if anything.)

When the sun set that evening we knew we were safe, for not a plane or ship had been sighted all day. Java was now less than two hundred miles away, and we would arrive off the entrance to Surabaja early the next morning.

I was halfway through my watch the next morning when Java was sighted. By the time I was relieved we were preparing to enter the channel into Surabaja harbor. In fresh uniforms and cleanly shaven, the crew looked as if they had just finished a practice exercise at sea. The tension was gone from their faces and most of the talk was about liberty in Surabaja.

By ten o'clock we were tied up alongside the Dutch naval barracks pier. Liberty did not commence immediately for there was a lot of work to do. First we had to refuel. Working parties were required to bring supplies aboard. The gunner's mates and their strikers were busy cleaning the guns and getting them ready to fire again. The engineers were pulling apart pumps and air compressors and renewing valves so that we would not have a repeat of the casualty we had at Balikpapan. Stagings were rigged over the sides so a much-needed coat of paint could be applied. We did not know how soon we would have to go to sea again and were trying to make the most of our time in port to get the ship back in condition. Captain Blinn had gone ashore to a conference of commanding officers to report to Admiral Hart on the battle. He and Antrim had been busy all morning getting together the information for the report.

That afternoon Admiral Doorman, the senior Dutch admiral afloat, came down to the pier and stood gazing at the four dingy-looking destroyers tied up there. His facial expressions seemed to reveal his thoughts: are these four obsolete ships the same ones that fought the Japanese forces at Balikpapan? It is impossible.

A little later he was joined by Admiral Hart and Admiral Glassford, and they visited informally each of the four destroyers. Admiral Hart, who had a reputation for being stern and forbidding, was smiling and looked in an affable mood. After all, the plan for the night attack had been his, and it was more successful than he had hoped.

Liberty was granted later that afternoon, but before allowing the men ashore, Antrim called them together and passed on instructions that no mention of the battle was to be made in public. Antrim and the rest of us were somewhat surprised a few moments later when we turned on the radio in the wardroom and heard a Dutch announcer broadcasting in English a summary of the battle. (The enlisted men, when they came back aboard that evening, told us that the first Dutchmen they had met ashore had wanted to know if they were from the ships that fought at Balikpapan. It must have been disappointing to the sailors and baffling to the Dutchmen when the sailors had to reply: "We have orders not to discuss the battle.")

Apparently there had been a mix-up in the higher echelons. Unquestionably the news of the battle had to be broadcast as soon as possible because it was the first victory for the anti-Axis forces since the beginning of the war with Japan, and a boost to morale was badly needed. It was unfair to the personnel of the ships to order them not to discuss a subject that was rapidly becoming common knowledge, but the object of silencing the ship's complements was probably to prevent information from reaching the Japanese regarding the location of our naval units. (Fifth-column activity in Java was well organized and was abetted by the native Javanese who had not learned to love their Dutch masters.)

We had also tuned in Radio Tokyo to hear what reports the Japanese would have about our action. They completely denied that an action had even taken place. I could not follow the reasoning behind this type of propaganda, unless the desire was to make the people at home doubt our reports. The entire Makassar Straits action lasted three days—air raids by Dutch and American planes the day preceding our surface attack and air raids for the two days following. Dutch and American submarines were in the area the entire time. The final results indicated that about thirty-four Japanese ships had been sunk or badly damaged in the three days.

The attitude of the Dutch in Surabaja had become much more hospitable since our previous visit in December when we had come down from the Philippines. The success of our naval action had much to do with that, but another point was the proximity of the war. Surabaja had already received its first air raid.

While our four destroyers were still alongside the pier, I went over to the *Ford* to see what damage had been done by the 3-inch shell hit she had received at Balikpapan. Burned paint was about all that was visible, but one of the men told me that the auxiliary radio gear in the after deckhouse was ruined. A signalman who had been transferred before the war to the *Ford* from the *Pope* was among the few casualties. When I saw him on deck and asked him where he had been wounded, he seemed annoyed and embarrassed. He finally said that he had trouble sitting down. The signal gang from the *Pope* had already been to see him and ride him about getting his "fat duff" in the way.

Also tied up to the same pier were some of our old type of submarines. "Harry Dog" Forbes, a classmate from the naval academy who was assigned to one of the submarines, invited me aboard. His submarine had recently returned from a patrol in the Lingayen Gulf and had had bad luck on that run. Whenever the submarine had fired a torpedo, severe depth charge attacks from Japanese destroyers followed. A battery explosion followed one of these attacks. (Saltwater mixing with battery acid produces a gas that, in proper concentration in air, results in an explosive mixture.) I wondered how the submarine had been able to make the long trip back to Surabaja. A rest camp for submarine crews had been established in the mountains near Surabaja, and there was no doubt that this crew needed it.

The Dutch naval barracks on the pier had a beer canteen. As soon as the crew heard about it, the ship's work suffered a setback—and so did the beer stock. By periodically clearing our men out of the canteen we managed to keep a fair proportion of the crew at their jobs. Liberty was granted later for a quarter of the crew. Enlisted men's liberty started early in the afternoon and expired early in the evening. Officers' shore leave began when the enlisted men's liberty expired; officers had to be back aboard ship before midnight. This arrangement left much to be desired. In order to give all hands one liberty, the ship would have to be in port at least four days, and even then the liberty amounted to only a few hours. (Our stay in port was always indefinite, and the ship remained on twelve hours'—or less— notice at all times.)

Most of the enlisted men would return from liberty with shopping bags bulging with chocolates, cakes, fried chicken, and other food. Because it was unlikely that the officer of the deck would inspect the entire bag, a few bottles of beer or stronger drinks were also carried aboard. (This I learned after the beer had long since been consumed.)

When my turn for shore leave came around, I went ashore with Jack Fisher. Our first stop was the Orange Hotel, which was being used as a headquarters for U.S. Navy personnel on duty ashore in Surabaja. We had heard that Chuck Osborne, a classmate of Jack's in supply corps school, had arrived by submarine from the Philippines and was staying at the hotel.

Chuck had his usual cheery greeting and an amusing story for us. Shortly after his arrival in Surabaja, the city had its first bombing raid. At the time of the raid Chuck and another officer just down from Manila were having a drink at one of the bars in town. When the air raid siren sounded, he and his friend dived under the nearest table, taking their drinks with them. This procedure brought forth hearty laughs from the Dutchmen seated in the bar. A few minutes later bombs started to drop on the city, and the Dutchmen dashed out of the bar for the nearest air raid shelter. Not so Osborne and friend; they merely shifted their position from under the table to behind the bar, and at frequent intervals refilled their glasses. When the air raid was over they were the only American "casualties" in Surabaja.

Chuck, who had been quite a man about town in Manila, lost no time in adjusting to his new surroundings in Surabaja. When I asked him to get me a date for that night, he gave me the telephone number of a girl who he assured me was "terrific." He and Fisher left before I had a chance to call. When I did call I had the wrong number and couldn't check again with Chuck. I'm still wondering what the girl looked like. Then I called the girl whom I had met during our stay in Surabaja at Christmas. Her parents would not let her go out that night, or so she said.

Feeling dejected, I made my way to the Tabarin nightclub; I hoped that the music and gaiety would cheer me. I met Les Geer, whom I had not seen since 1938 when he resigned from the naval academy. He had gone to Pensacola for flight training after leaving the academy and was now a PBY pilot. He had been at Pearl Harbor when the Japanese made their raid, and he told me that our losses there, although not as severe as the Japanese had reported, were more serious than our own report indicated. His squadron had come out to reinforce Patrol Wing 10, the PBY group that had been stationed in the Philippines and was now operating from Java. The PBYs were being used on what amounted to suicide missions; no fighter protection was available for them. So far we had lost a large part of our small force, but fortunately most of the plane crews had been rescued. (Frank Ralston, another classmate from the naval academy, had his plane shot down near Jolo in the Philippines, but with the help of Moros he made his way back by water and land to the Netherlands East Indies. However, he had to spend a few weeks in a hospital before going back to duty.)

Geer wanted to hear about our battle at Balikpapan, so I gave him the story as I had seen it. Later we joined Captain Robinson, commanding officer of the USS *Marblehead,* who asked me a lot of questions about the attack and expressed great disappointment that the *Marblehead* had been unable to take part in the shooting.

After the captain left to return to his ship and Geer was dancing with one of the hostesses, Antrim and Bassett arrived. They invited me to join the party at their table, and in a short time things were going at a merry clip. Every so often one of us would telephone the ship to find out if there was any need for our immediate return. In this way we added a few hours to our scanty shore leave.

One morning the *President Polk* arrived in Surabaja bringing troops and supplies from the States. That afternoon all destroyers were told to send over working parties for fresh meat. I went with our ship's cooks, partly out of curiosity and partly to see that we received everything that was due us.

The troops were still aboard, lining up for chow with mess kits in hand. This seemed strange on board ship, but there was probably no other cooking equipment provided. I was down in the cold rooms for a while; at first the change from the Java heat was pleasant, but the chill soon became uncomfortable. After some delay we managed to get our meat topside for transfer to our boat.

While we were waiting for this final maneuver, I asked a steward if there was any chance of getting some of the magazines I had seen about the ship. He looked at my naval uniform and asked, "Are you from one of those little old four-stacker tin cans?" I nodded. "Well, you can have all the magazines you can carry off this ship. We made this trip all alone and the only other ships we saw were the two tin cans that picked us up last week and stayed with us until we got here. We never saw two nicer looking ships."

I did not see him again until just before the *Pope* was ready to shove off. He handed me a pile of magazines and said: "Take good care of those little tin cans."

The *Pope* remained in Surabaja only a few days longer. We left in company with the *Ford* and two Dutch merchant vessels. Our orders were to proceed to Port Darwin via Lombok Straits to rejoin the main group of the Asiatic Fleet. We escorted the merchantmen more or less out of convenience.

At night the *Pope* would take a position well to the rear while the *Ford* remained with the other two vessels. This was an antisubmarine measure; our slow speed would have made it possible for a submarine to overtake the ships by running on the surface. Our job on the *Pope* was to see that this did not happen.

Ordinarily it would not have been too difficult to make out the black masses of the ships several miles ahead, but shortly before midnight a thunderstorm forced us to close up to within a few thousand yards of the convoy. Fortunately we did not encounter any enemy submarines while we were with the ships. The next day, however, one of the Dutch ships developed trouble with her steering gear and performed some erratic maneuvers. On one occasion the ship could steam only in circles, and we were forced to steam around her using our sound gear to detect any submarines that might be in the vicinity. Finally the Dutch ship got on course again, and shortly thereafter we received orders by radio to rendezvous with a group of our ships about midway to Darwin. We gathered from the message that most of our ships were leaving Darwin to return to Java. This time, however, the base would be Tjilatjap and not Surabaja. The *Ford* ordered the Dutch ships to proceed independently, and the *Pope* fell in astern of the *Ford* as she set course for the rendezvous point.

Wilson, our gunnery officer, began to complain of a "boil" on his back. The boil was actually an enormous carbuncle. We had no doctor aboard, but Hyde, the pharmacist's mate, did an excellent job of lancing. The carbuncle was teacup size, and it drained enough to fill several such cups. I had read that carbuncles can be fatal. After seeing Wilson's back and noticing his greatly weakened condition, I could understand how a person with low vitality could succumb. Wilson attributed the carbuncle to the Japanese food he had eaten for three years in Tokyo while he was a language student. (He had been aboard the *Pope* less than four months, having joined her immediately after leaving Japan.) He was very weak for a fortnight, and the wound was not completely healed until months later.

Wilson did not pick a good time to have his carbuncle. We were in the Indian Ocean; the sea was rough, and the *Pope* pitched and rolled endlessly. When Wilson went on the sick list, Jack Fisher relinquished his stateroom on the main deck, which was cooler and airier than the other staterooms on the ship. The room was also larger than the others because Fisher, being paymaster, had to have a large safe in his room. Wilson at least had a relatively comfortable recovery.

After several days steaming we sighted the force we were to join—the *Holland, Black Hawk,* and *Pecos* escorted by destroyers. The *Ford* and the *Pope* took station on the screen around the tenders. The next day we fueled from the *Pecos* while under way.

Fueling under way is often a tricky operation. The tanker and the vessel being fueled steam side by side at about ten knots (high speeds are not unusual; the choice of speed is governed by the circumstances). The distance between the two vessels varies constantly, but an effort is made to keep the distance steady at about fifty feet. Manila lines passed between the ships are used to help hold the ships together. The fuel line, a heavy corrugated rubber pipe, is passed over as soon as the riding lines are made fast. The great weight of the fuel line, especially when fuel oil is in it, requires special lines and booms to support it. Once the fuel line is secured and the oil starts to flow through it, both ships must be handled with great skill. The tanker must maintain a steady course and speed, and the destroyer tries to keep abreast of the tanker at a constant distance. This requires minute changes of rudder and speed, care being taken not to make any sudden changes. When the operation is not properly performed, the usual result is a parted fuel line, with a consequent bath of oil for both ships. Captain Blinn was an excellent ship handler; with the *Pope*'s well-coordinated detail for this operation, he made the entire maneuver seem simple.

Just as we finished fueling, one of the ships in the formation hoisted an emergency signal indicating enemy aircraft. Immediately the force executed the proper scatter plan to present a poor target. No planes materialized, however, and the ships re-formed, thankful that it had been a false alarm. Someone had been unduly influenced by the report of the *Houston* and *Marblehead* bombing.

When we arrived at Tjilatjap a day or so later, the larger units entered the harbor while the destroyers patrolled off the entrance. Toward evening we were allowed into the harbor. The channel was narrow and had a ninety-degree turn just past the entrance. This sharp turn and the thick foliage on the banks had concealed any view of the harbor from seaward. We were amazed to see the large number of ships jammed into this limited area.

The *Holland* was moored in midchannel upstream of pairs of merchant ships. An American destroyer was in a small floating dry dock that had been used to repair the *Marblehead,* which was now tied up to a wharf. The *Houston* was not in the harbor; I had seen her outside while we were waiting to go in. Although her number three turret was useless, she still had her two forward turrets (three 8-inch guns each) and still looked capable of dealing a few heavy blows. We went alongside the *Black Hawk,* which was moored close to the bank upstream of the main port area. The *Asheville,* a gunboat, was moored upstream of the *Black Hawk.* Small docks dug out of the marshy banks served the Dutch PBYs (Catalina flying boats).

This was the first time we had been alongside the *Black Hawk* since our overhaul in Surabaja during Christmas week, and we received a hearty welcome. We knew the reason: as long as the destroyers were out fighting, the *Black Hawk* would be safe.

While we were having our overhaul, a message came through confirming our skipper's award of the Navy Cross. The commanding officer of the 29th Destroyer Squadron read off the citation and made a few remarks to the assembled crew of the *Pope.* Upon completion of this "ceremony," Captain Blinn turned to the crew and said: "This Navy Cross has been awarded to me, but I want you all to feel that it belongs to you as well. A note will be made on your records to the effect that you were serving on this ship during the action for which this award was made."

After we had been in port a few days, we were permitted to send liberty parties ashore. The town was small and more "native" than

Surabaja. I took my crepe-soled sports shoes ashore and had them resoled in an Indian cobbler shop. Then I shopped around for white socks but could find only small sizes. My next stop was the local club, where the supply of Heineken beer was not yet exhausted. At the club were Dutch merchant marine officers playing billiards and drinking. Later, Dr. Connell, Commander Newsom—skipper of the *Otus*—and other officers from the *Otus* came in for drinks. I went over to speak to Commander Newsom and Jimmy Connell; I had come to Manila with them on the *President Grant*. They told me about the close call the *Otus* had had when Cavite was bombed. The *Otus* had been a Luckenback Line freighter that the navy took over in 1941 to convert to a submarine tender. The conversion was nearing completion when the war began. The *Otus* had been close enough to one bomb burst to get her bow riddled by bomb splinters.

In return for these details I gave a play-by-play description of our action at Balikpapan. In all our conversation, the talk touched only briefly on the *Marblehead* and the *Houston*. Somehow we did not want to talk about them. (The *Marblehead* was tied up just forward of the *Otus* and was a constant reminder of what happens to ships without aircraft support—and our aircraft support was becoming less evident by the day.)

The fall of Singapore was imminent. The Malayan campaign had apparently been a constant retreat. It had even been suggested that the British had sent out the Dunkirk Harriers to compete in the Singapore Handicap. Our own troops in the Philippines were holding out in Bataan. We puffed up a bit because our troops were putting up the best show against the Japanese, but in our hearts we knew the situation was hopeless. By the time we built a base with the proper supplies and sufficient troops to relieve the Philippines, the islands would be lost. This was not defeatist talk; it was cold logic. We still had a job to do though: we could try to hold back the Japanese as long as possible so that a secondary defense could be prepared. Meanwhile any loss to the Japanese we felt would mean more than a similar loss to us, for Japanese industry could not match our production.

I went back to the ship for dinner. The only decent restaurant in Tjilatjap was hard pressed to supply its regular patrons, and we had been asked to avoid eating there. The food on board ship was generally good (as the commissary officer I can't very well say otherwise). Our greatest drawback was the antiquated refrigerator box. Fresh meat if received well frozen could be kept in the box two weeks at most. Some meat we had received in Surabaja during our first visit there had lasted only a few days and had to be thrown overboard.

The weather in Tjilatjap was warm and sticky, but we did not mind the discomfort. Being in port gave the crew a chance to relax while many repairs and overhauls were being made to the *Pope*'s aged equipment.

One night Fisher, Spears, and I went over to the *Tjitalingka,* a Dutch liner moored in the stream. I could not understand why this ship and the other merchantmen were just sitting in the harbor, unless it was because the *Tjitalingka* had aboard the only good liquor in the area. The modern, air-conditioned cocktail lounge was a pleasant change from the *Pope*'s stuffy wardroom.

We ordered drinks and surveyed the room. Besides the regular passengers, some of our submarine officers were living on board while their ships were being overhauled alongside the *Holland.* Across the room we noticed an attractive girl sitting by herself. We were about to draw lots to see who would have the first chance to meet her when she was joined by two other girls. We sent over one of Bill Spears's cards with a note asking the young ladies to join us. The reply was: "Why don't you join us?"

In no time we were sitting at their table exchanging small talk. The girls were sisters who had just arrived from Singapore. Their father was the Swiss consul there and he was staying on in that city. The girls had left a few days before the fall of the city and proceeded by ship to Batavia and then to Tjilatjap by train. They expected to go to New Zealand on the *Tjitalingka* and from there to the United States. They spoke English fluently but with a slight British accent.

The pleasant evening was interrupted at midnight when the whaleboat from the *Pope* returned to pick us up. It was discouraging to have our acquaintance begin and end in the same evening, but we were scheduled to get under way the next day. Where we would go was a matter of conjecture.

4

When Singapore fell on February 15, it was no surprise. But it made everyone realize the seriousness of the situation in the Far East. The question in every mind was: how long before the attack on Java?

One of the immediate effects of Singapore's surrender was to make available to us a shipment of fruit consigned to that city; it was aboard one of the ships in the harbor. Jake Britt from the *Asheville* signed for the crates for all the U.S. ships because the regular supply officers could not find a rule authorizing them to make the purchase.

The next day we received orders to rendezvous with a Dutch force under Admiral Doorman; it was off the entrance to Tjilatjap. Late in the afternoon the *Pope* and the *Ford* got under way and headed downstream. Again we passed a long line of ships moored in midstream. This time, however, there were many small ships crowded with soldiers and civilians from Singapore. Many of the refugees were living on the open decks with their possessions at their sides. As we passed by, the soldiers, thinking we might be headed for Australia or some other haven, jokingly attempted to thumb rides with us.

As we were negotiating the minefield off the harbor entrance, the *De Ruyter*, Admiral Doorman's flagship, passed us heading in. Expecting to meet outside the harbor, we wondered about our next move when the admiral appeared on deck and saw us. He did not bother to send a signal but waved his arms vigorously, motioning us to follow his ship. We completed our run through the minefield, turned around in clear water, and headed back into the harbor.

By the time the *Pope* and the *Ford* were moored again, it was dark. Captain Blinn left immediately for a conference aboard the flagship.

59

The *Pope* was maintained in readiness to get under way again as soon as the captain returned. Meanwhile more Dutch naval vessels were entering the harbor; with so many ships moving about in that small area, the scene was lively. The Dutch disregarded the blackout regulations completely, and I couldn't blame them.

After several hours Captain Blinn returned. The conference itself had lasted less than half an hour, but they'd had to wait for the other commanding officers. Captain Blinn went over the plan with us: the *Pope* and the *Ford* were to accompany the *Java* and the *De Ruyter* with two Dutch destroyers, the *Piet Hein* and the *Kortenaer*. We would leave Tjilatjap that night to attack a Japanese force at Bali the following night. Our group would make the attack from the south and withdraw to the north to Surabaja. A second group made up of the Dutch destroyer leader *Tromp* and U.S. destroyers *Stewart, Parrott, Edwards,* and *Pillsbury* coming from Surabaja would make a similar attack one hour later.

The plan seemed a good one except for one detail: the *Java* and the *De Ruyter* would lead the attack while the destroyers followed behind. Some of us thought that the destroyers should lead. Being smaller than the cruisers, they would not be seen as easily, and using torpedoes would not disclose the positions of the ships. After an initial torpedo attack by the destroyers, the cruisers would have good targets at which to fire. However, the Dutch were running this show, and we were there to take orders.

According to the plan, we followed the Dutch destroyers downstream—at a good distance because of the darkness. As we neared the sharp turn in the channel, we saw a ship against the bank, apparently aground. We eased by her and made her out to be a Dutch destroyer. We were called over as we passed and asked if we had a pilot aboard—we didn't. The cruisers were coming down astern of us, using their searchlights, and we assumed they would give the destroyer the necessary aid.

At daylight the next morning, February 19, we saw that we were missing the *Kortenaer*. We deduced that she was the ship aground in the channel. To lessen the danger of a submarine attack, we commenced zigzagging. I was waiting for a signal from the flagship, the *De Ruyter,* telling us what zigzag plan to use; none came, but by watching the Dutch ships and turning when they turned, we were able to keep close to our proper position. Captain Blinn suggested that I try each zigzag plan until I found the right one. Luckily, the first one fit.

A little later there was a change of course and speed—without a signal. We may have looked sloppy to the Dutch with our time lag in changing course and speed, but we were rapidly losing confidence in the ability of our Dutch leader. If we were not getting any signals now, we certainly wouldn't get any in action.

At sunset we were close to Bali, and to the best of our knowledge we had not been sighted by any Japanese air patrol. On board the *Pope* we were making last-minute preparations for the coming engagement. There was not the same tension we all had felt on the eve of our first action. This time it was just an air of expectation.

Before darkness set in, we received a signal from the *De Ruyter* telling us to form a column. The order in the column was *De Ruyter, Java, Piet Hein, Ford,* and *Pope.* A better plan in my opinion would have been with the destroyers in column about two thousand yards on the *De Ruyter*'s port bow, the side toward Bali.

In this setup the destroyers would have made first contact and, when sighted by the enemy, would have presented a more difficult target.

As a precaution against fire in case we were hit, we jettisoned the drum of gasoline we carried aft for fueling the motorboats. Just before 10 P.M. we went to general quarters and were waiting for something to happen. I was in my usual station, the crow's nest. Bali was in sight on our port bow, and a fire burned somewhere ashore. I thought it was probably a tourist hotel, because that's about all there was on Bali.

The Japanese were already ashore, and their transports were no doubt somewhere close to the beach and not far from the fire. Suddenly a searchlight picked up the *De Ruyter.* The two Dutch cruisers turned on their searchlights, and there was an exchange of salvos with the Japanese ships. When the lights went out and the firing ceased, flames were seen on one of the Japanese ships.

The Dutch cruisers did not follow up their advantage, however. A little later the *Piet Hein* swung to the left ahead of us and opened up with torpedoes and guns. The gunfire was a tactical error, for it gave away the *Piet Hein*'s position. She was taken under fire immediately and burst into flame. The *Ford* and the *Pope* fired torpedoes to port at the *Piet Hein*'s opponent (probably one or two cruisers) and turned away, making smoke. It reduced the visibility, but I saw several fires, and they were not all aboard the *Piet Hein*.

As we swung away, it became apparent that we would not be able to proceed north through Badung Straits as planned. Furthermore, we were in a cross fire of heavy batteries. We fired more torpedoes to port; either these or our evasive maneuvers gave us a brief respite.

From the *Ford* via TBS (voice radio) came the word that we would head for the shadow of the shore to the east of us. This sounded like an excellent idea, but before we were able to lose ourselves in the darkness, the *Ford* was suddenly illuminated by a cruiser. Because we were by no means certain of the whereabouts of the *De Ruyter* and the *Java*, both the *Ford* and the *Pope* turned on recognition lights, a special arrangement of colored lights, the colors and arrangement changing each day. The cruiser fired a salvo at the *Ford* at a range of less than two thousand yards. The *Ford* disappeared from view, and everyone on the *Pope* watching the action knew that the *Ford* was finished.

The splashes from the shell fire subsided—and the *Ford* reappeared. A shout went up on the *Pope* and at the same time five torpedoes from our starboard battery fanned out toward the cruiser. (There should have been six torpedoes in the salvo, but one tube had a misfire.) As soon as the torpedoes were away, we commenced fire with our 4-inch guns. The range was so close that we couldn't miss, but our shells were hitting a bit aft. I spotted the next salvo to the right to bring the forward part of the enemy ship under fire.

Meanwhile the *Ford* disappeared and reappeared at regular intervals (as fast as the Japanese could fire). The *Ford* was firing her guns—she must have fired all her remaining torpedoes by this time—and began making smoke to elude the cruiser.

The *Pope* was not under fire, but everything seemed so bright around us that it was impossible for us not to have been seen. As we got off our third salvo—and at the proper time for our tin fish to have reached their target—the searchlight went out on the cruiser;

not another salvo was fired at the *Ford*. I do not think we were unduly optimistic in assuming we'd either sunk or severely damaged the cruiser. The *Ford* was apparently undamaged, and we fell in astern of her once again and headed in a southerly direction.

We seemed to be out of danger when a lookout reported torpedo wakes approaching us from astern. The wakes turned out to be the reflection of a bright star on the waves created by our own motion through the water. After this letdown there was a considerable release of tension on the ship.

As I was watching for any overtaking ships, I saw an exchange of gunfire. On the *Pope's* bridge the opinion was that the second group had joined battle ahead of time, or the *Java* and the *De Ruyter* were still mixing it up. The action was situated so that I could see the tracers (luminous matter in the base of the shells to allow the shells to be followed by eye) from both firing ships. The ship to the left as I looked aft seemed to be a cruiser; its adversary to the right was probably a destroyer. The exchange was rapid and heavy, with both ships using searchlight illumination. Both ships were being hit, but the one to the right was taking greater punishment. She was soon afire; after a series of explosions she retired from the battle. A third ship came up from the right (probably another destroyer) and engaged the cruiser. Both ships suffered hits, and when the action terminated, both ships were burning.

It was a strain watching the action and not knowing which side I was rooting for. My station gave the best view of the battle, and I made a continual report to the bridge of the progress.

About half an hour later I saw flashes of gunfire over the horizon. When I reported this to the bridge, I received the happy reply that according to the time schedule this should be our four destroyers and the *Tromp*. By now we were fairly certain that the three ships we had just seen exchanging salvos were Japanese. (Later, we received confirmation that the *Java* and the *De Ruyter* were already clear of the area and that our second group had not yet arrived on the scene.)

Our division commander on the *Ford* decided that our best move would be to return to Tjilatjap and refuel. The trip back was peaceful, and we had time to consider the effect of our phase of the attack. Several Japanese transports had been hit and possibly sunk, and at least one cruiser was damaged severely. Taking into account the damage that the Japanese did to themselves, two destroyers were sunk or badly damaged and another cruiser was severely damaged. Our own losses as far as we knew were the *Piet Hein* (destroyer) sunk and the *Ford*'s motor whaleboat lost overboard. We would have to wait and see how the second group made out.

We arrived off Tjilatjap early on the morning of February 21. A Dutch minelayer patrolling near the entrance seemed surprised to see us. There were fewer ships in the harbor now because most of the naval vessels had left. The USS *Pecos,* a tanker, was still in port. The *Pope* and the *Ford* went alongside her and commenced fueling immediately. We were informed that we would evacuate Royal Air Force (RAF) personnel from Java. This sounded good—we might get to Australia for that navy yard overhaul yet. An amplification of the orders was less encouraging: rendezvous with *Black Hawk* at Christmas Island, transfer RAF personnel, take aboard replacement torpedoes (four-stackers carried only the torpedoes that were actually in the tubes), and return to Surabaja.

The British troops came aboard late that afternoon. Each ship received about thirty officers and men; they were served the evening meal as soon as they got aboard. I was in the forward crew's compartment checking to see that they were being taken care of. Parkin, a seaman from my forecastle gang, was helping out: "Here, have some pickles, Limey." "I'm not a Limey." "OK, Limey, have some pickles anyway." For some reason the matter ended there.

After clearing the harbor that evening, we went to twenty knots. With a moderate sea and wind, we began to take a lot of spray aboard and the forecastle was wet.

About 7 A.M. the next day we sighted the *Holland* and the *Black Hawk* ahead of us. They were escorted by two destroyers and a submarine. As we approached, the *Holland* sent the message: "Congratulations" (referring to our action off Bali). The *Black Hawk,* our own tender with our squadron commander aboard, sent the signal: "Your gun shields are reflecting the sun. Rectify this condition." There was no reference to the battle. The cause of our bright shields was a thin coating of salt left by the spray, which we removed. One of the sailors sounded our sentiments when he said: "I guess that's the old bastard's contribution to this war."

About an hour or so later we sighted Christmas Island. Our plan was to proceed to the lee side of the island, transfer our passengers to the *Black Hawk*, and take aboard the torpedoes. As we approached the island, thousands of seabirds began flying about the ships. The island was a rocky mass clad in green foliage. Sheer cliffs rose straight out of the sea; one wondered how anyone could get ashore. Caves along the cliffs were the nesting places of the birds.

The lee side of the island proved to be only a slight improvement over the weather side. Fifty-foot launches arrived from the *Black Hawk*—an empty one for the RAF chaps and others with our torpedoes. The British were glad to see that they were going to a larger ship, but their transfer in the motor launch was wet. Aft on the *Pope* the torpedomen aided by a working party from the deck force were hoisting torpedoes aboard and sliding them into the tubes. For the torpedomen this was just preliminary work; the torpedoes had to be checked and then charged with compressed air (from our decrepit compressors), warheads (the explosive charges) had to be attached, and all preparations for putting the battery in readiness had to be made.

Jack Fisher had a chance to transfer to the *Black Hawk*, but he turned it down. As paymaster he merely "rode" on the *Pope*. His assignment was to the 59th Destroyer Division, and as far as pay was concerned there was little opportunity to spend money anyway. But Jack felt that he had come this far with the *Pope* and he might as well go the whole way. It was a big sacrifice, but he felt that any other course would be equivalent to running out on his shipmates.

During the loading, the crew of the *Black Hawk* looked extremely nervous and kept urging the *Pope* and the *Ford* to expedite the loading. There was something unseemly about this, like telling a condemned man to hurry with his last breakfast. It was annoying too because the men were working at top speed, and without the advantage of power-driven cranes.

At last the operation was completed and the *Pope* and the *Ford* parted company with the rest of the force. We were heading back to Surabaja, and they were going to Australia. The next time we would see the *Black Hawk* we would be in a good liberty port—if there was to be a next time.

It was night when we reached Sunda Strait. The only vessel we sighted was a Dutch patrol craft. After clearing the strait we headed east, keeping fairly close to the shore. The next day was sunny and hot. In the afternoon we encountered some Javanese fishing boats. Later a Dutch Dornier flying boat on patrol circled our ships. We steamed on through the night without interruption and arrived off the entrance to Surabaja harbor early in the morning.

As we steamed in toward the port area, a flight of B-17s (Flying Fortresses) passed overhead. It was a small group but the most sizable concentration of American planes we'd seen in some time. They were heading north, probably to attack a Japanese fleet. Seeing the B-17s was like a shot in the arm.

About ten minutes later the air raid sirens sounded ashore, and in a short while Japanese planes were overhead—in ten times the number of American planes we had just seen. We were almost at our berth at Holland pier but decided that the open harbor would offer greater safety. A few minutes later, bombs were falling on the port area. Warehouses were set on fire; a freighter at Rotterdam pier was hit, and her burning cargo of rubber gave off heavy smoke. Tugboats and small craft scurried aimlessly about the harbor. We tried to signal the tugboats to go alongside the ships at the piers and tow them away from the target. This effort was without success, but fortunately no more large ships were hit.

After a while the all clear sounded. Our original plan to tie up at the pier was changed, and we anchored out in the harbor. The destroyers that had taken part in the second phase of the action off Bali were in Surabaja. From them we learned that the *Tromp* had been badly damaged and would have to go to Colombo, in Ceylon, for repairs. The USS *Stewart* had taken an 8-inch shell hit in her steering engine room (in the stern of the ship), but somehow the steering engine had held up until she reached Surabaja. The *Stewart* had been put into a floating dry dock for repairs but was improperly shored. As the dock was raised, the ship tilted to port and the shores punctured her sides, making abandonment of the ship necessary. This brought our losses for the action to two destroyers lost and one destroyer leader damaged.

The second-phase group had had a lively battle in which they believed they had sunk several Japanese ships. We learned that the *Java* and the *De Ruyter* had gone through the first phase of the battle with the former firing only five rounds of ammunition and the latter none. We could very well have done without them.

We received word that because the *Stewart* was to be abandoned, any of her supplies that might be of use to the other ships could be had for the taking. I took a party over to the *Stewart* and picked up items throughout the ship. Walking on her decks was like walking on a sloping roof. The fact that there was no electric power and therefore no lights made moving about belowdecks difficult and dangerous. We had hoped to find camouflage paint in the forward paint locker, but all we could find were cans of white lead. A British army sergeant came aboard and said he'd been told to take any rifles he could find. We directed him to the armory, which was also forward, but the guns had already been removed. He was probably from an outfit that had been evacuated in a hurry from Singapore and had left most of its equipment behind.

I went through the CPO's living space into officer country. The wardroom was strewn with broken crockery, papers from files, clothing, and linens left behind by the *Stewart*'s officers. In some of the staterooms, uniforms were still hanging in the closets. Either the ship was abandoned in a hurry or a lot of people had decided to travel light.

By judicious scavenging we assembled a collection of many useful items, including a brand new Beauty Rest mattress for Fisher. As we were preparing to transfer the load to the whaleboat, the air raid sirens sounded. There was no time to load the boat and collect our group. The whaleboat left the dock to keep clear of any possible targets. Meanwhile I yelled to the men in my party to get off the ship and either go to the air raid shelters ashore, which were close to the dry dock, or get into the dry dock control room, which was protected by reinforced concrete.

As I entered the control room I saw that about half the men were with me; the others had evidently decided to go ashore. By this time the bombers were overhead and the antiaircraft battery of the *Houston* was firing from the Surabaja navy yard. Although the desire to rubberneck was strong, the instinct of self-preservation was stronger;

I flattened out on the deck with the rest of the people in the room. As the whistle of falling bombs grew louder, I held my hands over my head and clamped a few folds of my shirt between my teeth, which was supposed to prevent injury from the blast. Fortunately I didn't have to rely on this flimsy defense.

The bombs dropped just close enough to make the dry dock vibrate violently. I looked up after the first series of explosions and saw a Javanese near me trembling. I gave him what I hoped was a reassuring smile. It gave me unexplainable confidence to know there was someone else as scared as I was. He smiled back. Then we both ducked again as more bombs whistled above us. The sort of game we played, looking up and smiling as each explosion left the dry dock undamaged, made the bombs seem less terrifying.

The antiaircraft guns of the *Houston* were still firing, so we assumed that she had not been hit. Pieces of antiaircraft shell and debris from the bombs landed on the tin roofs of the sheds near the dock and on the dock itself. Landing as they did during the comparative lull between explosions, they served as deterrents to any sight-seeing even when the bombs were definitely destined for other targets. The Dutchmen in charge of the dry dock had a radio receiver on during the raid and gave us reports on the location of the bombers as the raid passed us. After a long period free from explosions, the Dutchmen announced that the raid was over. As we left the control room, the sirens were sounding the all clear.

I quickly gathered my group together and waved the whaleboat alongside the dock. When noses were counted we found that two of the party were missing. We were sure that they had not been hurt in the raid because there had been no serious damage near the dock. I went to the entrance to the dockyard and asked where to find the nearest bar. It was all the way into town, so I abandoned hope of finding the men in a reasonable length of time. Back aboard the *Pope* I reported the absentees to the executive officer, who did not seem overly concerned.

That afternoon there was another raid. Our ship steamed slowly about the harbor so that we did not present an easy target. The airfield and seaplane base, not far from our usual anchorage, were thoroughly worked over. Clouds of dust followed most of the explosions as the bombers systematically destroyed the field's usefulness. A mobile antiaircraft battery (British, we learned later) had been set up near the field, and though a steady rate of fire was maintained during the raid, we did not see any Japanese planes hit.

After the raid ended and the chance of another one that late in the day seemed remote (there was no need for the Japanese to resort to night bombing when the daylight raids met such little opposition), all American destroyers were ordered to fuel from a tanker alongside the quay near the seaplane base. As we finished fueling, the two absentees from my salvage party showed up in an exuberant mood. There was no question about how they had spent the afternoon. In view of the circumstances, it was decided that an oral reprimand would suffice as punishment.

We returned to our anchorage after fueling and awaited orders to get under way. Captain Blinn had been to a conference during the day and had received orders to stand by for operations that night. At dusk the orders came to leave for a sweep eastward in the Java Sea.

Our fairly large force—three cruisers and about seven destroyers—steamed east until midnight looking for Japanese forces; finding none, we retraced our course back to Surabaja. The return trip through the minefields was nerve-racking because all lighthouses and beacons ashore had been extinguished. Finally it was necessary to turn on running lights to minimize the danger of collision, and one of the ships ahead turned on its searchlight to pick out landmarks and buoys.

On February 26 we had our usual air raids, but the harbor area did not receive any particular attention. The *Pope* and the other destroyers stayed well clear of the wharves and other potential targets. The *Java* and the *De Ruyter* as well as the *Houston* seemed likely targets regardless of their locations, so they were tied up at the piers where air raid shelters were available for unengaged personnel.

At one of these piers was the *Op Ten Noort*, a Dutch hospital ship that, despite her markings, had been damaged in a bombing attack earlier in the week and was now undergoing repairs. Fortunately she did not receive any more hits. The *Soerabaja*, a coastal defense vessel, was sunk during one of these raids, but it was not a serious loss.

At sundown, HMS *Exeter*, a cruiser with 8-inch guns, and HMAS *Perth* and HMAS *Hobart*, cruisers with 6-inch guns, accompanied by destroyers, steamed into the harbor. Here before our eyes was the sort of thing we all hoped for. The *Pope*'s crew crowded the forecastle to get a clear view of the new additions to our force, and every pair of binoculars on board was focused on the new arrivals. One of the destroyers was painted in dazzle camouflage of an unusual design: the color scheme and pattern on one side of the ship was distinctly different from that on the opposite side, so that an observer seeing first one side and then somewhat later the other might well believe he had seen two different ships.

As if to initiate these new arrivals to their surroundings, the sirens sounded for another air raid. This one lasted only a short time for it was almost dark. Probably a group of planes was returning to base and getting rid of their last bombs for the trip back.

A hurried conference of commanding officers was held as soon as the British ships anchored. Before Captain Blinn returned from the flagship, the plan for the evening's events was announced over the TBS—a dubious procedure but perhaps expedient to ensure readiness for getting under way. We were to make a sweep similar to that of the previous night, but this time we expected to do some business. All ships were to prepare to get under way immediately.

Meanwhile Bassett, the engineering officer, came up to the bridge with disturbing news: our much repaired hot well (a tank for receiving fresh water from the condensers) had developed a bad leak along an old weld; we were losing more water than our evaporators could replace. It was now out of the question for us to take part in tonight's sweep, and if we could not have the hot well repaired, we would probably have to use saltwater in the boilers to make any long runs.

When Captain Blinn returned to the ship and received the report on the hot well, he requested permission from our division commander to remain in port for repairs. The answer came back to proceed to the navy yard, where welding facilities were available, and upon completion of repairs to stand by to rejoin the force.

We watched the rest of the force get under way and steam out of Surabaja harbor. The *Pope* remained at anchor until the harbor was cleared. Our run to the navy yard was short, but we were held up by lack of familiarity with the waters in that area. Finally we eased into a narrow channel and went alongside a wharf near an electric welding shop. Bassett brought aboard some welders from the yard, and, after a lengthy inspection of the damage, they went back to the shop to get the necessary equipment to weld the leak.

February 27 dawned bright and clear. The hot well was almost completely repaired, and the impatience of the previous night was gradually giving way to admiration for the skill and perseverance of the Javanese welders. Bassett said that Cavite (the U.S. Navy yard in Manila Bay) had never been able to do as good a job on the hot well even without being rushed.

A number of the men from the *Pope* were walking about on the shore, and I joined them to stretch my legs and look around. In a long shed near the water were a number of torpedo boats in various stages of construction. I learned that with the first air raids on the harbor area, most of the native workers took off for the hills. That ended that project. Not far away the *Soerabaja* rested on the bottom, and water lapped about her turrets. This place was inclined to instill a pessimistic outlook. We were soon called back aboard to get the ship under way. The welding job was finished.

Out in the harbor we felt a little self-conscious. Being the only warship in the harbor and having nothing to do but wait felt like playing hooky. The only other ship of any size left in the port was an oil tanker.

There was little activity in the harbor, but there was a distinct feeling of anticipation. The daily air raids would start on schedule; it was just a matter of waiting. And the invasion of Java would come soon; the combined Allied naval force could delay things only momentarily. How long could the Dutch army hold out? The Dutchmen said they would fight to the last man; even the women wanted to fight. A message had been sent to the Allied naval forces to the effect that no sacrifice would be too great for the defense of Java.

In the afternoon we got under way and stood out toward the entrance to the harbor, where we waited for further orders. Some change had apparently been made in the schedule, for the force did not return to port. Then we picked up our own destroyers on the TBS and learned that contact with the enemy had been made.

Before we could get any orders for the *Pope*, we lost contact with our ships. We knew that the force was heading away from Surabaja at high speed, so our chances of joining up were remote. Captain Blinn decided that his best course of action would be to remain at the harbor entrance until our ships headed back in our direction. Until late that night we patrolled back and forth off the harbor entrance, hoping to hear a report of the action and possibly rejoin our force.

A little before midnight we sighted a cruiser standing in toward the minefield. We supposed that it was one of the ships from our force, but we went to general quarters just in case. After our challenge was properly returned, we tried to make out which of our cruisers it was. A closer view of her silhouette identified her as the *Exeter*. She had a destroyer with her.

Some time later we picked up our own destroyers on the TBS. From the conversations we gathered that the destroyers had been ordered to Batavia but the orders could not be executed because the ships had insufficient fuel. The ships were returning to Surabaja and the cruisers and the British and Dutch destroyers (larger than our four-stackers) were proceeding to Batavia (Tandjong Priok). When our destroyers came in sight, the *Pope* was ordered to fall in astern the last ship in the column and return to port.

It was not until the next day (February 28) that we learned anything definite about the action that had taken place. HMS *Exeter* had been hit in one of her boiler rooms and had been forced to break off the action. The personnel who had been killed in the battle were buried in Surabaja. HMS *Encounter*, a British destroyer, had also returned to port, bringing with her the survivors from a torpedoed Dutch destroyer. The American destroyers had made a torpedo attack in the course of the battle and had expended all their torpedoes.

Apparently the Allied force had run into the covering force for the Japanese invasion fleet. The odds had been hopelessly against our ships, but they had fought courageously and had sunk several Japanese ships and damaged others. But it would be just a matter of time before the Japanese finished off our hodgepodge force.

Before long we received word that the *Java* and the *De Ruyter* had been torpedoed during their attempt to retire to Tandjong Priok (port of Batavia) during the night of February 27. The *Houston* and the *Perth* had apparently succeeded in reaching port. The total fighting force we could muster against the Japanese invasion fleet was three cruisers (one seriously damaged and another with only two-thirds of her main battery operative) and eight destroyers (five over-aged four-stackers—the *Pope* was the only one with any torpedoes left—and three newer types of which two were in need of repairs). To make matters more difficult, our force was divided.

During the afternoon of February 28, Captain Blinn went aboard the *Exeter* to attend a conference of commanding officers. When he returned he told us that the *Pope* and the *Encounter* had been assigned to the *Exeter* and would leave Surabaja that night via the north channel. The four American destroyers that had taken part in the Java sea battle were to leave by the eastern channel past Bali and then on to Australia. It had been decided that because the *Exeter*'s draft was too much for the eastern channel (by far the safer route), she and her escorts would have to go back into the Java Sea, swinging east and then north toward Borneo and finally heading southwest to the Sunda Strait (the exit that the *Houston* and the *Perth* were also to use). The object of this complicated course of action was to avoid the Japanese fleet, which we expected would be busy covering the landing on Java.

The immediate effect of this information on the officers of the *Pope* was to curse the Dutchman responsible for the order. The next things to be cursed were the torpedoes (without them we would have been ordered to proceed with our own destroyers out past Bali). The *Black Hawk* received her share of vituperation for having given us the torpedoes in the first place—and on general principles.

As soon as it was dark that evening, we headed out of the harbor with the *Exeter* and the *Encounter*. One of my boatswain's mates came up to me: "Mr. Michel, do you think we have a chance of getting out of this?" Rather glibly I replied: "It's a cinch. Our orders are to avoid action because *Exeter* is damaged. Besides, the Japs will be so busy with their landing that they'll never notice us." My answer seemed to satisfy him.

Condition watches were set as soon as we cleared the minefield, and I turned in to get as much rest as possible before my midwatch. When I took over as officer of the deck at midnight, we were steaming quietly, zigzagging as a safeguard against submarines. The *Exeter* had been making repairs to her boilers continuously; as a result her original speed limit of sixteen knots had been improved to twenty-one. The sea was calm and there was a fairly bright moon, which we could have done without.

A few minutes before I was due to be relieved, I saw objects on our starboard bow that might have been ships. I woke the captain, who was sleeping on the bridge, and reported it to him. While we were looking at the objects and trying to decide whether they were ships or islands, I turned around to check my position on the *Exeter* and found that she was not where I expected her to be. A quick search did not reveal her presence. Captain Blinn was not perturbed and told me to reverse course. As we steadied on our new course, the *Exeter* appeared out of the gloom ahead of us on a similar course. By this time Bassett had arrived on the bridge to relieve me, and I was glad to go below and turn in.

After a few hours' sleep I was up again. As I was finishing my breakfast, general quarters sounded. Passing the bridge en route to my battle station, I found out that the *Exeter* had reported sighting two enemy cruisers. Our force turned to a southerly course to avoid these ships. The *Exeter* was making about twenty-two knots; her engineers and artificers had been working all night to repair the damage received in the Java Sea engagement and had succeeded in adding about six knots to her speed. Later we resumed our westerly course to take us toward the Sunda Strait. We remained at our stations to be ready for action in case the cruisers had sighted us.

For a while it seemed that we had escaped detection, which gave us a reprieve from the growing tension. A few minutes later, however, we sighted a destroyer ahead of us. The *Encounter* was the first to open fire. We joined in with the two guns that could bear on the enemy ship. The *Exeter* opened up with her 4-inch guns, but our combined efforts did no more than raise some splashes near the destroyer. The enemy reversed course and returned our fire with her after guns.

We pursued the ship until we sighted cruiser mastheads over the horizon. Again we changed course to avoid this apparently superior force. The *Exeter* managed to increase her speed to twenty-five knots.

Our plan to slip around the Japanese was not working well. A plane was sighted, and as it circled the force at a safe distance we recognized her as a Japanese reconnaissance plane (as if there would have been an Allied plane in the area). The *Exeter*'s antiaircraft battery opened up, without any apparent effect.

We had secured from general quarters for a short while after our unsuccessful encounter with the Japanese destroyer, and when the plane was sighted I went aft to the 3-inch gun just in case we had a chance to fire. This gave me an opportunity to see how the crew was reacting to the morning's events. In general they seemed in good spirits. Chief Torpedoman Netter, who was standing by the after torpedoes when I passed, stopped me for a few words: "Say, Mr. Michel, didn't those guys get the word? We're supposed to be avoiding them and they're supposed to be covering the landing on Java." "Well, you can't expect these slant-eyed bastards to get the word," I said.

Before long we were back at general quarters again: more cruisers had been sighted. It began to look as if we had picked the center of a task force for our evasive tactics. This time the Japanese maintained contact, and at about 1015 our force was under fire from four cruisers. The range was about twenty thousand yards, and the cruisers were disposed on our port quarter.

At first the *Exeter* received nearly all the attention, but when the *Pope* laid a smoke screen to give the British cruiser a brief respite, the splashes began to advance toward us. Some of the splashes were within a hundred yards of our ship, and it began to look as if we might see just what a salvo of 8-inch shells would do to a destroyer. There were two factors contributing to our safety: first, our relatively small size offered a poor target; second, Captain Blinn was steering toward the splashes to throw off the Japanese fire. This seemed like good sport, but an uncomfortably close salvo told us that the game could not go on indefinitely. All this time we were not firing guns, for the excellent reason that our guns could not reach the enemy cruisers.

Meanwhile Japanese destroyers came up on our starboard beam and, running parallel to us at about twelve thousand yards, opened fire. The *Pope* took the leading ship under fire and the *Encounter* took the second in column, leaving the remaining two for the *Exeter*. This range was close to the extreme range of our 4-inch guns, and as a result our fire was not effective. The Japanese salvos were in small patterns, but they did not land close enough to us to affect the ship or crew.

At one point in the battle when the *Exeter* was being straddled with disheartening regularity but was not hit, the *Pope* fired its six port torpedoes at the cruisers on our port quarter. The range was about twenty thousand yards (the torpedoes would actually run about eleven thousand yards to reach the target), and it was difficult to determine the effect. However, the Japanese cruisers did alter course, and one cruiser was observed to drop out of formation. Whether we actually hit her is questionable. Meanwhile we continued firing at the destroyers on our starboard hand. I was spotting these salvos and ran into some difficulty when the splashes from the shells of the *Encounter* and the *Exeter* lined up with ours. Our shells straddled the leading destroyer several times, but we did not have the satisfaction of seeing a definite hit. I walked our salvos across the target a number of times to make sure that what I judged to be straddles were not all shorts.

Our forecastle gun crew reported that their magazines were empty. We slowed our rate of fire, and ammunition was shifted from the after magazines.

It was decided to fire our starboard torpedoes at the column of destroyers. The range was between ten and twelve thousand yards— close to the torpedoes' maximum range. We did not see any definite hits, but we did see most of the torpedoes explode as they hit the wakes of the Japanese ships.

It was surprising to us that the Japanese ships did not attempt to close the range on us. During this running battle, we were making at the most twenty-six knots, and the Japanese ships should have been capable of greater speeds. The destroyers that had come up from our starboard quarter did not advance more than a couple of points forward of our beam and stayed most of the time at about twelve thousand yards range. The cruisers kept their position to the rear at about twenty thousand yards. Apparently the Japanese felt that they would sink our ships eventually and there was no need to risk their own ships unnecessarily. The destroyers might easily have forced our ships back toward their cruisers by heading us off ("crossing the T") or by a torpedo attack from a point ahead of us.

At 1120 the action reached its climax: the *Exeter* was hit. There was not much smoke and flame, but the damage was critical. Her guns stopped firing, and before long she was dead in the water with all power lost. The *Encounter* dropped smoke floats to try to conceal the *Exeter* in her helpless condition.

The Japanese ships were hitting the *Exeter* regularly now, and we could see people abandoning ship. Meanwhile the *Encounter* and the *Pope* increased speed to attempt to get away from the Japanese force. Then the *Encounter* stopped. At first I thought she was going to try a gallant but foolhardy last stand by her disabled companion, but it was soon evident that she too was out of the action.

The *Pope* increased its speed to about thirty knots. It seemed as if we were deserting our comrades in arms, but a less emotional view indicated that our only logical course was to try to escape while the Japanese were diverted. In a short time we had put a good distance between us and the Japanese, and we were no longer under fire.

Not far ahead of us was a dark rain squall, and we found the visibility gradually decreasing around us. The cruisers' reconnaissance planes, similar to our own navy's cruiser-based biplanes (SOCs), kept us in sight until we reached the center of the squall, where the rain was so heavy that it was impossible to see more than fifty yards. Now I had nothing to do but think of our situation, and I realized that I was scared. Here we were—one little old four-stacker trying to run away from a large force of Japanese cruisers and destroyers. Our torpedoes were expended, and a check of our 4-inch ammunition revealed that a total of only twenty shells remained. Our only salvation was in flight.

I had been so engrossed in spotting and making various reports that the precariousness of our situation did not bother me. But now that we were trying to run away, I had an insecure feeling. Between thoughts of what the *Pope* would look like when those cruisers caught up with her, I prayed for a speedy recovery or the grace of a happy death.

The squall gradually dissipated. We had run into it as far as we could and were now running out of it, and in just a few minutes we were in bright sunlight again. I had begun to search the horizon for ships when the bridge called to say that Wilson would come up to help me. Just where Wilson would stand was not mentioned; the crow's nest was large enough for only one man.

Meanwhile the planes from the cruisers were sighted again. They circled us at a safe distance and then began to make approaches on us one at a time from various angles. When the planes were within range, we opened fire with our 3-inch gun and occasionally our 4-inch guns. The latter were designed only for surface targets, but we hoped to create an impression of greater antiaircraft strength, and it was good for our morale just to hear the guns go off.

Either our deception was too clumsy or the Japanese knew thoroughly our antiaircraft armament; at any rate the planes began to approach us from dead ahead (a bearing on which our 3-inch gun could not train), leaving only .50-caliber machine guns and Lewis guns (.30-caliber of 1918 vintage) to oppose them.

The planes would go into a dive at about three thousand feet and release their bombs, pulling out at between fifteen hundred and a thousand feet. Because they came in one at a time, the problem of maneuvering to avoid the bombs was relatively simple. Whenever a plane started its dive, I would watch her until I saw the bombs released and report it to the bridge. (The personnel on the bridge were watching for the bomb release too, but I continued to make my reports because it made me feel that I was serving some useful purpose on top of the mast.) As soon as the bombs were released, the captain would order the rudder put over hard right or left to avoid the bombs. Some of the bombs landed in the water close to the ship; the explosions threw water on the deck but caused no serious damage.

Wilson was standing on the ladder below the crow's nest (I had the door in the bottom of the crow's nest open so that we could speak to each other) when the bombing began. I tried to squeeze into the top of the nest to let him in the bottom in case the plane started strafing. Four planes had attacked us without causing damage when the fifth one put a bomb in the water right next to our port propeller. This gave the mast a terrific whip, and I thought Wilson might lose his grip on the ladder. As the vibrations continued, though they were less severe, Wilson went back down to the fire control platform. Meanwhile another plane dive-bombed us but caused no damage. Because of the explosion of the fifth plane's bomb, it was necessary to stop our port screw; the compartments in the damaged area were flooding rapidly. We had started to list to port, but our turn to avoid the sixth plane's bombs heeled us over to starboard, and there we remained. We slowed rapidly with only one engine in operation. The situation was now beginning to look hopeless.

Another explosion erupted and my telephone set went dead. This explosion was the demolition charge set off to destroy our submarine detection equipment. I called down the voice tube to the bridge and asked if I was still wanted at my station; with my phones dead I was serving no purpose there. The answer I received was startling: "Come on down. We're abandoning ship."

As I started down the ladder I could see the men throwing over the Carley life floats (only three remained; the fourth had been blown overboard in one of the bomb explosions) and lowering the motor whaleboat, which had escaped damage. When I reached the fire control platform, I found that the ladder to the bridge was missing; it had been carried away in an explosion. On the bridge Radioman First Class Frame was on a stretcher; his leg had been broken by fragments from the ladder. On the other side of the bridge Yeoman Davis (who had been the bridge telephone talker on my circuit) was lying face down. When I asked if there was a stretcher for Davis, I was told that he was dead.

I started down to my stateroom to pick up a few items I planned to take off the ship with me, but there was so much congestion on the ladder that I gave up the thought of going below. Instead I went aft, where Captain Blinn and Antrim were supervising the loading of the whaleboat with the wounded and supplies for abandoning ship—food, water, and medical supplies. Jack Fisher had the presence of mind to go down to the safe in the wardroom for the case of brandy the ship carried for emergencies. This was safely stowed in the whaleboat. With the help of a couple of men I managed to throw over wooden staging, which could be used for support in the water. Antrim meanwhile was yelling to the men to get off the ship; they seemed reluctant to leave even though the ship was obviously sinking steadily. The cruisers might catch up with us at any time now, so it would not have been wise to remain aboard until the last minute.

I went over to the hatch leading into the crew's after living space to peruse the damage, but I could see only debris-covered water. Bill Spears, who had gone aft to inspect the damage immediately after the bomb explosion, said that the situation had been hopeless from the start. Seams had opened up all along the port quarter, and it had been impossible to limit the flooding to only a few compartments. The repair party had attempted to stop the leaks with mattresses but had no success. These factors, along with our damaged propeller and depleted ammunition supply, caused the captain to decide to abandon ship before the cruisers reappeared on the scene.

A plane started diving toward the ship. Our 3-inch gun was lying useless on the fantail, the gun barrel having dropped out of its slide onto the deck. Bill Lowndes, who had been manning that gun, climbed up to the .50-caliber machine gun on the after deckhouse and began firing at the plane. Bill looked like a wild man; his helmet and eyeglasses had been blown off by the explosion that damaged the ship, and he had a cut on the side of his head. The machine-gun bullets were accompanied by a stream of curses, but neither had any noticeable effect on the plane. The gun finally jammed and Bill climbed back down to the main deck.

Meanwhile a plane was diving on the whaleboat and attempting to strafe it, probably to indicate the boat's location to the surface ships. Someone in the boat was firing at the plane with a Browning automatic rifle, which seemed futile at this stage of the game. To protect the wounded men on board the whaleboat, Rohletter, the coxswain of the boat, ordered the guns thrown over the side; then he stood in the stern sheets with his hands above his head to try to stop the plane from firing. The firing ceased.

Most of the men had left the ship, and I looked around for Jack Fisher to go over the side with him. The only other people left aboard were Wilson, Spears, Lowndes, Austin, and Matthews (from the engineering gang), who were waiting for everyone to leave so that they could set off a demolition charge. It would ensure that the *Pope* did not remain afloat long enough to be boarded by the Japanese.

Jack joined me at the whaleboat davits. I had just taken off my shoes preparatory to entering the water when we spotted a flight of seven single-engined bombers heading for the ship. We held a quick conference and decided that it would be safer on the ship than in the water during a bombing attack. (In the water, the bombs would not have to be very close to injure us; on the ship, only a direct hit would endanger us.)

I put my shoes back on; the steel plates of the deck were burning my feet. Then Fisher and I ran forward to tell Wilson not to set off the charge, because we were staying aboard until the planes were past. We looked for a safe spot to spend the raid and ended up in the galley, where we noted with satisfaction that the noon meal we had missed was Vienna sausage and sauerkraut.

Hearing the whistle of the bombs, we stretched out on the deck and waited. There were two quarter-inch thicknesses of steel to stop fragments from the sides, and there was a deck over us. Then we heard the explosions; although the ship vibrated, we knew that the first run was a complete miss.

We thought that the planes might break off the attack after seeing that the ship was sinking, but they circled and made another run. Having encountered no opposition on the first run, this time they came in at a lower altitude. Again all the bombs missed. The planes took position for another run but for some reason did not drop any bombs. When we stuck out our heads to see if they were finished, we found that they were starting another attack. Fisher and I were becoming a little impatient. We didn't begrudge them their attacks, but we wanted them to clear out before we got into the water.

The fourth run proved to be the last, with no improvement in marksmanship. Fisher and I left the galley and prepared to leave the ship. Before going over the side, we tried to float a wooden crate of canned fruit, but the crate tipped with the first wave and we did not have time for further experimentation.

The ship had a heavy list to starboard now, so we decided to go over the port side. This was the weather side, which would make it easy for us to get well clear of the ship before she sank. This time I left my shoes on until I was in the water. As I started to swim I felt heavy in the water despite my kapok life jacket. Then I noticed that I was still wearing my pistol. This seemed to be useless gear at the moment, so I unhooked my pistol belt and let it sink. The rest of my clothes and equipment I left on, including, for the time being, my helmet. I continued wearing my black socks because I feared that sharks would otherwise be attracted by my white feet.

As soon as Fisher and I were clear of the ship, Wilson and his party set off the demolition charges. The resulting explosion was a disappointment: a small hole was blown in the port side just above the waterline, and a puff of smoke came out of one of the stacks. There may well have been other damage that we could not see. The *Pope* was settling anyway, and the seemingly ineffective demolition was of no consequence.

We were about a hundred yards from the ship and slowly widening the gap. A Japanese plane circled the ship and occasionally dived toward the water. Each time we were sure that the plane was diving at us to do some strafing, so we would loosen our life jackets and duck under the water. We were relieved when something else diverted the pilot's interest.

We noticed that the Japanese cruisers had caught up with the *Pope* and were lying to about eight thousand yards away. They made no attempt to come closer but opened fire from that range. Fisher and I were now about two hundred yards off the *Pope*'s port quarter and between her and the Japanese ships. The rest of our people were on the starboard quarter, spread out over a wide area but clear of the firing. If the shells from the cruisers landed short, Fisher and I would be very close to the point of impact; in fact we might become points of impact. We swam as quickly as possible away from the line of fire, turning onto our backs when we expected the salvos to land. This was protection against a blast in case a shell exploded nearby in the water.

Fortunately, all the shells except the last salvo landed beyond the *Pope*, which was now sinking rapidly by the stern. The last salvo scored a hit on the bow just as it rose out of the water for the final plunge. Then the ship disappeared completely, leaving only swirling water to indicate where she had been. I felt relieved, perhaps because the cause for the shooting and bombing had disappeared beneath the waves.

Slowly Fisher and I made our way toward the rest of our ship's company gathered about a life raft. Bassett had left with the whaleboat to bring back two more Carley life floats that were drifting a short distance from the group. A survey of our resources showed that we had three rafts with a capacity of forty persons each, a whaleboat capable of holding about twenty people, and a wherry (a dinghy-sized boat), at present capsized and damaged but capable of holding four if it could be repaired. With this equipment we could accommodate all but a handful of men; they would have to cling to the side of the rafts or the whaleboat. Every man had a kapok life jacket, so it was not essential to be aboard a craft in order to stay afloat.

The wounded were all in the whaleboat. Because there were only a few seriously wounded, it was possible to make them fairly comfortable. All provisions and drinking water were in the whaleboat; they did not take much space.

Fisher and I were the last to reach the group, and room was made in the whaleboat for us. Antrim gave me a shot of brandy, which I promptly threw up. Apparently I had swallowed a lot of seawater on the way over, which made my stomach queasy. After I had rested awhile I went back in the water to give someone else a chance in the boat.

When it became apparent that the Japanese ships were not going to pick us up (they left the area immediately after the *Pope* was sunk, probably fearing a submarine attack), a plan was worked out whereby groups of ten would take turns in the whaleboat, each group remaining in the boat about forty-five minutes.

The life rafts were not designed for prolonged periods in the water; although they were more comfortable than a life jacket, they were tiresome to be in. The raft consisted of a rectangular tubular-copper frame covered with cork and canvas; from the frame was suspended a rope net supporting lightweight wood flooring four to five feet below the surface of the water. A raft of this type has a large capacity for its size because the occupants stand on the flooring and are supported by the water as well as the raft itself.

Of the *Pope*'s entire complement of officers and men, only one man had been lost, and he had been killed before the *Pope* sank. The remaining 143 men had left the ship safely and were now all in one group. It was our intention to keep the group together, and to this end anyone who began to drift away was either called back or pulled back. In this way the little food and water we had could be distributed equitably, and anyone who became ill or collapsed had a better chance for survival than if he'd been alone.

After leaving the whaleboat, I held on to one of the rafts for a while and then finally climbed into the raft. Having nothing solid to lean against in the raft was like being in a crowded subway with no hand strap to hold on to. Fortunately the sea was calm and the raft did not move about.

By the time everyone was settled in a raft or the whaleboat, it was almost dark. Biscuits were passed out, one to each man, and canteens filled from the water breakers were passed from hand to hand with the admonition to take only a mouthful. Feeling neither hungry nor thirsty, I passed.

As night came on, the people in the boat slept and those in the rafts dozed. Several times during the night I started to doze off and each time I started to dream. I was on the bridge of the *Pope* standing an officer of the deck watch; I was very tired and began thinking about the end of the watch when I could go down to my room and sleep. Whenever I reached this point in the dream, I would awaken and realize that I was in a raft, that the *Pope* was gone, and there was no stateroom to go to and no place to sleep. The accompanying feeling of frustration and hopelessness had me close to tears. Fortunately I was too tired to follow the train of thought for long, and I dozed again.

When morning came I found that I had rested a little during the night. Some people in the raft had slept soundly—standing on their feet in water up to their chests. How I envied them.

The morning was gray and drizzly. Despite the warmth of the sea—more than eighty degrees—I began to feel chilled. I got out of the raft and swam toward the whaleboat. The wherry was upside down in the sea next to the whaleboat, and Captain Blinn and Strouse, a shipfitter, were in the water repairing the wherry. They used strips of cloth from a blanket and pieces of wood and nails from the biscuit cases to repair the larger leaks in the bottom. When they decided to test the boat, about six of us in the water combined our strength and righted it.

Strouse climbed into the wherry and began bailing with a helmet. When it was apparent that he was more than holding his own against the leak, another man climbed in gingerly to help out. In a few minutes there were four men in the boat, three paddling (with paddles from the rafts) and one bailing. With this arrangement proving successful, the wherry was put into use taking people who had gotten sick to their stomachs over to the whaleboat where they could rest. It was also used to take the biscuits and water from the whaleboat to the rafts.

We discovered that at least half of the cases we had put in the whaleboat before she left the *Pope* turned out to be medical supplies (which we needed hardly at all) instead of the corned beef we thought they contained. We managed to content ourselves with the thought that the corned beef would have made us too thirsty to be satisfied by our meager water supply.

Toward noon I had another turn in the whaleboat. I was cold and tired and must have looked disheartened, because Captain Blinn put his arm over my shoulders and tried to offer warmth and encouragement. Antrim was in the stern sheets of the boat trying to talk convincingly about the currents carrying us back to Java. The sun came out, which cheered us up.

We discussed the possibility of being picked up by one of our submarines. Or perhaps a PBY would spot us from the air and set down on the water. If we crowded a little, a PBY should be able to take twenty to thirty of us for a short haul. Later a plane did appear, but it was a Japanese reconnaissance plane. We waved to the pilot—what could we lose?—and he waved back but continued on his way. If worse came to worse, the Japanese would pick us up. This thought kept morale high, and there was little or no pessimistic talk.

The cigarette smokers in the crew found it almost impossible to satisfy their craving for a smoke because nearly all their cigarettes and matches were wet. Occasionally someone in the whaleboat would manage to dry out a cigarette. After struggling with a lighter he would get about one drag before he was forced to relinquish it to his clamoring shipmates.

Time passed slowly, and the almost constant immersion produced a number of annoyances. My armpits and nipples were sore from the constant rubbing of my life jacket—my shirt was slight protection. The combination of sun and saltwater had already cracked my lips, and my nose was beginning to feel tender from constant exposure to the sun. I was thankful to have only these minor discomforts; the wounded were experiencing real suffering yet there was hardly a moan out of any of them. Frame, the radioman, lay quietly in the stern of the whaleboat, his broken leg clad in bulky bloody bandages. Chief Pharmacist's Mate Coggins, a veteran of the trenches of World War I and now in his fifties, made the rounds of the casualties, giving them water and dressing their wounds. We rigged a combination sail and awning (a blanket) to protect us from the sun and used an oar for a mast.

Sundown was the best part of the day. The sun no longer beat down on us and the evening chill had not yet set in. A biscuit was passed out as the evening meal. Then two of the rafts were tied astern of the whaleboat and the third one astern of the wherry. The motor of the whaleboat was run at slow speed and the rafts were towed gently through the water. The wherry was hard pressed to keep up with the whaleboat, so the speed was slackened until there was only the illusion of motion. This activity, although producing little effect on our position, did cheer everyone with the thought that perhaps we were going somewhere. The sea was calm and the moon was bright; under almost any other circumstances it would have been a lovely jaunt.

At about midnight we sighted four ships that we soon identified as Japanese destroyers. They had to be Japanese; there were no other surface vessels in the Java Sea. We thought we still had a chance of being picked up by our own submarines, so it was decided to avoid being sighted if possible. The whaleboat's motor was stopped and everyone was cautioned to remain perfectly quiet. I sank down in the water up to my chin to be a little more inconspicuous. The destroyers steamed by about a thousand yards away without noticing us. We would have been an easy shot.

I spent the night in a raft and had dreams similar to those of the previous night. People around me were sleeping soundly and were occasionally a source of annoyance, for they would lean forward and backward as the raft moved with the motion of the sea. Some people still had shoes on, and when they kicked or moved in the raft the rest of us suffered.

The next morning was bright and clear. The brisk wind picked up the sea a bit but not enough to cause difficulty. I was given a place in the wherry with Sperandio, my chief boatswain's mate, and a couple of other men. The whaleboat's gasoline had been exhausted during the night, but an improvised sail and a pair of oars gave her some forward motion. The motor was dismantled and thrown overboard to provide additional room in the boat.

In the wherry we paddled around between the rafts and occasionally dropped back to bring a straggler into the group again. People in the water were becoming exhausted, and we would draw them out of the water for a short rest. When these cases became too numerous, we merely towed them over to the whaleboat, where they were taken care of.

One of the men we had in the boat was beginning to lose his mind. We had given him a drink of water from our canteen, but he wanted more. When we refused, he squeezed water out of his life jacket into his helmet and then drank it. I asked him what he thought he was doing, and he replied that the kapok filtered the salt out of the water and made it all right to drink. He finally stopped this mad practice when I told him either to stop or get out of the boat. As on the previous day, a Japanese plane circled us, and we searched the horizon for ships but saw none.

Antrim tried to divert our restlessness by suggesting that a cloud bank on the horizon was land, but the uneasiness persisted. Everyone knew that our food and water would be exhausted that day. The general opinion seemed to be that the wherry should be sent to the nearest land (wherever that might be) to get a native sailing vessel and return to pick up the others.

Sperandio, Mattila (a chief petty officer), Fisher, and I decided that we would make a good crew for the wherry and began to prepare for the trip. We collected money from those willing to help pay for the native sailing vessel if and when we reached land, then we went alongside the whaleboat to get water and food. When we asked Antrim to give us the approximate direction of the nearest land, he advised us strongly not to leave. Captain Blinn did not want us to go but felt that the decision was up to us. The ensuing conference canceled the expedition. The water and food were returned to the whaleboat, and the money was given back to the donors. We all got out of the wherry to give another group of four a turn out of the water.

Although canceling the trip was a letdown, we decided that the scheme was ill considered: the direction and distance to the nearest land were unknown, and there was no guarantee that we would find a vessel large enough to hold the crew of the *Pope* and then be able to return without navigational instruments to a tiny spot in the Java Sea.

I climbed into one of the rafts and tried to rest. Paddling the wherry had been more tiring than I had realized. The men in the raft looked worn out; their sunburned faces gave a false impression of ruddy health. The water had seemed cold after being in the sun, but being in the water seemed to have eased my thirst.

We considered ourselves fortunate not to be bothered by sharks. The gunfire and other explosions may have scared them away, or maybe our large group made enough noise to discourage their attention. When I was in the wherry we saw a snake about six feet long and attacked it with our paddles. Although we did not kill it, we managed to drive it off. Sea snakes of this type are peculiar to the Java Sea area and are extremely poisonous.

The day had been a hard one, for the sun had shone relentlessly. At sunset the remaining water—one mouthful each—and the last biscuits were distributed.

I took a place in the wherry again and was glad for the opportunity to spend most of the night out of the water. The people in the rafts were settling down for the night, and only occasionally would there be singing or conversation. The bright moon made it easy to see everyone and prevent anyone from drifting away.

At about 1030 someone in the whaleboat sighted ships ahead of us. We knew they had to be Japanese; the question was whether or not to signal them to pick us up. Antrim called over from the whaleboat and wanted to know the wishes of the people in the raft near us. Upon hearing that everyone favored taking a chance with the Japanese, I took the wherry to the whaleboat to join the discussion in progress. Our lack of food and water, the exhaustion of the entire ship's company, and the fact that we had seen no Allied planes or submarines in the past two days determined our decision to signal the ships. One of the signalmen took a battle lantern (a waterproof battery-powered lamp) and signaled to the lead ship using international Morse procedure, which the Japanese would understand.

The ship slowed and turned on its recognition lights. They may have thought we were one of their own ships challenging them. Soon they were within hailing distance, and a voice called to us in Japanese. Wilson's Japanase language course in Tokyo was about to bear fruit.

To their question of who we were, Wilson replied that we were survivors of the American destroyer *Pope* ("Popu-ga" was how he rendered the name). This did not seem to impress the Japanese, but Wilson and he continued to exchange Japanese rapidly. Occasionally Wilson would translate a few words to let us know what was going on. When the Japanese realized that we were Americans, he said he would take the officers aboard. When Wilson informed him that we had some wounded men, he agreed to take these too. After a few more exchanges Wilson told us that everyone would be taken aboard. The destroyer, for that's what it turned out to be, came alongside us, put over a Jacob's ladder, and turned on lights so that we could climb aboard. The wounded were taken out of the whaleboat first, then Wilson went aboard the ship to translate as the rest of us came aboard.

The prolonged period in the water had weakened everyone, and climbing up the ladder was a major effort. The wherry was the last to discharge its passengers. By the time I reached the ladder the Japanese were becoming impatient and shouted at me to hurry, or so I presumed. At the top of the ladder two Japanese sailors grabbed hold of me while another sprayed me with a carbolic acid mixture and a fourth went through my pockets and relieved me of my wallet and a string of rosary beads. Then one of them gave me a shove and I started to stagger aft. Wilson called to me to turn around and go forward. The Japanese were separating the officers from the enlisted men, and because I was wearing dungarees and no insignia they thought I was one of the crew.

I was led up to the forecastle, where the rest of the officers from the *Pope* were already assembled. Some Japanese sailors were rigging a canvas screen while others spread canvas on the deck for us. The

Japanese motioned us to sit down, and I was happy to comply. In a little while a bucket of a warm, sweet drink with a slight lemon flavor was brought to us, and we were allowed to drink a cupful apiece. We were also given hardtack, which was much superior to ours. This was not a princely repast, but it was wise to eat and drink sparingly until our shrunken stomachs could accommodate more.

Then we all lay down on the deck to sleep. Wilson was not in our group, and we assumed that the Japanese were questioning him.

5

The next morning I awoke a trifle stiff from sleeping on the deck. Bassett had just awakened too. "Call room service, Mike, and tell them to send up breakfast," he said sleepily.

In a little while everyone was awake and sitting up. We all needed shaves (except Austin, who had to shave only once a week) and our faces were sunburned. Bassett and I had badly cracked lips. Captain Blinn and Fisher were both a little deaf from the gunfire and bomb explosions. None of us had shoes and most of us were wearing dungarees. All in all we looked a disreputable lot.

The ship was headed in a northeasterly direction and was in company with a cruiser and several other destroyers. The destroyers seemed huge compared to the *Pope,* and the cruiser was much larger than our heavy cruisers. Japanese people were smaller than Americans, so I guess that made things even.

Two sailors with rifles and fixed bayonets stood guard over us. They did not bother us except to motion us to sit down whenever we stood up to stretch. A sailor brought our breakfast: warm milk and hardtack. The food was sufficient, and I suppose that milk was one of the best foods we could have had in our condition. After breakfast the smokers in the group began cadging cigarettes from the sentries and any other Japanese who happened to come within reach.

One of the differences between the Japanese ships and our own was the large pairs of binoculars mounted on their bridge. The object glasses were about six inches in diameter, which should have made them excellent night glasses. The decks of the Japanese destroyer were covered with a composition similar to linoleum, whereas

91

our destroyers had plain steel decks. Japanese uniforms included knee-length khaki shorts and short-sleeved shirts, canvas shoes, and hats similar to baseball caps. It was a sensible uniform for the tropics, but it didn't offer much protection against the flash of explosions. In the *Marblehead* bombing most of the casualties were due to bomb flashes, which badly burned any exposed body parts of personnel in the vicinity.

At about 1100 the destroyer we were on stopped and another destroyer came alongside. Cane fenders were rigged over the side, and sailors stood by with bamboo poles to keep the ships from coming together too rapidly; they came together without a bump. Although this method worked, none of us was impressed enough to think it should be used in our navy. A plank was put between the ships and our enlisted men were brought forward and sent across to the other ship. When they were all transferred, we were sent over and placed on the forecastle of the new ship. Wilson was not transferred with us. We saw him on the bridge of the destroyer before we left and shouted to him to try to retrieve our wallets, which had been taken from us when we first came aboard.

We once again headed in a northeasterly direction. Life on the new ship seemed a little more easygoing than on the first one. We asked for food and were given a bowl of what looked like corned beef. When the smokers asked for cigarettes, sailors passed their packs around, and an officer threw a pack down from the bridge. Instead of matches, a brass urn was supplied; its top had a hole in the center through which a piece of tarred rope was rove, with the burning end inside the urn. This must have been the Japanese version of the "smoking lamp" of the old navy.

We never lacked an audience on the deck. One sailor who spoke a few words of English began telling us lies about his athletic prowess; we dubbed him "Champ," which seemed to please him. Austin, who did not smoke, asked for candy. When we kidded him about this, he replied with unassailable logic: "Well, the people who smoke are bumming cigarettes; I don't smoke so I'm bumming candy." A sailor gave me mentholatum for my lips, and I was touched by his solicitude.

As evening approached we settled down for another night on deck. We were awakened several times and led belowdecks into the crew's living space. The first time this happened I thought it had begun to rain, but I soon realized that the ship had been alerted either by a submarine contact or by the sighting of some suspicious object. The compartment into which we were taken had no bunks or hammocks; rather it had several large, low platforms upon which the sailors spread their bedding. There was a distinctive odor to the place—not unpleasant, just different—and we came to regard it as typical of the Japanese.

After midnight the number of alarms decreased considerably, and we managed to get several hours of uninterrupted sleep before morning. For breakfast we had more "corned beef," Japanese potatoes, and Japanese coffee. Apparently we were being well treated, but I didn't like the potatoes and coffee. Everyone else seemed to enjoy the meal.

Almost four days had elapsed since the sinking of the *Pope,* but it was still hard to realize that the ship was gone for good. Our present situation was more difficult to deal with; we never thought it would happen to us. As Bassett remarked: "They can't do this to us—we're American citizens."

That afternoon, March 5, we sighted land. Later it became apparent that the ship was heading into port. Before the ship entered the channel, we were taken below again. Perhaps there was a minefield here and the Japanese were afraid we might notice the channel and reveal it to our own forces.

The guards in the compartment kept us amused with books made up of news photographs of the war and the Japanese home front. One of the guards offered us vitamin tablets in a bottle with a German label.

Finally we heard the rumble of the anchor chain running out, and the guards motioned us to go back on deck. We were in a harbor filled with ships of all types, including two large hospital ships. I spotted the steel mast of a sunken yacht near the breakwater, which confirmed our general opinion that we were in Makassar, on Celebes.

As we waited to embark onto a landing barge that had come alongside the ship, one of the ship's officers came over to try out his English. "I am sorry we could not make you more comfortable aboard this ship. When you go ashore you will learn true Japanese hospitality." We thanked him for his interest and for the kind treatment we had received. If this was indicative of the general attitude of the Japanese, maybe being a prisoner of war would not be too bad.

We scrambled into the landing barge to join our enlisted men. Most of them seemed to be in good spirits, and the wounded had been shown as much consideration as the circumstances permitted.

The sun was setting as the barge left the ship, and by the time we reached the landing, night had fallen. At the landing the sentries were impatient and seemed to shove us needlessly. Again the officers were separated from the enlisted men; they marched off first and we followed. It was now dark and there were no streetlights. The town seemed deserted; probably the Japanese had a curfew. We could make out an occasional demolished building and gutted stores. We learned later that this was the work of Dutch demolition parties and native looting parties—equal credit to each.

The sentries in charge of the enlisted men ordered them to double time, and our sentry tried to get us to run too. We protested and pointed to our shoeless feet; after a while he gave up and we continued at a walk. We halted in front of a large, dreary-looking building, and our guard shouted to someone inside. The door opened and we were led in. An open court was enclosed on all four sides by cells. We were taken to an empty cell, given some hardtack, and left for the night.

There was no light in the cell, but enough light came through the window to allow us to make out the layout of the cell. A wooden platform along both long walls served as sleeping accommodations. At one end of the cell was a barrel of drinking water. At first we were hesitant to drink, but thirst overcame our qualms. At the other end of the cell was a large covered bucket that served as a toilet.

We were all tired and immediately stretched out on the bunks to sleep. It took a while to drop off. I kept thinking about our predicament. The farther away from the ship we got, the worse our situation seemed to become. The guards were less cordial and the surroundings less pleasant. I imagined all kinds of insects inhabiting the cell. I worried that I'd be awakened by a rat nibbling my toe. Just as I was beginning to feel sorry for myself, I fell asleep and didn't awaken until morning.

Captain Blinn and Bassett were already up and were washing with water from the barrel. By daylight the cell looked less sinister, and I saw that the courtyard was covered with grass. My fears of the previous night seemed childish.

Outside we heard shouting and screaming, and we all crowded around the window to see what was happening. A native youth was tied to a post near our cell and a Japanese soldier was belaboring him with a club. Each time the soldier hit the youth, he would scream like a woman; the louder he screamed, the harder the soldier hit him. Finally the soldier stopped, but the boy continued sobbing.

At breakfast we were given one bun with a hint of butter. We kept waiting for the rest of the meal to appear. At noon we were still waiting; then we learned that there were only two meals a day—one bun in the morning and fish and rice in the evenings. We filled up on water.

Bassett found a twig broom in the cell and decided to sweep it out. When he finished he did not want to sweep the dirt into a corner, and there was no rug handy—so he pushed the dirt through the wide crack under the cell door. A few minutes later a Japanese soldier found the dirt and came into the cell shouting and waving his arms. When we realized what he was saying, we swept up the dirt. This seemed to calm him down, but as a parting gesture he whacked a couple of us with a stick.

The cells around the courtyard seemed filled, but we could not make out who the occupants were. We did learn that two young fellows who passed close to our cell were from HMS *Exeter*. They were surprised to hear that we were from the *Pope*, for they thought that we had gotten away after they were sunk.

In the course of the day we acquired mattresses, blankets, towels, and soap—Lux toilet soap at that. These new possessions gave us encouragement because they indicated some interest in our well-being.

The evening meal arrived: plain boiled rice and dried fish. The rice was unappetizing but edible; the fish was too rank for anyone to get near enough to eat it. The general opinion was that someone with a perverted sense of humor was playing a cruel joke by expecting us to eat such food. That night we all slept in our clothes and covered our heads with towels as protection against the mosquitoes.

The next day we were shifted to another cell across the court, putting us next to the cell containing some of the *Exeter*'s officers. In the afternoon we were allowed outside the cell for exercise and a shower under a hose. The daily shower came to be the best part of the day.

One morning the prisoners were shuffled again, and the British officers from the *Exeter* were moved into our cell. This was most welcome, because we had exhausted most of our topics of conversation. Gunner White had been on HMS *Prince of Wales* during the engagement with the *Bismarck*. Sublieutenant Jenkins, who had been serving on the *De Ruyter* as liaison officer, had been on the cruiser *Southampton* when it was bombed off Crete. Midshipman Hilton-Finn (we soon shortened that to Mickie) had been sunk twice on merchant ships in the North Atlantic and twice on naval vessels in the Far East (the *Prince of Wales* and the *Exeter*). Sublieutenant Bennett could not match these experiences, but he was able to tell us tales of undergraduate life at Cambridge. We in turn told them of our war experiences and about life in the United States—as we remembered it.

When Jenkins and Bennett took a sick officer to the hospital the previous day, they learned that the majority of *Exeter*'s personnel were in a prison camp on the outskirts of Makassar. Somehow the two had received permission to see a Japanese officer about being transferred to the camp. The officer had been pleasant enough, but no change was made. Jenkins and Bennett did bring back some novels (Penguin editions) from the Japanese headquarters; we read them avidly.

The fact that Jenkins and Bennett had been able to get out of the prison to visit the hospital gave our people some ideas. Fisher and Captain Blinn were both suffering from broken eardrums, and Lowndes had a cut that needed a dressing. They made arrangements through a native who was acting as interpreter for the Japanese to visit the hospital for treatment, then were told to be ready the next morning. We discussed the trip to the hospital, the main purpose of which would be the purchase of fruit, tobacco, and food from the street vendors whom Jenkins and Bennett had mentioned seeing.

During this discussion, a large group of Dutchmen was brought into the compound. About twenty of the new arrivals were put in our cell, which brought the total number to more than thirty; the cell was intended for half that many. The Dutch were all naval officers who had been captured in the Indian Ocean in an unsuccessful attempt to reach Australia. They had left Tjilatjap on a merchant ship, and the night before their capture had had a gala evening celebrating their "escape" from Java. The following morning two Japanese cruisers steamed over the horizon and signaled their ship to heave to. A prize crew was put aboard and the ship was brought to Makassar. The officers looked crestfallen, but at least they had decent clothes and had been permitted to take one handbag of personal effects from the ship. They were told that their heavy luggage would be sent on later.

The Dutchmen were quick to note that we had mattresses and they had none. They wanted us to share the mattresses, which we did if one of us was using a double mattress. We did not feel constrained to give them anything: they were evacuating Java whereas we were defending it; they now had full kits of clothing whereas we were in rags; and some of them smoked cigarettes endlessly (Chesterfields from vacuum-packed tins) without offering any to the American and British officers who obviously possessed none.

At the evening meal when the buckets of rice appeared, we were at a numerical disadvantage and might well have starved had we not held a council of war after our initial experience. Because our suggestion that we devise a system instead of everyone grabbing at once met with no response, we adopted a campaign of vigorous shoving and vociferous damning of the Dutchmen. The effect of this was that no matter how many Dutchmen were crowding around a bucket, at least one American would receive unobstructed access. In this way we managed to hold our own.

Despite the friction between the groups, we did manage to make some friends individually. Gongrip and Halsdingen were especially friendly toward the Americans. They both spoke excellent English (most educated Dutchmen spoke several languages). They would sit by the hour with us exchanging views on all subjects.

Although we were crowded (a number of people had to sleep on the floor) and had to struggle for food, there was a definite improvement of morale—among the Americans at least—because we now had a larger group sharing the same predicament. The old saying that "misery likes company" seemed unquestionably true.

The next morning Fisher, Lowndes, and the captain were taken to the hospital. The Dutchmen had told them the Malay words for various articles and the proper prices to pay for them. Just before noon they returned, their clothes bulging. The Japanese sentry allowed them to buy what they could eat outside the prison or carry inside the prison whatever they could conceal on their persons.

They emptied their pockets first, then began the "heavy" load. From inside their clothing they pulled out several dozen hard-boiled duck eggs, bananas, brown sugar, oranges, tobacco, and small doughnutlike cakes. It was like Christmas and a couple of birthdays rolled into one. We shared various articles with the British officers and gave part of the sugar to some of the Dutch officers. With the British we had the common bonds of language, of a battle fought together, and of survival from "shipwreck." We lacked these bonds with the Dutch.

After a few days in the prison, a sort of routine evolved. The arrival of our daily bread was the first event of interest; later we would be permitted a brief period of exercise outside the cell. During this time the drinking water barrel was refilled and the latrine bucket was emptied. In the afternoon we had a shower; then there was only a short wait until the evening meal. The last official item of the routine was evening muster, at which time two sentries came to count us. This was often a tiring business, for we remained in ranks until the two sentries agreed on the count.

The routine somehow made the monotony bearable. The rest of the time we stretched out on the bunks. Occasionally we could borrow a deck of cards for bridge or rummy. Whenever we attempted to get off the bunk, we would black out, a symptom of our weakened condition due to lack of food. We could still walk around all right, but any sudden changes of position were not advisable.

One evening after we had settled down for the night, we heard a great commotion outside in the courtyard. Looking out the window we saw a large group of prisoners being led into the yard. One of the sentries passed our cell and threw handfuls of cigarettes and candies to us. Antrim, Fisher, and I were at the window and intercepted most of the items.

The Dutchmen to the rear naively expected us to leave the window (which was at the head of our sleeping space) so that they could have a chance at the gifts. We had several packs of cigarettes and some "penny" cigars about the size of cigarettes. The habitual smokers celebrated their momentary prosperity by indulging in a whole cigarette apiece. Because I did not care for cigarettes but did enjoy a cigar occasionally, I felt within my rights to smoke one of the cigars. We later learned from the new arrivals that they were Dutchmen who had been captured evacuating Java. The surrender of Java was the cause of the sentry's jubilant spirits and generosity.

The Dutchmen did not seem particularly surprised that Java fell within a week of the first invasion, but to us it was a shock. The only reason for such a speedy defeat was that Java must not have been defended. We had been told that no sacrifice was too great for the defense of Java. Dutch military personnel whom we had encountered in Java boasted that it would be defended to the last man. Apparently the Dutch in Java did not have themselves in mind when they were talking about sacrifices and last stands.

One day Wilson was brought into camp and put into a cell by himself. He brought a canvas bag containing most of the wallets that had been taken from the *Pope* personnel aboard the Japanese destroyer. Fisher, being a paymaster, was put in charge of the funds. Most of the wallets were still damp. We took the wet bills out of the wallets and put them in a book to dry. Fisher kept track of the amounts from the wallets, but there were rolls of bills without any identification. These we grouped together, and the sum was used later as a welfare fund administered by a committee of enlisted men. The wallets were turned over to their owners later. My wallet was missing, but most of the other officers found theirs in the bag.

After almost two weeks in the prison, we were transferred to the prison camp on the outskirts of Makassar. I still had no shoes; I wore socks as a protection against sharp stones and the heat of the road. Fortunately it was cloudy during most of the hike, and the heat of the sun was not unbearable.

We passed many attractive houses and hotels, which indicated that the city in peacetime was both prosperous and well planned. A number of houses and shops bore signs to the effect that the owners were Indonesians. As an additional precaution the Japanese flag was displayed. We did not pass many people on the road. It was apparent that those who had not taken to the hills upon the arrival of the Japanese were staying indoors. We were surprised to see a middle-aged white woman pass by on a bicycle; the Dutchmen had told us that the Dutch women and children had been evacuated to Molino, a hill station. This woman had a Red Cross armband, but the Dutchmen said that it was just a blind because the woman was really a German.

I bought bananas from a passing native. The fruit was not quite ripe but I ate it anyway, glad to ease my hunger. The sentries tried to prevent these transactions, but the column was a long one and the sentries were few.

At last we arrived at our destination, a former Dutch army post. The buildings looked substantial and the camp, even at a superficial glance, seemed well laid out. It was surrounded by a high barbed wire fence that was obviously part of the original installation. With only slight alterations the camp served the purposes of the Japanese admirably.

We entered the camp through the archway, which was part of the administration building. Just inside the gate were two buildings of similar shape and size, one on each side of the road. The Dutch officers were marched to the building on the right, which was unoccupied. The American and British officers were halted in front of the other building, which was apparently occupied by British officers.

To our surprise we recognized some American naval officers among them. They were from the USS *Perch*, a submarine, which had been sunk in the Java Sea about the same time as the *Pope*. I recognized (with difficulty, for he was fully bearded) my classmate from the naval academy Jake Vandergrift and also Lieutenant Commander Hurt (skipper of the *Perch*), who had been one of my instructors at the academy. The other *Perch* officers—Schacht, Van Buskirk, and Ryder—I had known by sight but not by name. They all looked bedraggled and unshaven, and it was evident that they had not been faring any better here than we had in the jail. After a great deal of consultation, the Japanese decided that we could all move in together.

One morning toward the end of March, shortly after we had made our rearrangement of billets in the building assigned to the British and American officers, Wilson returned from a conference with the Japanese with news that permission had been granted for the Anglo-American group to move into the cottages situated along the southern side of the camp. The cottages had been the quarters of non-commissioned officers of the NEI Army before the war, when the camp was a Dutch army post. We had all passed by the unoccupied cottages and peeped through the shutters, noticing furniture and the desirability of the quarters in general. I remembered the morning well, for we had received a whole dried fish that we had ordered through the officers' "canteen" and were boiling it in a five-gallon tin over a fire we had built outside our quarters.

We moved to the cottages immediately; one trip was sufficient to transfer all our belongings. The American officers were assigned two adjacent cottages near the east end of the row. The remaining cottages were assigned to the British. There were fourteen of us, so the division was simple—seven to a cottage. The senior officers occupied one and the junior officers the other. Because Jake Vandergrift and I were "cooks," it was decided to set up the galley in the junior cottage, and we soon had our fish back on the fire.

The arrangement of the cottages was well planned and represented a good compromise between utility and economy. Four cottages were built as a unit of three basic structures: two cottages with a mutual wall faced one street and a similar arrangement in the rear faced another street. A structure between the pairs of cottages housed four water closets, four washrooms, and four kitchens, an economical arrangement for the piping.

The cottage proper was joined to the kitchen unit by a cement walk, which was separated from that of the adjacent cottage by a partition about seven feet high. The walks were covered by a common roof. The side away from the partition was open to a plot of ground that could be used as a garden. Each group of four cottages was separated from the next group by ground that formed part of the garden space. The gardens were fenced with barbed wire, either as a deterrent to housebreakers or to prevent the theft of the fruits of the garden.

Our cottage had a lime tree in the garden with sufficient fruit for limeade (when we had sugar) or with papaya (when we had papaya).

We also had furniture, which gave us welcome relief from sitting on the floor. The few mattresses we had brought from our former billet rounded out our bedroom suite, which also had a large mirrored cabinet. We never did learn why there was no bed.

In the kitchen of our cottage we found a tin containing flour. Jake added some to the fish "soup" to thicken it. While we were getting ready to serve the meal, Beriontes and Sarmiento, two of our Filipino mess attendants, told us they would work for us in the cottages. (Wilson had received permission from the Japanese to have them come over.) We explained that we had little to compensate them for their work, but they said that they would be glad to get away from the barracks and would find something to do. They immediately took over the "galley"; they removed the shreds of fish from the soup (constant boiling had pulverized the fish), mixed the fish with egg and flour, and produced delicious fish cakes. These were served after the soup, which we drank with the hope that it had some food value.

There was a distinct improvement in morale with our move to the cottages. Gradually we accumulated a stock of brown sugar (goela djava) and bananas (pisang), which served as dessert. We could occasionally buy coffee and peanuts from the officers' canteen. In the evening we would sit around drinking coffee and eating peanuts and feel almost civilized. The smokers in the group would roll cigarettes and smoke them with intense enjoyment.

On these occasions Captain Blinn would often announce that he was going to the kitchen for "a glass of water." Later we caught on to his forays into the communal sugar jar, which we then hid. After several unsuccessful attempts to find the "water," the captain seemed hurt to think that we did not trust him.

Among the other improvements in our lot was the establishment of a separate mess for the American officers (we had previously drawn our rations with the British officers). This is not to suggest that the British were shortchanging us—the food distributors were watched with eagle eyes—but it did give us a chance to get our food more quickly, and it established us as a distinct group in the camp setup.

Occasionally we were able to supplement our rations with trading over the fence that was near the cottages. Our Filipino stewards were able to make themselves understood to the natives who lived in the *kampong* behind the camp, and for a while we had a regular supply of duck eggs. One day they brought back a mess of fresh fish, which they duly fried to make the most delicious fish dinner I can remember. The medium of exchange was Dutch guilders, which we had in modest amounts.

Some of the British cottages that faced the fence did a lot of trading. Only a few of them had Dutch money, but they made the most of it. Often at twilight we would hear British voices struggling through Malay words and the native voices answering. Then there would follow a steady barrage of canned goods into the gardens of the British cottages. Until late into the night the Britishers would be picking up their purchases, feeling about in the dark under bushes and among the weeds for the stray cans. We often wished that we were as well off with finances and location.

About a week after we moved to the cottages, we received notice that some of the British and American officers and men were to be transferred to Japan: from the American group all the *Perch* officers and Wilson, Bassett, Spears, and Captain Blinn from the *Pope*. The radiomen from both ships were also included in the party. Those of us remaining behind had mixed emotions; we did not want to part company with our shipmates and friends but more emphatically we did not want to go to Japan.

The makeup of the party left little doubt as to its purpose. All commanding officers of ships were included as well as communications and gunnery officers. These were the people most likely to have knowledge of war plans, secret publications, and codes. That the Japanese should take these people to Japan for interrogation was not surprising, but that they allowed an entire month to go by before making a move was inexplicable.

On the day of departure Wilson came into our cottage with a bottle of vermouth that one of the Japanese had given him. Wilson poured a glass for each of us, and we drank a toast to our reunion under happier circumstances.

While the party was being mustered, we who were remaining went to the gate so that we could say a last good-bye. The men looked nondescript, wearing cast-off civilian clothes that the Japanese had collected in town, perhaps from the looted homes of Dutchmen. Most of the men were bearded, which heightened the hobo effect of the ill-fitting clothes. As they passed through the gate we shouted our farewells and wished them a safe voyage. Then we walked slowly back to our cottages in silence.

Because there were now only five American officers left in the camp (Antrim, Lowndes, Fisher, Austin, and myself), we moved into one cottage. We transferred some of the better chairs and the mattresses from the other cottage and made ourselves as comfortable as possible.

One evening soon after, van Brockel and Krauss paid us a visit. We apologized for being out of coffee and having nothing to offer them but water. Krauss left, saying he would be right back. When he returned he handed us a package of coffee. We accepted it gratefully but reluctantly, for coffee was hard to find.

During Krauss's absence, van Brockel informed us that he had been telling Krauss that the American officers had a native girl come into their cottage each night. To lend substance to his story he had taken Krauss to our backyard and shown him a hole in our fence and pointed out another hole in the fence at the edge of the camp a few yards from our cottage. "Notice," he said, "how one of them will get up and leave the group and pretend he is tired and going to bed. Don't be fooled; it means that the girl has arrived and it is his turn that night."

During their visit it just so happened that Fisher got up and announced that he was tired and would turn in early. Van Brockel immediately caught Krauss's eye and nodded toward Fisher; Krauss answered with a knowing wink.

The next day van Brockel came around and told us of the success of his hoax. When he and Krauss had gotten back to their quarters, Krauss was excited and somewhat annoyed. "Hell's fire, what's the matter with us? Those Americans don't even speak Malay and they've already arranged to have a girl come in from the *kampong*. Why don't we do something?"

Later that day Krauss came for a casual visit but soon broached the subject. Because we were all well primed, we just picked up where van Brockel left off. First, of course, we made him swear that he would not tell anyone. We told him that we had made arrangements with the girl's mother (to give the story a genuine ring), who understood a few words of English. The girl's name was Tina, and she was fairly attractive; the mother was heavy but a good sport. Krauss wanted to know what precautions we used; we admitted that we took a risk by relying solely on a good washing. We added little particulars to make the story more authentic. When Krauss left that afternoon, he was convinced that Tina and her mother were real.

When we saw van Brockel a few days later, he had more to tell us. Krauss talked so much about our "arrangement" that a couple of the other Dutchmen decided to have a little joke. Van de Pool said, "Krauss, if you really want a woman, I'll make the arrangements with the native policeman who has been bringing in the whiskey. If he can bring in the whiskey, he can bring in a woman." Krauss thought this would be just fine. To string along with van de Pool, some of the others said they wanted to be included. After supper, van de Pool informed the group that everything had been arranged but that they would have to draw lots to see who would have the girl first. Van Brockel was first and Krauss second. It might be well to mention that each man had a mosquito net, which gave almost complete privacy, at least visually.

Shortly after taps that night, when the men had gone to bed, a knock was heard on the window. Van de Pool, who was waiting for this signal, whispered, "There she is; I'll go out and bring her to the right bunk."

A lively conversation ensued between van de Pool and the girl (actually Gongrip, one of the Dutch officers). Gongrip, mimicking a native girl's voice, indicated reluctance to go through with the plan. More whispering followed. Then van de Pool came back into the room and said that the girl wanted to be paid first because she was afraid a sentry might come. After collecting the money, van de Pool went out and brought the "girl" to Brockel's bunk.

For the next ten minutes ecstatic sighs and groans came from van Brockel's mosquito netting. Krauss called over, "God *verdamme*, van Brockel, don't take so long." Finally van Brockel informed Krauss that the girl would be right over. Just as Krauss was ready to receive her, however, van de Pool, who was supposedly keeping watch, announced that a sentry was approaching. The girl left the room with a cry of terror. Gongrip returned a little later and found Krauss still berating van Brockel for taking so long. Not only that but the girl had gone off with his money.

Van Brockel took great delight in telling us the story, and our amusement was by no means forced. A few days later Gongrip dropped in to see us. I mentioned that we enjoyed hearing about the joke that he and van de Pool had played on Krauss. He asked how we had heard; when we informed him that van Brockel had told us, he had a good laugh. According to Gongrip, van Brockel was just as excited about getting a girl in as Krauss was, and when Gongrip went into van Brockel's bunk, van Brockel was ready and waiting. Only by clamping his hand over van Brockel's mouth did Gongrip prevent him from giving away the show.

Krauss did not suspect the truth for a while. In fact one day when I told him that we had never had a girl into our cottage, he was annoyed that I should try to deceive him about something for which he had almost positive proof.

Krauss was always good for a laugh, whether or not the joke was on him. He told us about a pen club he had joined before the war. While living in South Africa he had written to a pen club column in an American magazine stating his age and weight and general appearance (he was powerfully built though a little heavy) and that he was planning to return to Holland for a visit via the United States. He did not mention that he was married and had four children; he did mention that he was engaged in gold mining, which indeed he was.

Letters poured in by the hundreds, mostly from women, pictures enclosed. Krauss showed his wife the letters containing platonic sentiments and unattractive pictures; the others he arranged according to towns he planned to visit on his trip across the States. One girl from the southwest said she would take her trailer out to California to meet the steamship when it arrived on the West Coast and drive Krauss across the country. Krauss had her address with him but would not give it to us, although we offered to look her up on our return and tell her what a fine fellow Krauss was.

A few days after the men had left for Japan, we were sitting in front of the cottage when an automobile drove up and stopped in front of our door. A Japanese warrant officer and a white man got out. The white man was short and heavy and was wearing white trousers, a blue sport shirt, and shoes. By our standards he was well dressed. The Japanese bid the man good-bye and drove off. The man asked us if we were American officers and identified himself as Lieutenant Commander Donovan from the *Langley*. Introductions were made; he sat down with a cup of coffee and proceeded to tell us his story.

We all knew that the USS *Langley* had been sunk in February somewhere south of Java, but we had understood that all survivors had been picked up by our own destroyers. What, then, was Donovan doing here as a prisoner of war?

The *Langley* had picked up a load of American fighters in Freemantle, Australia, and was en route to Tjilatjap, Java, when a flight of Japanese bombers spotted her. Direct hits were scored on her and immediately she was afire. Attempts to control the fires were fruitless, and the captain ordered the crew to abandon ship. Two destroyers who were in company picked up survivors. The burning hulk was sunk by gunfire and torpedoes from the destroyers.

Because of the crowded conditions aboard the small destroyers, it was decided to rendezvous with the *Pecos*, a naval tanker in the area, and to transfer the *Langley*'s crew. The transfer was to be made off Christmas Island. Upon arriving at the island Donovan went aboard a pilot launch that had come from the island, intending to go to the *Pecos* and make arrangements for getting the survivors transferred.

As the launch passed astern of the *Pecos*, out of sight of the destroyers, Japanese planes were sighted. The ships immediately scattered, the destroyers thinking that Donovan was aboard the *Pecos*, and the *Pecos* not knowing he was coming. The launch was headed for the island, and as the planes passed overhead the boatmen beached the launch and disappeared into the jungle, leaving Donovan by himself. When the raid was over the boatmen returned but the ships did not.

Donovan was eventually taken to the small town on the island; he met the British governor, who made him feel at home. The population of the island consisted of four or five British government and mining company officials, a garrison of Indian troops with British officers and noncoms, and many Chinese coolies, who supplied the labor to work the phosphate mines.

Donovan reported his whereabouts to American authorities in Australia by means of the island's radio transmitter. A few days later Japanese bombers raided the island and destroyed the radio station, cutting off all communication to the outside world. The inhabitants could still keep abreast of the rapidly deteriorating war situation in the NEI by means of radio receivers on the island.

Donovan planned to join some Britishers who were preparing a boat for a sea voyage to Australia. Before their preparations were complete, however, a situation arose that made it impossible for them to leave. One evening as they were discussing their plans, the Indian troops began singing and chanting loudly outside. The British officer in command told them to keep quiet and to return to their barracks. The troops mutinied and killed the British officers and noncoms. The remainder of the white men were saved through the intercession of the Indian officer attached to the garrison, who claimed no knowledge of the mutineers' plans.

Donovan and the Britishers were confined in one of the buildings, and the troops took over the administration of the island. The next morning a white flag was raised in place of the British emblems to prevent further bombing by the Japanese. In spite of this, a Japanese naval force bombarded the island a few days later. The following day, transports arrived and the Japanese landed. The prisoners were released from their confinement and taken to the beach, where they helped the coolies and the Indian troops unload the Japanese landing barges.

When the Japanese learned that Donovan was an American naval officer, he was taken off the detail and put aboard a cruiser, where he was told that he was fortunate to be alive. The Japanese had seen the white flag and had decided that if a single shot was fired from the island during the landing they would kill whomever they found there.

Donovan's treatment aboard ship was humane. It was a novelty to have an American naval officer aboard, and he received a great deal of unsought attention, especially from men eager to try out their high school English.

By this time Java had fallen. After leaving Christmas Island, the cruiser put in to Batavia to refuel. Donovan was transferred to a merchant ship and in due time was put ashore on Makassar.

Donovan was a welcome addition to our group. Just for his story alone we were glad to have him, but besides that he was easy to get along with and a good bridge player to boot. His arrival helped take the place of our shipmates who had gone to Japan.

Donovan's views about the war agreed with ours. In six months or so the American juggernaut would be rolling back this way and all would be well. When I asked Donovan if he thought we would be sent back to the States on leave when we were liberated, he replied, "Why? We'll all be in good shape. They'll just stick us in an officers' pool until they can assign us to a ship." I remember feeling chagrined at this answer.

Shortly after Donovan arrived, Dutch troops who had been holding out in the hills of Celebes surrendered. They were brought into camp at night amid great precautions. Sentries were tripled, and we were required to keep our door and windows closed. Evidently the Japanese were expecting treachery of some sort.

The next day we saw some of the new arrivals. The officers looked very military in complete uniform including sabers, which they were permitted to keep under the terms of the surrender. They seemed to swagger a bit, but I could not understand why unless, in April 1942, they were the last group of Dutchmen to give up. I felt that they looked down on us barefooted ones, or perhaps I was merely feeling naked in the presence of the fully dressed.

In time we learned the details of the surrender. The detachment had retreated to the hills in central Celebes shortly after the Japanese landing in the Makassar area. (The Stadts Waacht, made up mostly of elderly Dutch businessmen and untrained youngsters, was left to surrender with the fall of the city of Makassar.) The size of the group made it of little military importance, but the fact that the rest of the NEI had surrendered caused the Japanese to be particularly anxious to mop up these holdouts.

Because of the detachment's inaccessibility in the hills, the men could not be captured without disproportionate losses on the part of the Japanese. The Japanese therefore resorted to a low but characteristic trick: they threatened to kill all the Dutch women and children (who had been sent to Molino, a hill resort south of Makassar, for safety) unless the detachment surrendered. This left the group with no alternative; nevertheless they were stiff-necked enough to demand terms such as humane treatment for all prisoners on Celebes, maintenance of administration within the camp by the Dutch army, and the transfer to the camp of medical and food supplies still in their possession. These terms were kept by the Japanese as long as it pleased them. When they no longer wished to abide by the agreement, they transferred the Japanese officer who had negotiated the surrender, and his sucessor refused to be bound by terms not agreed to by him personally.

The internal administration of the camp was now theoretically in the hands of Lieutenant Colonel Gortmans, who had the nickname of Johnny War. He had spent a colorful life in the army in the Indies and had taken part in numerous battles of subjugation of natives in Sumatra and Borneo. At the beginning of this war he had participated in skirmishes with the Japanese in British and Dutch Borneo. He reminded me somewhat of a fighting cock, lean and tough, though on in years. He was respected by all the Dutchmen, especially the younger ones, who viewed him with awe and admiration.

Each morning, Johnny War held a conference, which the senior British and American officers attended. The needs of the various groups were discussed: the Americans and the British were survivors of sunken ships and had come into camp with only the clothes on their backs, whereas the Dutch had come with spare clothing and in many cases possessed full kits. The orders of the Japanese authorities were also transmitted. These conferences, like most international conferences, did not always go smoothly, but some agreements were reached, and conditions in camp gradually improved.

Our funds were running low. We had the money that Wilson had gotten back from the Japanese aboard the destroyer, and the loose cash that had been turned over to the welfare committee of the enlisted men for the use of both the *Pope* and *Perch* crews. The money belonged to the *Pope* men of course, but we had decided that it should be used for both groups. We didn't want the *Perch* men (who were now without officers from their ship) to feel that they were a separate group. This action drew comment from a few *Pope* men, but on the whole the men thought it was the proper thing to do.

Meanwhile we officers arranged for a joint personal loan from one of the Dutch officers to buy soap, fruit, sugar, tobacco, and other items available in the officers' canteen. The arrangement was as follows: we submitted a list of what we wanted each week; when the native merchant brought the goods into camp, they were allotted on a pro rata basis. A decent supply of soap and fruit arrived each week. We stocked up on soap, because we did not know when the supply would be cut off.

The enlisted men did not have a canteen, but through the persistent efforts of Antrim and Donovan, the Japanese finally agreed to let a merchant come into camp on Sunday, the rest day, so that the men could make purchases. They would no longer have to rely solely on the working parties for goods.

The working parties were drawn from all nationalities in proportion to their numbers in camp. In the beginning the Americans supplied thirty men from the total group of two hundred. On this basis the group could be made up of volunteers. Later, the call for working parties increased, and it was necessary to run a roster and in some cases to send all men not on the sick list.

The American working party was eventually picked to work at the hospital in town each day. There they did odd jobs such as cleaning up rubbish, cutting grass, unloading supplies, and anything else the Japanese thought of. The Dutch and the British had previously been assigned this detail; when the Americans were put on the job, it was decided to keep them on it permanently. The story went around camp that "the Dutch were too lazy, and the British were too dirty. The Americans stole everything in sight but at least they did some work and were clean."

Seldom did the working parties come home empty-handed. Because "shakedowns" were not infrequent, "loot sacks" were made to conceal the contraband. Bags with strings at each end were tied to the legs. For the most part the loot sacks were highly successful, though they gave the wearers a strange gait.

The men did not usually consume what they brought into camp; they sold it for whatever the market would bear. In this way they accumulated capital for purchases from the natives while out of the camp. By employing this Yankee trader spirit, the Americans who had entered the camp in rags and almost penniless were in time well supplied with cash and the luxuries of life—such as they were.

One day Fisher went to the American barracks to listen to our swing band practice. (Some musical instruments had been found in camp—relics of the Dutch army band of the garrison—and the Japanese had given permission for the various nationalities to use the instruments.) While Fisher was there, one of the Japanese sentries tossed a stone in the window of the barracks. Our men paid no attention at first, but when the Japanese started shouting, they put their instruments in the cases and started to leave the building.

The Japanese singled out Fisher and began to swing at him with a club. Fisher told him he was an American officer and that the men had been practicing their music. This infuriated the sentry, and he grabbed Fisher's arm and led him toward the guardhouse. Meanwhile one of the men ran to our cottage and informed us of what was taking place. We found Fisher at the gate trying to talk to this madman of a sentry. Donovan and Antrim attempted to find out what the difficulty was, and Fisher told them what had happened.

I was sent to get the Dutch interpreter, but he had gone with a party of patients to the *Op Ten Noort,* the Dutch hospital ship that the Japanese were holding in Makassar. When I returned, the Japanese had taken Fisher to the guardhouse, where a native interpreter was translating what the Japanese said to a Dutchman, who in turn was translating into English for us. Finally we were told that the sentry intended to give Fisher forty lashes across the buttocks with a four-foot length of manila hawser, the method used in the Japanese navy for administering corporal punishment. Because there was no means of stopping the Japanese now, Antrim told me to go to the gate and bring the interpreter as soon as he arrived in camp.

I watched the procedure with morbid curiosity. A chair was brought for Fisher to hold, then a basin of water arrived to revive him in case he should faint before the punishment was completed. The Japanese swung the hawser like a baseball bat, hitting Fisher across the buttocks. Fisher took the punishment bravely.

At about the tenth blow, Ketal, the Dutch interpreter, arrived in camp. I told him to come to Fisher immediately. Ketel, who was feeling fine from the Bols gin he had had aboard the hospital ship, was as fearless as a lion. We reached Fisher at about the fifteenth stroke, at which time he was knocked off balance and fell down. Ketel tried to speak to the sentry, but he would not listen. Meanwhile another sentry aimed a kick at Fisher's head. Fisher saw it coming and caught it on his shoulder instead.

Antrim offered to take the remainder of Fisher's punishment. His intention was obvious to the crowd of prisoners looking on, and they began to applaud and cheer. At this the Japanese guards rushed out of the guardhouse, fixing bayonets as they ran. The crowd dispersed. One of the sentries vented his rage by bayoneting a basketball that had been left nearby. Meanwhile Ketel told Fisher to stand behind him and pay no attention to the Japanese.

Antrim's offer to take Fisher's punishment put the Japanese at a loss. Yoshida, as we later found out was the instigator's name, refused to accept Antrim as a substitute and tried to pull Fisher from behind Ketel. Eventually a Japanese petty officer, Hatayama, the senior petty officer of the guard, arrived from town. He called a halt to the proceedings and, after listening to the interpreter and Yoshida, told Fisher to return to his quarters.

Back at our cottage we put petrolatum on Fisher's buttocks to prevent severe bruises. He was tired and tried to rest; he was in pain and in shock. That evening some of our Dutch friends visited us to give Fisher their sympathy. Gongrep, one of the Dutchmen we had met in the cell at the Makassar jail, brought some Chesterfield cigarettes, a rarity in the camp, to help Fisher forget his pain. To our surprise a number of Japanese sentries came to see Fisher. He had to take down his shorts to show his bruises while they made sounds of sympathy. Several of them brought gifts of cigarettes for him. This unexpected gesture indicated to us that the Japanese guards in general did not approve of the afternoon's beating.

We finally received an explanation for the beating. It seems that the Japanese had issued orders to Johnny War not to play the musical instruments during working hours. The orders had not been passed on to us. Because Fisher was an officer, he was seen as doubly at fault because he should have known the regulation and should have been an example to the men. Yoshida's logic was not flawed, but the punishment did not fit the "crime."

In time Yoshida came to be known throughout the camp for his sadistic beatings, and he was called "Gold Teeth" and "The Mad Monk" (the latter applying to his simian rather than his religious attributes). When he was angered he would fly into a rage and deliver summary punishment to anyone who happened to be even remotely involved.

One day the American enlisted men had done something to annoy Yoshida. He called out our entire group and said he was going to give each man ten blows with his club. The first man got the full measure, but with each swing Yoshida became more tired. The perspiration poured off him, and he had to stop to catch his breath or remove his shirt. By the time he had dealt with twenty men he was exhausted, and in disgust he gave up and chased the men back into the barracks. It was possible to find him amusing, if you were not one of the first twenty in line.

A short time after Fisher's beating, a sentry at the barracks beat some of the men because they had firewood that he thought they had stolen from the galley. They had actually bought it from Dutchmen who had brought it from town. These transactions were so involved that it was no wonder that the Japanese became confused and tried to settle matters by giving everyone in sight a blow.

Donovan, who investigated the beating but spoke no Japanese, tried to explain by sign language that the men had bought the wood. He must have used the wrong signs, because the Japanese motioned him into position and beat him across the buttocks with a baseball bat. We gave Donovan the petrolatum treatment that had worked so well with Fisher. Then those of us who were still "virgins" joked nervously about who would be next.

We did not receive much news in camp, and each day was much like the previous one. It was sunny all day but became warm around noon, so we would take a siesta after lunch. The evenings were cool and the stars were bright—much brighter than in the temperate zones. Stars shining through the trees seemed to be hanging from the branches.

It seemed that whenever the monotony of our existence was about to become too annoying, something interesting happened. One day a new group of prisoners was brought into the camp—one

Australian and the rest Dutchmen. The group had come down from Menado, in northern Celebes. The Aussie, Ted Howard, was an aviator who had been shot down over Minahasa and managed to swim ashore at Menado. He never saw the rest of his plane crew again. He and the Dutchmen from Menado told us about American naval personnel who had come to Menado from the Philippines.

Grover De Long (a classmate of Lowndes's), several CPOs, and some Catholic missionaries escaped from the Philippines just before the capitulation and made their way to Menado. They were met by Japanese troops as they beached their boat. In the encounter, shots were fired from the boat, and one of the Japanese soldiers was killed. Because flight was now impossible, the American group surrendered and was brought to the local jail in Menado. The Americans were placed in a cell next to the Dutch prisoners—civil servants and area troops. A day or so later the Americans were removed from their cell and did not return. The Dutch later learned from natives who were working around the jail that the Americans had been beheaded.

A few days after this, the Dutch themselves were taken from their cells. They thought that beheading might be in store for them. As they left the jail, mobs of natives pelted them with stones and refuse to drive them out of the town. The Japanese put them aboard a small interisland ship and brought them to Makassar. The demonstration by the natives had been instigated by the Japanese, but the natives had sufficient latent hatred for the Dutch that they required little urging.

The Dutchmen from Menado told us another story about an American sailor, this one lighter in tone. But first, the background of the story. When the war started, the *Pillsbury* and the *Peary,* two destroyers of the Asiatic Fleet, were in the navy yard at Cavite undergoing repairs. In the first daylight raid on Manila, these ships suffered damage and loss of personnel, so they were not able to leave Manila Bay until January. The ships finally made their way south to the Dutch East Indies taking separate routes: this was a hazardous undertaking because the Japanese controlled the air and sea around the Philippines. The ships traveled by night; in the daytime they anchored close to shore camouflaged with palm fronds. In some cases this was as perilous as detection by the Japanese, for many of the men contracted malaria from the mosquitoes.

Now for the story. The *Peary* had reached the coast of Celebes just off Menado when she was attacked by aircraft. The previous day, Japanese bombers had attacked her; this time the planes were Australian. To scare off the planes the *Peary* fired her 4-inch guns. These surface guns could not be expected to hit the planes, but it was hoped that the flashes would give the impression of strong antiaircraft armament that would deter the attacks.

The ruse was successful, but the blast of one of the salvos blew a seaman, Billie Green, over the side. The ship could not stop to pick him up while under attack, so he was given up for lost. But Green made the beach near Menado. He was taken in by the Dutch, who had seen the engagement and who also had a memento of the episode—a 4-inch shell in the wall of the Menado Hotel.

When the Japanese took Menado, Green was among the captives. The Japanese interrogated and registered all the prisoners. When Green told him that he was an American sailor, the interpreter told him to go back to the cell and reconsider his impossible story. When he was called again he told the interpreter that he was an American typewriter salesman who had been stranded on Celebes by the war. The interpreter accepted the story, then gave Green a short lecture on the wisdom of telling the truth. So Green was placed in the camp with the civilian internees because he was obviously a noncombatant. When the Menado group was brought to Makassar, Green remained with the civilians who occupied cottages around the outside of our camp. That was the last I heard of him.

Austin made the acquaintance of Ted Howard, the Australian in the group, almost as soon as he entered camp. He took Ted to meet the senior British officers in the camp and then brought him to our cottage. Because we were not too crowded and the British had not given Ted a particularly warm welcome, we asked him to live with us.

After Ted moved in, we realized that our action had unintentionally put the British in a bad light. Some of them felt that we had not given them a fair chance to ask Ted in. We merely thought that Ted would rather be with an English-speaking group than with the

Dutch, and because the British had not made the first move it was up to us to extend an invitation.

Our life in camp went on in a fairly even tenor. The quantity and quality of food had picked up. We were now getting three meals a day. The morning meal was usually bread, duck eggs, and coffee; the noon meal was rice, vegetables (usually bean sprouts), and beef (carabao) or pork with a sort of gravy. The evening meal consisted of bread, cooked eggs or a hash of some sort, and coffee. Because we were a small group and drew our ration separately, it was usually generous. (The galley help was used to measuring fifty rations at a time.) As a result we ate our meals family style, each one taking as much as he wanted. There were no complaints about anyone taking more than his share.

Beriontes and Sarmiento, our Filipino mess attendants, prepared our breakfast eggs and toast and even made jam for us out of brown sugar and papaya rinds and fruit. When we had canned milk they made rice pudding from leftover rice. They also cleaned up the cottage for us.

We had little to offer in return other than gratitude. We gave them fruit and tobacco and our extra food. Occasionally we gave them money, but more often than not they would use it to purchase a spice or something to add to our menu. Perhaps they enjoyed working around the cottage because it gave them something to do and lent some purpose to their existence, but more likely it was a sense of loyalty.

Sarmiento was the comedian of the pair and always had a wise-crack. Beriontes was serious and a bit timid. On board the *Pope* he had seemed slow and constantly bewildered; around the cottage he seemed to find himself. He offered suggestions when a household problem confronted us. When Fisher had a bad infection in his foot, Beriontes dug an herb out of the garden and made a poultice, which brought the infection to a head as we watched. In a few minutes the foot was draining. It seemed like black magic, so sudden were the results.

Our duties in camp were light. We took turns at mustering the en-listed men and making the report to the guardhouse. As for inspecting the barracks for cleanliness, it was hardly necessary. The men set up their own cleaning schedule and held regular field days without any urging on our part. Most of our time was spent reading and playing bridge. Donovan got hold of some paint one day and painted an acey-deucey board on a small table. Buttons were used for counters, and we bought a pair of dice from the canteen.

6

Whenever we began to think that life was agreeable, the Japanese would beat up someone or impose a new regulation. Then, realizing that we were subject to the whims of our captors, we would experience again the frustration of our inability to alter the circumstances.

For some time it had been a source of annoyance to the Dutch officers that the British officers were living in quarters more desirable than their own. By some means they persuaded the Japanese to move the British officers to a building near the British enlisted men's barracks. The camp was partitioned into Dutch, British, and American sectors by erecting wire fences around the British buildings and around the American barracks, leaving the rest of the camp to the Dutch.

This order emanated from the Japanese authorities, but there was little doubt that it had been instigated by the Dutch. It was decided that because we American officers occupied only one cottage, it would not be necessary to move us into the American sector. Instead we moved into a cottage at one end of the row—to maintain the illusion of separate camps. With this new arrangement Ted Howard had to leave us to move in with the British.

The change was an improvement for us because our new cottage had a garden with beautiful flowers and a guava tree. We also had a phonograph with a good selection of records, and a shower hose, which the British midshipmen, the former occupants of the cottage, left us because they would have no use for it in their new quarters. There was a birdcage with a parrot, but this was not among the desirable features.

119

Before leaving our old cottage, we stripped the lime tree of all ripe fruit and exchanged some of the furniture to make sure we had comfortable chairs. The latter action brought some sharp words from Donovan, who wanted to adhere to the order of taking only our personal belongings. We won him over by pointing out that we had to take the acey-deucey table, and the mere exchange of chairs was not an infraction.

The division of the camp isolated us and curtailed most social intercourse with our friends among the British and the Dutch. Each nationality was now forbidden to visit with the others, but we got around that. We could visit the British or the Dutch, which was easier than for them to visit us. If a sentry counted more than six in our cottage, he knew someone was there who did not belong.

Shortly after the change, a truckload of books was brought into camp from the Dutch houses in town. We had been asking the Japanese for reading material, which they probably did just to stop us from bothering them further.

With typical Japanese logic they decided that, because the camp was divided into nationalities, books printed in English were to be used by Americans and British only. This was a blow to the Dutch, because most of the best books were printed in English and nearly all the Dutchmen could read English. (Because of the comparatively small population of Holland, few books are published, but the price of books is high because the market is limited.) We now had a library of about 2,500 volumes to share with the British. Some of the books were pirated editions of American and British best-sellers; others were expensive limited editions. The range of subject matter was broad enough to satisfy the most catholic tastes.

Jenkins, the British librarian, set up a system of distribution and book repair. A catalog of all the books was made up for general information. Each man in our cottage made up a list of ten books that he would like to read; with these lists as a start, Jenkins arranged to reserve the books for us so that we would always have one book apiece from our lists.

For our enlisted men we drew a miscellaneous lot of about 150 books. Each week the man designated librarian for the barracks would pick out 40 to 50 books for the men. Every week we would return to Jenkins whatever books needed repairs and the unpopular books, receiving in return an equal number of new books. The system worked well.

Late one afternoon more prisoners arrived in camp; among them were two Americans—Walt Haines, an army pilot, and his gunner, Collins. Walt joined us in our cottage and Collins became the only soldier in the American barracks.

After we gave Haines supper (we had finished eating a few minutes before), we began popping questions at him. Though he was tired from his trip, he sat up with us and told his story. He had arrived in Australia in January 1942 with a dive-bomber outfit. It was one of the army's first dive-bombing squadrons; the planes were navy dive-bombers converted for land-based operations. After shaking down in Australia, the squadron was ordered to Java to reinforce the Allied air forces there. The planes were to be flown in short hops through the islands because they did not have the range for a direct flight from Australia to Java.

While landing at Soemba (one of the NEI islands), the plane ahead of Walt's cracked up in the middle of one of the runways. Walt was forced to use the remaining runway, which ended in a marsh. Walt's plane hit the runway safely, but before it stopped rolling it hit the marshy ground and overturned. The accident broke Walt's collarbone, and he was placed in the local hospital. The pilot of the other wrecked plane was uninjured, and he took Walt's plane, which was easily repaired. The group could not wait for Haines to recover and left him in Soemba with Collins.

When Walt recovered, there was no way for him to get to Java, so he joined the local defense unit. He and Collins stripped the wrecked plane and set up its machine guns on a wharf near the town to be used against Japanese planes. During a raid they managed to shoot down a plane with these .30-caliber guns.

When news of the surrender of Java reached Soemba, Haines and Collins planned to escape from the island in a small boat with some Dutchmen. After traveling for a couple of days, they learned that the Japanese had already reached Soemba in landing craft; they decided that they could not make good their getaway. They proceeded to the nearest town and surrendered with the Dutch forces there.

They were locked up in the local jail. One of the Japanese guards came to Walt's cell and asked if he was an American aviator. When Walt replied in the affirmative, the guard threw Walt to the ground and his arm was broken; while he was down the guard kicked him and broke several ribs. Then the guard left him there and refused to allow him any medical attention. A Dutch doctor came to see Walt that night and put his arm in splints and taped his ribs. The next morning the Japanese guard returned. Upon seeing that Walt had received medical attention, he kicked Walt's arm and then sought out the doctor and beat him unmercifully. In spite of his beating, the doctor returned to Walt that night to make sure that he was all right.

After a month or so, the Japanese decided to transfer the prisoners from Soemba to Celebes. They were put aboard a small ship along with Dutch women and children. One of the women had been raped by a Japanese officer and was carrying his child. (Japanese men did not usually molest female European prisoners; they supposedly did not find them attractive.) The prisoners were all brought to Makassar, where the women and children were placed in the civilian camp and the men were brought to our camp.

Walt brought with him some cigarettes of the type smoked by the natives of Soemba. The "tobacco" was a kind of wild grass; it was enclosed in a piece of palm leaf and rolled into a cone shape, which was tied with a bit of string. After trying one of these, we felt that not all of the atrocities of the war could be attributed to the Japanese.

Walt's arrival into our group gave us cause for a number of bull sessions. We had been to Australia, but only to Port Darwin, a place most Australians would be happy to disown. Walt had spent time in Brisbane and could tell us all about Australian women and beer. Both reports were good. We had many laughs over Walt's tales of his flight training days.

One day we got Holleven, a Dutch army officer who had a good sense of humor and a talent for art, to do a watercolor of Walt having his picture taken in a plane. The picture showed Walt seated in the cockpit, a photographer in the foreground and sighing damsels looking on. Walt was depicted wearing helmet and goggles and a six-foot silk scarf. A small fan was shown forward of the cockpit blowing the scarf out straight to give the impression of flight. On the side of the fuselage was tied a panel bearing a flaming skull. We presented this watercolor to Walt with due ceremony, and then forcibly restrained him from tearing it to bits.

Until now we had no serious illnesses in our group. Then one day Antrim came down with a severe attack of malaria, and the doctors decided that he should be taken to the hospital ship, where he would get proper medicine and care. When he left we wondered when we would see him again. Judging from the initial violence of the fever, we expected that it would be a while before he returned.

We received reports each week when the interpreters made their trip to take and bring back patients. After a few weeks Antrim was out of bed, but he was kept aboard ship to convalesce. From one of his notes we learned that Frame, one of the *Pope*'s radiomen, who had broken his leg in our final battle, had contracted tuberculosis. His case presented a serious problem: he needed to walk to give his leg exercise, but his tubercular condition demanded a maximum of rest. The doctors were not too optimistic.

Occasionally news of the outside world filtered into camp. Sometimes a Dutchman would get hold of a Japanese newspaper printed in Malay and pass on a translation to us. At least one native was listening to shortwave news broadcasts from San Francisco, and these reports were somehow smuggled into camp.

In June we had reliable reports of the Coral Sea and the Midway battles and of the repulsed attack on Dutch Harbor. In general the news was good, but the opinion grew increasingly in camp that the war would last much longer than had originally been expected. Most of us thought that it would be at least a year before we were liberated.

Austin was our most persistent news hound. He would make the rounds of the camp several times a day picking up a rumor here and "straight dope" there. The source of the latter was usually something like this: the working party was told the "news" by a well-dressed Chinaman on a bicycle, or one of the guards "who never discussed war news" told the "news" to the men who were cleaning out the guardhouse. It was always surprising to find out later that some of these rumors were based on fact.

When the Dutch moved into the cottages vacated by the British, the cottage adjoining ours was occupied by Lieutenant Colonel Gortmans (Johnny War). He and Donovan became close friends, and soon Gortmans was spending as much time in our cottage as he spent in his own. It was through this friendship that Donovan was able to get adequate clothing and soap for our men. (The Japanese occasionally brought into camp odd lots of clothing and shoes—all used but serviceable—and sometimes soap and tobacco, the results of rummaging through some previously overlooked warehouse.)

Sometimes Johnny War would call Donovan to have a drink, usually a gift bottle sent over the fence by a friendly native. The quality of the stuff would make the friendship suspect, however. On one occasion Johnny War came back with Donovan late at night and insisted on playing the phonograph. After a couple of numbers (we expected a sentry to appear at any minute), Johnny War left. The next morning we found out that he had made a tour of the cottages, throwing eggs into the open windows. Donovan, who had tried to dissuade him, received most of the blame from the irate Dutch officers. When they learned who the culprit was, they thought it was a good joke.

Among Johnny War's troops were a number of soldiers who were expert in making bamboo furniture. They had made a bamboo bed for Johnny War, and we asked if they would make a bed for us. They used heavy bamboo sections for the legs and split bamboo for the "spring." It was large enough for four and did not sag with all of us on it. They also built a shed with a tin roof in our garden so that we did not have to move our mess table (a tabletop set on two trestles) every time it rained.

When the guavas began to ripen, Beriontes made guava jam, which went well with our French toast at breakfast. The guava tree with its fragrant fruit would draw the fruit bats at night. Before we had the shed built, our mess table was located in the shade of the guava tree, and each morning we would find evidence that the bats had been eating fruit during the night.

Ants were another source of annoyance. They would find our bread and sugar in the cabinet and do their best to carry them off. After a little experimentation we finally thwarted this threat to our food supply by putting the bowls containing the food in dishes filled with water. Occasionally we were careless and allowed a piece of bread to touch the side of the cabinet, and our next visit to the cabinet would disclose a horde of ants on the bread.

Flies were also a bother. They were particularly annoying when one was trying to take a nap during the day. Our fly-killing sessions provided temporary relief, but we were never entirely free of them. The only insect that we successfully deterred was the mosquito. When playing bridge in the evening or reading, we burned Chinese punk under our chairs; when sleeping we were protected by netting.

Somehow we had acquired a stock of paper that we used as toilet tissue. One day the Japanese put out the order that paper no longer could be used for this purpose, because it was allegedly interfering with the operation of the septic tanks. This presented a new problem. One solution would be to take a shower instead of using toilet tissue, but this seemed unsatisfactory, especially if one happened to have an attack of diarrhea. We finally went native and used a bottle of water, the custom in the Indies. It required a certain amount of dexterity and good sense of balance, but in time we learned the knack.

A few weeks after his arrival in camp, Walt Haines had an attack of appendicitis. It was at times like this that the detention of the Dutch hospital ship in Makassar, though contrary to international law, was a godsend. Walt was taken to the ship for the operation and was kept aboard until he recovered completely.

In Walt's absence our bridge game suffered a setback. Lowndes did not know how to play, and Donovan did not like to sit up every night playing cards. Lowndes responded to the situation nobly and sat down with us to learn the game; he had tried once before but had lost patience with our method of teaching. This time he saw it through and before long he was avid. When we did not feel like playing cards in the afternoons, he would go over to the British officers for a game and play again with us in the evening.

When Haines returned from the *Op Ten Noort* about three weeks after his operation, he brought new topics for conversation. Antrim was up and around but had apparently lost a lot of weight. Walt had noticed a number of Dutchmen aboard the ship who looked well enough to return to camp but for some reason were kept aboard.

There was a good canteen aboard the ship, but prisoners other than Dutchmen were restricted in the use of it. This was especially annoying because the canteen sold Mascot cigarettes, a brand not unlike American cigarettes.

Other instances also produced friction among the prisoners. When a British patient complained of not getting a full ration, he was told by the Dutch, "Remember this is a Dutch ship and you are just a guest." In addition, the doctors and nurses did not feel that they were in the same category with the rest of the prisoners; they were noncombatants and should be allowed to proceed with the ship to Australia. They periodically brought up this proposition to the Japanese, who apparently had no intention of letting the ship go.

Let me explain how the *Op Ten Noort* came into Japanese hands. At the beginning of the war the ship was stationed in Surabaja. During one of the bombing raids the ship, though plainly marked as a hospital ship, was hit although not seriously damaged. She was ready for duty again at the time of the Java Sea battle and was sent out to pick up survivors of the sunken Allied warships.

While on this mission the ship was captured by the Japanese, a breach of international law but of no particular consequence at the time to the Japanese, who were confident of victory. The ship was taken to Banjarmasin in Borneo, where the Japanese put aboard some of the *Exeter* survivors. The Dutch in command of the ship refused to feed the prisoners of war for fear that this would jeopardize their status as noncombatants—and their chances of being released.

The British prisoners were extremely frustrated, for by looking through the skylight of the main salon they could see their Allies eating full-course meals while they starved. Their hunger was relieved by rations supplied by the Japanese.

From Banjarmasin the ship was taken to Makassar, where the British and some of the Dutch were transferred to the camp and jail. The fact that the ship's personnel were kept aboard gave them hope that their stay at Makassar would be brief.

Haines had gotten on well with the people aboard the ship. But he could not help note that it was always the same group of convalescing patients who volunteered to help the staff while certain Dutchmen who were well enough to go down to the canteen were always too sick to do any work. Walt helped wash dishes as soon as he was able to get out of bed, but when he realized the attitude of the other patients he asked to be sent back to the camp as soon as the doctors considered him fit.

We all wanted to know how the nurses were. According to Walt some were young and some were young and attractive. We were surprised that Walt made this distinction; we were at the point where almost any woman would have been attractive, but then we had been away from the States longer than Walt had. He said that almost all the nurses were kind to the patients and in general were unselfish.

In addition to our occasional bits of excitement in the camp, we had long periods of monotony, varied only by the fact that we read different books. The enlisted men, who felt the monotony more than the officers did, suggested getting baseball equipment from the Japanese, reasoning that if baseball bats were available for beatings, there might be some available for baseball.

After several tries we were able to get bats and leather with which to make a baseball. Because no gloves were to be had, it was decided that a softball should be made. Before long a team from the *Pope* and a team from the *Perch* took the field, with Fisher and Haines as the opposing pitchers.

I have never determined who enjoyed the baseball games more, the Americans or the British. Whenever the Americans had a game, the British would line the fence of the athletic field to listen to the "chatter" of the players. To the British this was the main attraction, for they did not understand the game. (Nationality dictated the game played on the field. The Dutch and British usually played soccer, and the British occasionally played cricket.)

With the permission of the Japanese, we were allowed to have concerts on Sunday afternoons. The *Exeter* band played on these occasions. At times like these we could relax and almost forget the prison camp. The sound of music floating on the warm afternoon air reminded me of Central Park ten thousand miles away.

For some reason the Japanese forbid us to play our phonograph except on Sundays from four to six. This was intended as an annoyance, but actually it worked to our benefit. We reasoned that if we could play the records anytime we wanted, we would soon tire of them and not play them at all. In fact, before the restriction had been imposed, we had played the phonograph so much that everyone was tired of hearing it. The restricted playing time reawakened our interest in the machine.

On Sunday afternoons long before the designated hour, we prepared the records for our program. Our library was surprisingly broad in scope. We had both Gounod's and Schubert's "Ave Maria," selections from *Carmen*, selections from *Irene*, some Viennese waltzes, two records by Ray Noble and two by the Dorsey Brothers, several German pieces, and a host of *krandjong* (native music) records.

We each had favorite numbers, and every Sunday we included all these. The programs lacked originality but they contained something of interest to everyone. I liked to listen to the German records and tried to pick up the words. Our phonograph had to be cranked, and the supply of needles was limited, which necessitated reuse of the same needles. The records were not improving with age either. But the music took us out of ourselves, for a while anyway.

One day when camp life seemed not too bad, we were brought sharply back to reality. Three Dutchmen had attempted to escape; they had gotten out of the camp without difficulty but were captured by natives and turned over to the Japanese.

Long before this, the Japanese had placed a price on the head of every white man; the idea was to encourage the natives to inform on any who might still be at large. The reward of the Japanese as well as the natives' natural hatred of Dutchmen made escape unlikely. The fugitives were back in the camp within twenty-four hours. Three Dutchmen who had previously escaped from Celebes to Australia were captured attempting to bring arms and radio equipment to a guerrilla band (led by de Jong) holding out in the hills of Celebes. The six of them were kept in cells near the gate awaiting trial.

One day the Japanese ordered all prisoners to assemble before their barracks. I went up to a point near the gate with Donovan where certain officers were required to fall in. A detail of Japanese soldiers came in the gate and deployed, fixing bayonets. A couple of motorcycles arrived, with mounted light machine guns in their sidecars.

I felt nervous with all this activity and wondered whether the Japanese intended to mow us all down. The soldiers conducted a rapid inspection for firearms and other weapons, then we received orders to assemble in two groups—one Dutch and the other British and American.

Our group was addressed by Lieutenant Ota, a member of the staff of Admiral Mori, the senior naval officer in the area. In picturesque English he read an announcement describing the offense ("desertion from the Japanese military forces") and the punishment ("'shooted' to death"). The language was odd, but the import had a sobering effect on all of us. We learned later that the execution had taken place during our assembly and that the men had not been shot but beheaded. Six graves were dug, so we concluded that the men who had attempted to aid de Jong's forces were executed with the men who had tried to escape.

We also learned that up to the present we had been considered "captives," but now, "through the graciousness of the Emperor," we were to be treated as prisoners of war. Our existence had been much more precarious than we realized.

Although the absence of the fugitives had been reported as soon as it was known (the next morning), and notwithstanding a note by one of the fugitives explaining that no one had knowledge of the planned escape, the Japanese locked up all the friends and neighbors of the men who had made the break. These people were kept in cells long after the execution, perhaps as a deterrent to anyone else who might be considering escape. The Japanese stated that the reason these people were not executed along with the others was that the escape was reported as soon as it was.

Following this episode the Japanese held the evening muster later at night and, where previously they had accepted the report of an officer POW, they now sent a sentry to make the final check. The Japanese seemed to have taken the escape as a personal insult, and the charge of "desertion from the Japanese military forces" indicated an irreconcilable viewpoint.

Surprise inspections became frequent. During one, we were at a loss for a place to hide a radio set that our enlisted men were building. As an original precaution they were working only in our cottage and building it into a small wooden stool. We decided that if we left it in an obvious place it would not be noticed. The stool was left in plain sight in our sitting room and was undisturbed while the Japanese searched the attic, the water box in the toilet, and all of the out-of-the-way places.

At this inspection, Donovan had to be present at the barracks. The search there uncovered a broken shotgun and handmade shells. The Japanese who found them was a friendly petty officer who had visited the States as a ship's cook. He gave Donovan the shells and told him to get rid of them after the inspection.

The camp eventually quieted down again, and those who complained of the monotony were reminded that we had had enough excitement. On warm evenings we would stroll about the camp discussing in low voices the news and our prospects of returning home. Sometimes the conversations lagged because we were lost in our own thoughts or in the beauty of the tropical night.

There was beauty all about us; the palm trees swayed slightly in the soft breeze, the camp buildings took on new outlines in the moonlight, and the love call of the gecko was, for the moment, musical. On such occasions we thought of our families, but more likely—with the mellow moon—we thought of the girls we had known at home. One of us would say, "Well, I guess Jane is married to some young air corps colonel now," or "By the time we get back, Rosemary will be married to someone—not me, thank God." The next morning we would be reprimanded by Donovan for getting in so late, not because we were late but because our bamboo bed squeaked when we climbed into it.

After two months on the hospital ship, Antrim returned to camp. He felt fine but looked pale and thin. We told him that Beriontes's breakfasts would put him back on his feet, and we weren't joking.

Before Antrim had gone to the ship, he was studying Malay and had tried to interest the rest of us in the language. We stayed with it long enough to learn that *mata hari* meant the sun—literally the eye of the day—and that *orangutan* meant man of the forest. Now, on Antrim's return, he was interested in Spanish and wanted us all to study it with him. Studying a language in this way was an excellent idea, but I had no desire to study anything. I had tried to learn Dutch, thinking that my knowledge of German would be a help, but I found the German a hindrance and gave up.

My lessons were not without their interesting points. I learned the way the Dutch detected German fifth columnists during the invasion of the Lowlands: at the various roadblocks, civilians and troops were handed a card with the word *Scheveningen* on it. The Dutchmen pronounced the word properly ("skayvaninga"), but the Germans said "shavaningen," much to their regret.

In July 1942 the Japanese ordered lists to be made up for each man in camp, including educational background, previous occupations, and technical abilities. We surmised that the Japanese were planning to send a draft away from the camp, perhaps to the mining district of Celebes or even to Japan. Typewriters and the necessary paper were made available, and we took the opportunity to make complete lists of the American officers and men to keep as records for our own use.

Rumors about parties leaving the camp flourished for a while, but when nothing happened the rumors faded. A small party of Britishers was sent to work on an airdrome not far from Makassar, but this was only a temporary detail; the men returned to the camp after a few weeks.

Toward the end of August the Japanese designated a number of men who were to leave the camp at some later date for a secret destination. The Americans were to provide twenty-four enlisted men and one officer. Lowndes was originally picked to fill the officer billet, but he was suffering from a foot infection and was excused.

I was chosen to take his place. Donovan explained to me that I had been picked by a process of elimination: Lowndes had an infection, Fisher was supply corps, Haines was army, Austin was U.S. Naval Reserve, Antrim was senior officer from the *Pope,* and Donovan was senior American officer in the camp. I was the only officer left.

Up to this time I had given little thought to leaving the camp. I was happy enough where I was. The living was easy and the Japanese bothered us only occasionally. Besides, there were a lot of books in the library that I wanted to read.

The idea of being the only American officer in the party was not encouraging. The British were sending 10 officers and 215 enlisted men; the Dutch 12 officers and 738 enlisted men. Another American officer in the party would have ensured companionship. Having a change of scenery would be balanced by the possibility of a change in living conditions, not necessarily for the better. There was a possible advantage: we might be able to send and receive mail at the next place. And we might get aid from the Red Cross.

A week or two later the Japanese announced that the members of the special party were to be available in the camp at all times and were not to be detailed for working parties. Then the Japanese started an indoctrination program. The party was mustered each morning after breakfast and marched to the athletic field, where we did calisthenics to improve our physical condition. It was not necessary for any of us to reduce our waistline, except for a few of the Dutchmen.

Later we turned to squad drill with a new twist: all commands had to be given in Japanese, and the maneuvers had to be executed in the Japanese manner. The possibilities for error were countless; for instance, if I were drilling my men, I had to remember the Japanese command, pronounce it correctly, and expect the men to understand it and remember how to execute it. The Japanese petty officers in charge of the detail were good-natured about the proceedings and got as many laughs out of them as we did.

After a week of these drills, the men began to ask when we would draw rifles and go to the front. The Japanese must have sensed that they had been emphasizing the military too much, for they began to acquaint us with "high Japanese culture." This consisted of instruction in the proper way to enter a room. A Japanese petty officer would stand in the middle of the field with the prisoners about him in a wide circle. He represented a "high Japanese official" in his office. A prisoner was picked to demonstrate how he would behave in this august presence. With elaborate gestures a prisoner would approach an imaginary door, knock on it, hear someone say come in (in Japanese of course), turn a nonexistent knob, remove the cap he was not wearing, bow, take two steps, bow again, receive a bow in return, bow again, back away to the door, bow again, turn, and leave.

After several prisoners had gone through this pantomime, instruction was halted for the day and a sports period began. The hardy types would run about in the heat of the sun while the rest of us reclined in the shade of a tree and smoked.

On the whole our indoctrination period was fairly enjoyable, but I would have preferred to stay in our cottage reading a book. One drawback to the detail was the necessity of wearing shoes. As with all the drilling, "go-aheads" (Japanese slippers without backs) were impossible to walk in, especially backward. My shoes were brand new and of excellent quality, but the left one was a 10C (just about right) and the right one was a 12D. Antrim had been given the shoes by Hatayama of the Japanese petty officers, who apparently thought one size was as good as the next as long as you could get your foot inside the shoe. When Antrim got hold of a pair of shoes, I inherited them. Later when I got hold of two other shoes, a 10B and a 9C, both the same color, I gave the previous "pair" to Hyde, the pharmacist's mate in my party, who knew someone who had shoes to swap.

When the Japanese started drilling us, we thought we would leave in the near future, but we remained in Makassar. At times it seemed as though we would never leave, but nobody seemed to mind. Because of the delay, we concluded that the Japanese shipping losses were so great that there were no ships available to take us.

One day we received notice that we should prepare to leave shortly. Later we were told definitely that we would leave in two days and that blankets and articles of clothing would be issued the day before we left. Johnny War came to our cottage and gave me a mosquito netting, a piece of cotton cloth large enough to use as a bedspread, and the canvas for a camp bed. He drew a sketch to show me how to make a bamboo frame on which to spread the canvas to make the bed. Whatever faults Lieutenant Colonel Gortmans had, and some people thought he had plenty, with Americans he was always generous.

Johnny War told me that if by chance I escaped on the trip, I should inform Allied forces that the island garrison was small and that a landing in the Parepare area (just north of Makassar) would split the island as well as control the food-producing region.

The day before we left we lined up to draw our going-away kit. It included two cotton blankets of fair quality, several pairs of cotton socks, two undershirts and underpants, two cotton KPM sailor uniforms (officers received only one), and tennis shoes for those having no shoes at all. The undershirts were made of a fabric similar to cheesecloth, only heavier, and came in one size—too small. Most of the items looked like Chinese goods, or were at least manufactured for the coolie market. The KPM suits, from the Royal Packet Company, a Dutch steamship line, came from the stores of some captured Dutch ship.

After all the gear was issued, Yoshida called the officers of the party to his private storeroom, where he had a special cache of clothing. He allowed each officer to take a winter-weight jacket and pair of trousers as well as a linen "suit," a shirt, and a tie. We didn't know if he gave us the clothes out of the goodness of his heart or whether he had received orders from above, but we were grateful for the warm garments because rumor had it that the party's destination was Japan.

The clothes were in piles on the floor like so much dirty laundry. After rummaging, snatching, and swapping, I ended up with an Australian officer's tunic (whipcord, olive drab) and a pair of civilian dress trousers that bore the label of a tailor in Nice. I also found a linen coat with trousers to match, a light blue shirt, and a solid blue Palm Beach tie. Some of the men were able to find merchant marine officers' uniforms that approximated their own naval uniform. Although my outfit was somewhat bizarre, it was not without a certain elegance. There were not enough clothes to outfit the enlisted men in the party, and we concluded that was the reason Yoshida had called us over so quietly.

That night while I was packing, I felt like a Horatio Alger rags to riches boy. I had entered the camp with the rags on my back and no shoes on my feet; I was leaving with a sackful of clothes, towels, bedding, and soap. (My share of the common supply was seventeen large pieces, enough to last the duration I hoped.) A special meal was prepared that night for the people leaving the next day. Smith, our ship's cook from the *Pope*, brought a whole roasted fresh ham to our cottage. I had no appetite and, to my eternal regret, ate only a small portion. The others made short work of it.

The next day, when it was time to leave, the parting was gay but strained. Our officers wished me luck and made a lot of cheering remarks to make me feel that I was going to enjoy the change. Everyone had a farewell gift for me. Austin gave me Dutch money, Fisher and Antrim cigarettes, Donovan three cakes of Lux soap, Haines a pair of cufflinks for my shirt, and Lowndes two brand new decks of playing cards.

When I went to fall in at the athletic field for muster, I stopped to say good-bye at our barracks. Galicia, one of the Filipinos from the *Pope*, gave me a cap to wear because I had none. I said good-bye to my friends in the crew and then joined my party on the field. Fortunately arrangements had been made for trucks to carry the luggage.

While we were lined up, the Japanese warrant officer in charge of the camp came down the line and personally handed each man a pack of cigarettes. We appreciated the thought behind the gift and were surprised that he made the effort, but a few explained it away: "The Nips have a terrific inferiority complex [with this much I concurred] and they want people to think well of them. We're going away and he gives us a lousy pack of cigarettes so we think he's a good guy." Examining every generous deed in this light is the road to cynicism. I prefer the words of one of my professors at the naval academy: "Beware of glittering generalities." There is no subject on which they are more freely used than nationalities.

Although everyone was ready to go, we waited for almost two hours before we received the order to get under way. The officers led the column, and a strange-looking column we were. Most of us were wearing our tropical civilian suits and looking smarter than we had in months. The Dutch army officers wore complete uniforms, as did most of their enlisted men. (The NEI Army seemed to dress and salute smartly, but like Ferdinand they had never learned to fight.) Most of my men and the British enlisted men were wearing their going-away sailor suits. When I saw all the men in the same uniform, I realized how far a uniform goes toward changing a mob into a body of men.

As we passed through the gate, we shouted and waved to our friends who were waiting to see us off. It was a beautiful day to be leaving; the sun was bright but there was enough of a breeze to keep us comfortable. Before we had gone a hundred yards from the camp, we were in sight of the sea. It was a strange feeling to look out to the horizon again and see how big the world was. The wind off the sea braced us all.

The road swung back from the water as we approached the town proper. The road seemed deserted and so did the houses. It was not until we passed the first house that we realized that the Japanese had apparently issued orders to clear the streets along the line of march and to close the shutters on all the houses.

From behind the shutters we could hear women and children weeping and wailing. These were the families of Indonesian boys who were leaving in our party. To most of us Americans and British it did not make much difference whether we left or not, but many in the Dutch group were leaving their homes and families, some never to return. We could not tell how the Indonesians among us were bearing up under the strain, but knowing how emotional they were, we guessed that the sounds of their womenfolk weeping shattered most of them.

The scenery became more interesting as we marched farther into town. The shops along the way had food and wares on display. It did not seem real that some people were going on about their business much the same as before while we suffered such an interruption in our lives. A couple of hard-faced Japanese prostitutes in gaudy kimonos crossed in front of us in a pedicab, the Makassar version of the ricksha, and drew a number of ribald remarks.

We swung back to the waterfront again to avoid the center of town. In the distance we could see several large ships tied up to the seawall. The *Op Ten Noort* was still in her berth. The port area had fine business buildings, but most of the *godowns* (warehouses) were in ruins, the result of demolition charges set by the Dutch army.

I had not heard of Makassar before the war; it seemed surprising that a city of its size and commercial importance was not better known. The term *antimacassar* is connected with this city. Makassar oil was used in hair dressings; an antimacassar protects the fabric of the headrest of a chair or sofa from hair oil.

At the seawall we were assembled before a platform on which a number of Japanese naval officers stood. It was evident that we were about to be addressed, and Budding was called to the platform to translate the speech into English and Dutch. The speaker introduced himself as Admiral Mori. He was big for a Japanese and very heavy, probably well over two hundred pounds. He would have been grotesque were it not for his intelligent face and dignified bearing. He told us that we were going to Japan and that we should take care of ourselves and keep healthy so that we could all return home when the war was over.

Why a Japanese admiral would want to address a group of prisoners was beyond me. Deep down the Japanese must be hams, always wanting to get into the act. Had he been genuinely interested in our welfare, he would have dropped by the camp occasionally and checked on Yoshida's activities.

At last we reached the point of embarkation. Our ship was the *Asama Maru*, a prewar luxury liner. After the usual wait we finally went aboard, where we encountered another delay. Its cause, we later found out, was Budding, the Dutch interpreter, persuading the Japanese to make some changes in the berthing arrangement. The original plan was to put some of the Dutch in the hold and the rest of the party in third-class accommodations. Budding convinced the Japanese that it would be better to put the British and Americans in the hold because there were fewer of us and we would all fit there.

The officers were put in third-class "staterooms." I went in with the British, and the eleven of us shared the six bunks and transom. Because I was the only American officer, I was given the courtesy of a single bunk to myself. We designated the extrawide bunks as double bunks and paired off the smaller people to share them. This arrangement left two or three people to sleep on the deck. The British enlisted men were shunted into the hold. I told my twenty-four men to stay on the stateroom deck at the foot of a wide ladder leading to the upper decks. Here at a clear space in the companionway they would have room to spread out and would not be far from my cabin.

The Dutchmen filled the remainder of the third-class cabins and overflowed into the passageways. Budding was given the room that had formerly been a purser's office. He had a real mattress on his bed and a washstand with running water. Wijzviss, a Dutch army doctor, later joined him there. Wijzviss never passed up an opportunity to improve his own condition.

Meanwhile a number of the British enlisted men came up from the hold and bedded down in the passageway near our cabin. The

Dutch protested to the British officers about this but were told that if they wanted to put the men back in the hold, which was hotter than hell, they would have to do it forcibly. It seemed typical of the Dutch to get the best of a deal and then complain of someone else trying to better his situation.

Nobody said anything about my men, and they quietly settled down in the place they had staked out. Long before we had left camp I had instructed the men to stay together, and that if anything should happen on the voyage—we expected to be attacked by submarines—to keep out of the way of the mob trying to get topside, to wait until we could leave without being trampled to death. (Most of us had inflatable life preservers, which the British had brought into camp with them.) If we got off the ship, I wanted them to stay in a group so that if, and when, the submarine surfaced, we could all be picked up together. Being picked up by a submarine presupposed a number of happy coincidences, but I felt that if the chain of events started, we should place ourselves in position to help the coincidences as much as possible.

The ship got under way before sunset, and we thought we were on our way. The rumble of the anchor chain a few minutes later informed us that we were still in Makassar. The meal that night was food brought from the camp—coffee, eggs, and bread. It was not a sumptuous repast, and our hike and the sea air gave us grand appetites, so before bedtime we were thinking of the next meal.

When we awoke in the morning, the ship was standing out of the harbor. A steam frigate was leading the way as antisubmarine protection. At breakfast we were introduced to shipboard fare—rice and a tasty stew. The rations were meager so we wiped the plates clean. Some meals were accompanied by fresh scallions. Although the camp food had been served in bigger portions and had more food value, this food tasted better and looked as though it had been prepared in a real galley by professional chefs.

Outside the harbor the ship sailed on a glassy sea but nevertheless began to roll slightly. This proved to be a boon to the American and British sailors, who went around collecting food from seasick Dutchmen. I noticed that when a Dutchman passes up food, he is really sick. Some of the Dutch naval ratings were among the seasick, but in most cases this was excusable, because for many this was their first sea duty.

My men, I later learned, spent their first few hours in true navy fashion—getting acquainted with the ship. They found a large empty room in our part of the ship. Because it was locked, they assumed it contained something of value. In a few minutes they had the door open and concluded that the room had been either nurses' or stewardesses' quarters. Now it contained only mattresses and blankets—and plenty of space. After sleeping shoulder to shoulder in the passageway, where the traffic to and from the head was incessant, this space was enticing. Their first concern was to make sure that no one else moved in; this they did by bolting the door from the inside. They would send a couple of men at a time to draw their rations, always leaving someone inside to hold the fort.

It was hot belowdecks, and Budding obtained permission for the prisoners to go up on the forecastle for fresh air. It was pleasant topside, but the brief respite merely intensified the discomfort when we went below again. At least we had plenty of water for drinking and washing. At first the fresh water was on all day; later, water hours were instituted to limit consumption, although saltwater was available anytime for bathing.

We shared our washroom with a crated monster that was being shipped to a zoo in Japan. The beast was a poisonous reptile that looked like an enormous lizard. Its food supply, which was stowed on top of its crate, was a cage holding live chickens. One day's ration was a live chicken dropped into reptile's crate. The stench was overwhelming, and we prayed regularly that the awful thing would die and be tossed overboard. Our prayers were about as successful as most of our prayers to date: the reptile remained healthy to the end of the voyage, and our efforts were repaid with a stronger stench. In time all the chickens were consumed, removing at least one source of the annoyance.

We spent most of our time reading, sleeping, and playing bridge. Activities didn't change much from camp life except that we did them in a more confined space. Our meals were made a little fuller by such extras as tea and *goela djava* (brown sugar), which the British officers had brought along. My contribution, a jar of jam that Beriontes and Sarmiento had made for me as a going-away present, was finished the first night to make our dry bread more palatable.

Whenever we had tea, part was always sent to the Dutch officers, who expressed their thanks but never reciprocated. (They had coffee several times but neglected to send over a single drop.) To us this seemed completely in character.

One morning we passed a number of islands that we did not recognize definitely but judged to be part of the Philippines. Our course seemed to be somewhat east of north, as if we had swung out of the archipelago into open sea. This we did the next day, dropping our armed escort. The wind was cooler and the ship became more comfortable belowdecks. The ship's speed was a steady fifteen knots with only occasional course changes. It looked as though our submarines were not as ubiquitous as we had hoped. At any rate the Japanese were not perturbed.

While on deck for an airing we noticed that the other passengers were naval landing force troops returning home to Japan. Their accommodations seemed a little better than ours, but we did not envy them.

At the beginning of our voyage we had thought we might stop at Manila en route to Japan. I had a list of the Filipinos from the *Pope* and the *Perch* and the addresses of their families, which I planned to pass to a likely looking Filipino on the pier. I also planned to ask the Japanese to permit me to send for my winter clothing, which was in storage ashore. I realized that none of these things might come to pass, but I was prepared to allow no opportunity to go by unexploited. In a few days it was obvious that Manila was not on the itinerary.

Summer 1941. Tawi Tawi, southern Philippine Islands. Author in *Pope's* wherry enjoying a busman's holiday. The boat survived *Pope's* demise and was used to take exhausted men to the whaleboat to dry out; also used to distribute food and water rations to men in the life floats.

Aboard USS *Salt Lake City,* Pearl Harbor, July 1940. Author is standing beneath guns of an 8-inch turret. These guns had an extreme range of close to twenty nautical miles.

July 1940. Pearl Harbor. Author aboard USS *Salt Lake City* heavy cruiser, 9100 tons, ten 8-inch guns. Shortly after war started in Europe in September 1939, the *SLC* was ordered to Pearl Harbor as part of the Hawaiian Detachment. In the spring of 1940 the Pacific Fleet was based at Pearl Harbor over the objections of the fleet commander, Admiral James Richardson.

USS *Pope* (DD 225), 1190 tons, built 1919, four 4-inch guns, twelve 21-inch torpedo tubes, maximum speed 35 knots. This class of "four stackers" was similar to the fifty destroyers lent to Britain in 1940 for the lease of bases in British possessions. (Courtesy the U.S. Navy)

March 1941. SS *President Grant* in heavy weather en route to Kobe, Japan, shortly after leaving the lee of the Hawaiian Islands. Note American flag painted on hatch cover.

Author with Moros at Tawi Tawi, southern Philippines, 1941. Moros like these later helped rescue downed PBY aircrews and keep them from capture by the Japanese.

Summer 1941. Jolo, Southern Philippine Islands. Battlefield strewn with dead and wounded Moros after an unsuccessful attack on the Philippine constabulary post. The Moros were armed with bolos and krises; not very effective against rifles and shotguns.

Close-up of one of the dead Moros. These Moros were believed to be "juramentados" who as Moslems had taken vows to kill Christians (thus ensuring a quick trip to paradise if killed themselves).

FUKUOKA CAMP N°. 2
KOYAKIJIMA
NAGASAKI   JAPAN

MERRY X-MAS AND

HAPPY NEW YEAR

FROM

JOHANNES J. BUDDING
CAPTAIN ROYAL NETHERLANDS INDIES ARMY

Milletstraat 34
Amsterdam Z.   HOLLAND

SUMIOKA
HARUTARO
1173   CIV.
SUGAMO PRISON
18 NOVEMBER 46
INTERPRETER

(BEETHOVEN)

✝

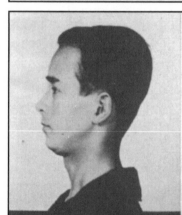

MURAI
MASAAKI
1175   SGT.
SUGAMO PRISON
19 NOVEMBER 46
OFFICE CLERK

(NAPOLEON)

IWATA
YAGOHEIJI
NO. 1118
SUGAMO PRISON
30 SEPTEMBER 46

GALLEY-HANCHO

(FLIP)

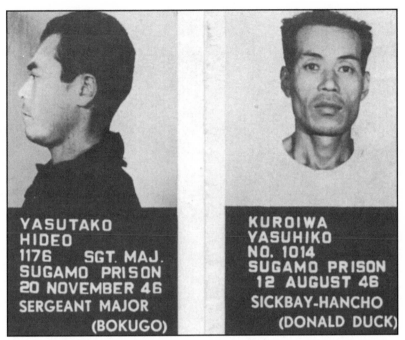

YASUTAKO HIDEO 1176 SGT. MAJ. SUGAMO PRISON 20 NOVEMBER 46 SERGEANT MAJOR (BOKUGO)

KUROIWA YASUHIKO NO. 1014 SUGAMO PRISON 12 AUGUST 46 SICKBAY-HANCHO (DONALD DUCK)

Captain Budding, RNIA, sent this out as a 1946 Christmas card. He had been the Fukuoka Camp #2 interpreter and later participated in the War Crimes trials for these honchos. Sumioka, the Japanese civilian interpreter, committed suicide while out of prison on bail.

Ex-POWs debarking from APA *Colbert* Buckner Bay, Okinawa. The *Colbert* brought ex-POWs from Manchuria to Okinawa.

Presentation of Bronze Star Medal to author by Vice Admiral Aubrey W. Fitch, USN, Superintendent of the U.S. Naval Academy, in Memorial Hall, June 26, 1946. (Courtesy the U.S. Navy)

Author shaking hands with Sam Evans (HMS *Exeter*), who was in the foundry working party at the Kawainami shipyard. Near Portsmouth, England, summer 1947.

7

As the days grew cooler we began to wear other clothes in addition to the usual shorts. Fewer people went on deck during the allotted periods. The novelty of the trip was beginning to wear off, and most of us were looking forward to a less transient existence.

The British sailors who were camping in the passageway outside our stateroom lent variety to our daily routine. In the evenings they had animated discussions about the prowess of Arsenal (a British football team, I soon learned). These discussions usually ended in the flagrant use of earthy Anglo-Saxon monosyllables. This would give way to group singing, during which a song would sometimes be made up. Here's one evening's creation.

> Heigh ho, heigh ho, we're off to Tokyo.
> Oh, okey dokey, hokey pokey, Tokyo.

Although the song had only one verse, in our simple way we liked it.

In the next week the weather turned definitely chilly. We were not surprised to learn from one of the sentries that we would reach Japan the following morning. The sentries had not bothered us much on the trip. We figured that they felt so good about going home that they had no desire to annoy us.

That night we turned in early so that we would be ready to leave the ship first thing in the morning. None of us slept well except Blain, who could sleep anytime regardless of the impending event. Aside from the tension, the steady blast of cold air into the room from the ventilator (which could not be closed) had most of us shivering too much to sleep anyway.

In the morning we were awakened by chatter in the passageway about sighting land. We loosened the metal shield over the port and gazed out to see a number of uninviting mist-shrouded islands. The ship anchored well out from the city of Nagasaki, which we could see in the distance. We were not far from the shore and could see groups of small houses and a road along the seawall with an occasional pedestrian or a bicycle. Off to one side were camouflaged oil tanks. These were the most encouraging things in sight: if the Japanese camouflaged the tanks they must be afraid of our bombers, and if they were afraid of our bombers, they could not be too far away. The scenery, especially on this drizzly gray day, was dull and muted, in sharp contrast to the rich tropical hues to which we had become accustomed.

After breakfast we were told that we would not leave the ship until the next morning because the camp was not yet ready for us. The day dragged on, and the general mood of the prisoners seemed to match the weather. It was too cold and wet to stay topside, and most of us passed the time sleeping.

The morning of October 24 was a continuation of the previous day's weather. We were told to fall in on the forecastle deck with all our gear for muster. While waiting for our transportation to the beach, my men showed me some woolen blankets they had acquired from their special room.

By the time two ferry boats came alongside the *Asama Maru,* we were thoroughly chilled. We were herded into the boats, where we were guarded by Japanese naval petty officers. At first I thought they were policemen; their blue uniforms were different from the uniforms of the U.S. Navy. The blinds were drawn on all the windows of the ferry, perhaps to prevent us from becoming familiar with the area through which we were passing or to conceal a secret zone from our view. Both ideas seemed equally ridiculous.

We landed at a pier that was just inside a shipyard. The buildings in the immediate vicinity of the landing were small, weather-beaten shacks with filthy windowpanes (when they weren't missing). The sound of riveting and the flash of electric welding came from the concrete building nearby.

We were led along a muddy road away from the yard. Japanese women and men gaped at us from the buildings along the way. After a short walk we came to an open square before buildings that had obviously just been completed. They were painted white with green trim and looked inviting. If this was to be our future home, we thought, it might not be too bad.

We assembled before a platform in the square, and while we waited for the inevitable address, we witnessed the naval sentries turn over our group to an army detachment. Up to now we had all been under navy control; having heard about the Japanese army mostly through reports such as the "Rape of Nanking," we were not enthusiastic about the change.

Eventually a group of Japanese mounted the platform, and we received a series of speeches about our new life. We were to work hard and keep healthy, presumably so that we could continue to work hard. If we tried to escape or were disobedient, we would get "heavy, heavy punishment." If we worked hard, in ten years or so we might be permitted to go home. We got the idea that the hardest-working, most obedient ones would be allowed to take Japanese wives. One of the speakers perpetrated a stirring non sequitur: "You have fought bravely for your flag; now you must work hard for Nippon." An army officer who seemed to be the master of ceremonies spoke English well; he was probably an alumnus of one of our West Coast universities.

While the speeches were going on, a steady stream of prisoners came and went; the cold weather was affecting everyone's kidneys. The speeches ended with Lieutenant Commander Chubb, the senior British officer and senior engineer of HMS *Exeter,* being required to sign a paper to the effect that no one would try to escape. As Chubb later remarked, "I didn't care what the hell I signed. I just had to get out of that damned cold wind."

Shortly afterward, we fell in for room assignments. The commissioned, warrant, and chief petty officers were in the first group. When we marched away from the square, we saw that the white buildings with green trim were not for us. We climbed a slight rise and then went down a steep path to our new home.

The camp, which we later learned was designated Camp Fukuoka No. 2, was located on the water's edge a quarter mile from the square and about half a mile from the shipyard. It was so new that it wasn't finished. At the moment it was in the shape of a large F with seventeen rooms down the long side; the galley, still uncompleted, in the middle; and the officers' room and storerooms along the top. The camp occupied land created by dumping rocks and dirt from a nearby hill, which was leveled in the process. (This filling in was still going on when we arrived and did not stop until two years later.) The building was wood with a cement finish.

The rooms were designed to accommodate fifty-six men each. A double-decker sleeping platform about six and a half feet wide ran the length of the room on both sides; each level accommodated fourteen people. The sleeping platforms were covered with a thin straw mat, which gave a deceptive appearance of comfort. Down the center of the room, from the door to the window at the opposite end, was a row of wooden tables with a row of benches on either side. None of the woodwork in the room was painted; in fact, none of the woodwork in the camp was painted. The floor was cement—mostly sand, we later found out. The room was not unattractive. The fresh, new look of the interior was a successful antidote to the depressing effect of the gray day outside.

We chose our sleeping spaces so that we could start to unpack our gear and get settled. Blain and I took places on the upper tier at the window end of the room, where there was extra space. The officers' room was not filled to capacity. Although it was the same size as the other rooms, it housed only forty-five instead of fifty-six: twenty-one officers, four warrant officers, and the remaining twenty sergeant majors and chief petty officers. Vanneste and Johnson, my two CPOs, were in the officers' room with me; the rest of my men were in room 5 (I was in room 1) with British sailors.

After everyone was settled, preparations were made to serve a meal. Japanese women were busy washing crockery and setting the table—a rice bowl, a teacup, a soup bowl, and a wooden box containing chopsticks at each place. Later they brought in small loaves of bread and gave each of us a loaf; it tasted something like French bread and was the best we had eaten in more than six months. Buckets of rice and trays of fish and Japanese pickles were placed on the tables. It was a fine beginning, and the consensus was that our stay here wouldn't be too bad.

The women, we soon learned, would not be regular servants; they had been brought in to help for the day. And it was several months before we had bread again. Because the galley in the camp was not yet in operation, the food was cooked in a galley near the square where we had assembled before going to the camp. Because it was brought in by cart we seldom received a hot meal, but we were usually too hungry to mind.

The next morning, group photographs were taken so that the Japanese would have a picture of everyone in camp for identification. We were also required to fill out forms giving particulars about our education and technical experience.

The unfinished state of the camp became increasingly apparent. The only water supply within the camp was a shallow well; the water was not fit to drink without boiling (in Japan most water must be boiled before it is drunk, which may account for the national custom of drinking tea), and it was not good for washing because it was slightly brackish and did not lather well. The *benjo* (latrine) was a hastily erected shed with two rows of stalls; below each row was a trench in the ground. In keeping with Japanese ideas of sanitation, the *benjo* was located less than fifty feet from the galley. We were fortunate that it was too late in the year for flies to become a serious nuisance. Another defect that became more noticeable as the weather grew colder was that none of the rooms had ceilings.

In time water was piped into the camp, the galley was completed, ceilings were put on the rooms, and a new *benjo* was built, but it was well into the next year before these improvements were completed.

About three days after our arrival, we were all given papers to sign swearing that we would not attempt to escape. My men asked me if they should sign, and I told them to do so in order to avoid any trouble with the Japanese. In our room, however, I joined the British officers in a protest to the Japanese. The Dutch officers signed, saying, "What difference does it make?" From a practical standpoint it did not make any difference. Escape from Japan was impossible, and if we did attempt to escape the Japanese would kill us, paper or no paper, the way they killed the three Dutchmen in Makassar.

Nevertheless we refused to sign, and at first it seemed that we were going to get away with it. A half hour after we had given the camp commander our refusal, sentries came to the room for us. They curtly ordered us to a place behind the guardhouse where tables had been set up. A number of sentries were stationed around us, and at the order from a Japanese warrant officer they loaded their rifles and fixed bayonets. At this, most of us exchanged glances and shrugged our shoulders. The warrant officer, speaking through Budding, asked us to sign the papers. We demurred, saying that it was equivalent to giving our parole, which was forbidden by naval regulation. This had no effect on the officer who addressed us, who again said that up to the present we had received kind treatment but if we did not sign, our treatment would be much different. He was becoming increasingly annoyed at our delay, and the sentries acted restless. Budding advised us to sign, and when one of the British officers observed that because we would be signing under duress the paper would not be legal anyway, we stepped forward to sign. As a last gesture we tried to have the wording changed slightly, but the warrant officer, realizing that he had broken our resistance, pressed his advantage and refused to allow any alteration of the oath.

When we were dismissed, we returned to our room, definitely relieved. Our protest had not accomplished its objective, but we had the satisfaction of having been forced to sign. Of course a few uneasy moments accompanied that satisfaction. The Dutch officers must have found us unbearable in the days immediately following the incident.

A day or so later we marched down to the square, where we were divided into working groups. Although papers had been filled out in Makassar and here giving our technical abilities, the parties were formed according to the whims of the prisoners. A Japanese interpreter got up on the platform and asked for all men with experience in welding, drilling, riveting, and so forth. Most of the men put in for what they thought would be the easiest jobs. Officers were assigned to each party. It was obvious that we were going to spend most of our time in the shipyard.

We protested in camp that this was contrary to the Geneva Convention, to which Japan had agreed to adhere. The Japanese indicated that they didn't know what we were talking about. Because having a job was inevitable, I tried to get assigned to the draughtsmen's party, because it would be clean work and out of the weather. Van

Marle and Jenkins got the job by claiming to be experts in this line of work. Van Marle had some background, but Jenkins couldn't tell a T square from a triangle and thought French curves were something one saw in the Folies Bergère. I ended up with the drillers. Thank God it wasn't the riveters.

Either these particular Japanese thought we were thick, or they left nothing to chance. At any rate we spent two days making sure that each man knew the number of his work party. The drill went as follows. All the prisoners stood in a mass. Men holding signs with the numbers of each party took positions off to one side of the group. A signal from the Japanese in charge told everyone to dash off to join his group in front of the sign. After we displayed a satisfactory degree of proficiency in falling in with our work parties, we were taken to the shipyard to see our working area.

The drillers were divided into two parties, the ship party and the shore party. I was in charge of the latter and Blain had the former. The shore party was told that they would start drilling as soon as the working area was cleared off; then we were taken to the place where we would make our contribution to the Japanese war effort. Here was a monumental pile of scrap iron that must have been the result of years of dumping. The means provided for removing the iron were straw mats slung from poles and carried by the prisoners. The American sailors called this method of carrying "yo-yoing" because of the up and down motion of the basket or mat.

There were two type of yo-yo poles: the one-man pole, which was light and flexible and designed to carry a weight at each end to give a balanced load, and the two-man or multiple type of pole, which was much heavier and bent only under heavy loads.

The men were paired off and each pair was given a mat and a pole. Several men were designated to load. As a *honcho* (boss) I was not expected to yo-yo; I was supposed to supervise and keep the men moving. Our Japanese honcho was a tall, shifty-eyed individual with a large black mustache and, as we soon found out, a nasty disposition. For no good reason except that they did not know his name, the men gave the honcho the nickname Louie.

Even on the first day, he was shouting at the men for not taking bigger loads. By the end of the day most of the men had sore feet and shoulders from the yo-yoing, and they all were looking forward to the day when they could start drilling so they wouldn't have to carry any more scrap iron. (Later, when nearly everyone could drill, some people said they preferred to yo-yo.)

Some of the yo-yoers started working in the morning and then would go aboard one of the ships and find a quiet, inaccessible place that the yard police and naval sentries would consider too much trouble to inspect. Here they remained until lunchtime, when they returned to the group to eat lunch. Occasionally the honcho or the police found these people loafing and administered a few kicks in the shins and a rain of blows about the head to discourage their practice.

The routine that gradually evolved was as follows: 0500 reveille followed by *tenko* (muster); 0530 breakfast; 0640 assemble for work; 0730 commence work in yard; 1200–1230 lunch; 1700 knock off and return to camp; 1800 evening meal; 2030 *tenko;* 2100 taps.

Although it took only fifteen minutes at the most to march to the shipyard, we seldom reached there before 0730. The reason for this was the counting of the prisoners by the yard policemen. Some mornings we were counted as many as five times, and no two tallies were the same. When the weather was warm we did not mind losing a half hour of work, but in cold or rainy weather it was annoying to stand around getting chilled or wet, or both, while a group of morons tried their hands at arithmetic. *Hands* is the proper word, for they used an abacus to add the totals.

The fact that we did not have a galley in camp and therefore could not bring lunch to work with us led to the arrangement whereby we were each given a box lunch in the yard at noon. The lunch consisted of cold boiled rice, pickled seaweed, and, occasionally, fish. After lining up to get the box, there was just enough time to eat the food and smoke a cigarette (if you were fortunate enough to have one). Later when the camp galley was in operation, we had more time for lunch. We brought our lunch to the yard in tins that looked like painted sardine cans. They were generally satisfactory but did not stand up well when we tried to heat their contents over open fires, a practice that the Japanese unsuccessfully tried to discourage.

We had our first death in camp less than a week after our arrival.

One of the Indonesians, an old man who had grown morose about leaving the Indies, died as the result of an attack of malaria. A funeral party was arranged for Sunday, which was our first free day since we started working in the yard. The party was mostly Dutch; Bennett, Jenkins, and Chubb went along to represent the British; and I represented the Americans.

The procession followed the road that ran on an embankment behind the camp. It led to the shipyard in one direction, the part with which we were familiar, but none of us had been in the opposite direction toward which we were now going.

We soon came to a small village of wooden houses and stores. The streets were narrow and unpaved and wound around the buildings, seeming to lead nowhere in particular. Just beyond the village we came to a grand sight: a wide stone stairway that climbed the face of a steep hill. Halfway up was a schoolhouse and at the top of the hill in a grove was a temple with a large stone *torii,* or gateway, before it.

Our procession, to my disappointment, did not go all the way up the hill to the temple. At the halfway point we turned left on a road crossing the stairway. Stops were made frequently to rest the body bearers, for the climb was tiring even without a burden. We passed several tiny cemeteries and many small garden plots. Everything was in miniature, and we seemed to be in another world where shipyards and prison camps were unknown.

At last we began to descend, and as we rounded a bend in the road the open sea came into sight. From this height (about two hundred feet, I estimated) we had an excellent view. The day was clear and sunny, and in the distance we could see another island a little smaller than our own. Below us near the water's edge was a brickyard. Off to one side of the road were Japanese men and women working in one of the small fields; the wind was from their direction, so we knew that they were spreading fertilizer.

A halt was called again, and this time it was apparent that the Japanese petty officer in charge of our party had no idea where he was supposed to take the body for burial. We retraced our steps back to the entrance of the camp, where we waited while the officer made arrangements to dispose of the corpse.

This time the party went toward the yard but stopped at the square. The body was taken into one of the buildings on the square, and we all filed into a room with a mat-covered floor (after first removing our shoes), where a short funeral service was held. Then we left the body and returned to camp. On the following day the body would be taken across the bay to Nagasaki, where it would be cremated. We arrived back in camp late for our noon meal, but this slight inconvenience was more than made up for by the pleasure of getting out of the camp and shipyard duty.

Although we continued to enjoy warm days, the weather was growing steadily colder. As soon as the sun went down in the afternoon, a chill began to work its way into our bones. The colder weather was especially hard on the enlisted men, who had been issued only cotton clothes in Makassar. We asked the Japanese for warm clothes for the men, but there were always excuses and no clothes.

With the steady work and the colder weather, the number of sick in the camp increased rapidly. At first all the sick remained in their bunks, but later the doctors managed to convince the Japanese that a sick bay was necessary for the more serious cases.

Now, a death occurred in the camp every other day or so. This was extremely bad for morale; within a short time the camp as a whole displayed a hopeless attitude. There seemed no chance for improvement and the winter had just begun. I blamed Lieutenant Commander Visser for most of this because, as senior officer, he failed to show proper leadership and always accepted the Japanese decisions without argument. His favorite phrase was: "What's the use?" When the officers were detailed to work in the yard, Visser did not protest even though the work was contrary to the Geneva Convention. If the first breach is not protested, those that follow are much harder to oppose.

On December 7 a group of 88 Americans and 212 British POWs arrived from Singapore. In the group were five American army officers, one American civilian, and one British Royal Air Force (RAF) officer. The American enlisted men were all army with the exception of three sailors (Rafalovich, originally from the *Houston* but serving as a liaison signalman aboard the cruiser *De Ruyter* when she was sunk; Connor, from the *Houston;* and Hopkins, from the *Marblehead*).

The senior American officer was Major Horrigan, of the army air corps. Lieutenant Michie was another pilot. Slone, Allen, and Straughan were lieutenants in the National Guard (131st Field Artillery, Texas). The civilian was Dave Hicks, an employee of Douglas Aircraft. The British officer was Pilot Officer Tweedie of the RAF.

The arrival of this new group was a shot in the arm to most of us, the Americans especially, because we were the smallest group in the camp. Now at last I had American officers to keep me company. This is not being derogatory to the British officers to whom I'd attached myself in the absence of any other American officers. The British were also happy to receive reinforcements to overcome the predominant Dutch influence in the camp.

Although the British sailors referred to the RAF contingent as the Brill Cream Boys (Brill Cream being a hair oil that British advertisements indicated as one of the secrets of the RAF's success), they nevertheless greeted them with open arms. The new group seemed to be in good shape and well clothed. All had woolen clothing (British battle dress or RAF uniform) and good leather shoes.

Although the new enlisted men were supposed to be quarantined, that is, not in communication with the rest of the camp, people were visiting them almost as soon as they arrived. The officers were put right into our room. They too were supposed to be in quarantine; they were told not to discuss any news with the other prisoners.

Because Horrigan was a major, we saw a means of deposing Visser from the position of senior officer. In the Dutch services a major in the army is senior to a lieutenant commander in the navy; Horrigan was a major in the army; therefore, he was senior to Visser. (Actually Visser had had several years in the rank, whereas Horrigan had just made the rank.) Chubb was also a lieutenant commander, and in Britain the navy is the senior service; he, realizing the importance of getting Visser out of the position, maintained a discreet silence.

Horrigan, a tall red-headed Irishman (half German, we later learned, which explained why he was twice as stubborn as most Irishmen), looked like a good one to oppose the Japanese. At any rate, after Visser, he would look good no matter what he did. We informed Horrigan of the setup, and he said he would be glad to take over.

Meanwhile the other Dutch officers prepared Visser for the change by mentioning casually that because Horrigan was a major, he would have to take over the duties of senior officer. The next day Visser gracefully accepted Major Horrigan as senior, glad perhaps to be rid of the dubious honor.

The new group brought the good news that the North African campaign was progressing well. The concensus seemed to be that we would be home by next Christmas (1943). The new officers spoke with such conviction that we were sure they were right. Besides it felt good to realize that we had only a year more away from home.

There was not time the first night to get all the news from them and the stories of their capture as well. For the next week or so we spent evenings after work swapping experiences. Horrigan, Michie, and Dave Hicks had been captured together in Java. Horrigan and Michie had been in the Philippines with a B-17 outfit at the beginning of the war and had moved down to Java just before their bases on Luzon and the other islands fell into Japanese hands.

In Java they were attached to Allied headquarters in Bandoeng, which they admitted was as lovely a place to fight a war as could be found in the Far East. Michie had pictures to prove it. We called a beautiful girl who was in every picture with Michie the "Bandoeng Babe" because Michie wouldn't tell us her name for fear that one of us would get back to Java before he did when the war ended.

Dave Hicks had been on his way to Java aboard a Dutch ship accompanying Douglas planes he was to have assembled in Tjilatjap. When Dave arrived in Java, most of the Dutchmen who could get transportation had left, but he assembled planes as fast as he could. Bombing and strafing raids on Tjilatjap harbor slowed him down, and after the Japanese landings in northern Java he was told to quit.

Dave made his way to Bandoeng, where he met Horrigan and Michie, who had been left stranded there when all the strategic personnel took off for safer territory. With Dave's technical knowledge and the flying ability of Horrigan and Michie, they hoped to get a damaged B-18, a two-motor bomber, in operation and fly it to Australia.

Dave worked on the plane for several hours and made it ready for flight. They waited until a little after sunset to take off; there was still enough light but the likelihood of detection by enemy aircraft was improbable. The plane took off without incident, but once it was airborne they found that the landing gear would not retract. It was too late to turn back to check it, so they risked the reduced speed and range. They had to pass Bali while several hours of darkness remained because the Japanese had a fighter base on Bali and would probably send out routine patrols at dawn.

During the flight, which was going well despite the initial setback, someone broke a bottle of bourbon that Horrigan had brought along. Being a native Kentuckian, this was a sharp blow to his morale. The other effect of the broken bottle was to fill the plane with alcohol fumes, which made some of the party giddy. This may have been the cause of the report that a Japanese night fighter was approaching from astern. After some radical evasive tactics, the night fighter turned out to be a planet.

A check of the plane's position indicated that they would have trouble clearing Bali before dawn, and even if they did, the chances were slim of their fuel holding out until they reached Australia. It was decided to return to Java to refuel.

They landed on a beach near Malang. As soon as they got out of the plane, they saw the reason for the failure of the landing gear to retract: the pins used to prevent an accidental retraction of the wheels while the plane was standing on the field were still in place. Ordinarily these would be removed by the ground crew, but when they took off they had no ground crew; indeed, they were lucky to have the plane.

Natives had gathered when the plane landed, and Horrigan inquired about getting gasoline. One of the natives said he could arrange to bring gas to the plane; when he returned to the plane an hour later he brought with him not gas but Japanese soldiers. The men learned that Java had been surrendered by the Dutch without a fight; in fact, the Dutch in carrying out their surrender disarmed the American and British soldiers who were trying to make a fight of it.

In time the men joined the Americans and British in the prison camps that the Dutch had set up. When the Japanese placed the Dutch in with them, the Dutch expected the internment to be temporary. The Dutch felt sorry for their allies because they would have to remain in prison camps whereas the Dutch would be paroled, or so they thought. It was in one of these camps that Horrigan and his party met up with the 131st Field Artillery, of which Slone, Allen, and Straughan were officers.

The 131st Field Artillery (Texas National Guard) had left Pearl Harbor en route to the Philippines just a few days before the surprise attack. Their transport, along with the rest of the convoy (a convoy system had been started several months before the war actually started because of the critical situation in the Far East), headed south to avoid any Japanese task forces that might be in the area. The outfit's 75mm guns were set up on deck for use against submarines. This move probably helped morale, but I think they were lucky not to run into any subs.

The USS *Pensacola,* a sister ship of the *Salt Lake City,* the ship I had left to go out to the Asiatic Station, escorted the convoy all the way to Australia. It was too late to try to run any troops into the Philippines because of the Japanese naval blockade. The soldiers, most of whom had not seen the sea before their embarkation at San Francisco, were amazed at the size and speed of the *Pensacola,* but most of them were glad to get their feet on solid ground again.

At Brisbane they debarked and set up camp at a racetrack, where these Texans with a background of cowpunching were delivered their worst insult: the only meat they could get for the mess was mutton. After a week or so ashore, the outfit was put aboard the *Bloemfontein,* a Dutch merchant ship, for transport to Java. The *Pensacola* escorted the ship as far as Torres Strait, where the *Houston* and some destroyers took over and brought her into Port Darwin. From Darwin the *Bloemfontein* went to Surabaja, where the soldiers went ashore. The *Pope* left Darwin the same day and was part of the escort until detached and sent to Timor. This was about ten days before our raid on the Japanese forces at Balikpapan in January 1942.

The various batteries of the unit were deployed in the vicinity of Surabaja to support Dutch forces in case of a landing. Some of the machine gunners volunteered to transfer to a B-17 outfit that needed gunners to replace the casualties in the plane crews. For the rest of the Texas outfit were to begin shortly a series of air raids on

Surabaja and its environs. The actual combat did not begin until March, after the Japanese defeated the combined fleet of the Allies. Then the landings began and the Japanese poured troops ashore from their transports without fear of interruption from Allied surface or air forces.

Whatever opposition, if any, the Dutch offered at the beaches was rapidly overcome, and the Japanese troops streamed inland. Lieutenant Allen's battery was given the task of covering a road leading from the coast toward Surabaja. A machine-gun post was set up several hundred yards forward of the guns to prevent infiltration and to provide a point from which to designate targets and spot the fall of shells.

It happened that the machine gun at the post was manned by Sergeant Fujita, half Japanese and half Mexican but 100 percent American. After tense moments of waiting for the enemy to appear, the battery opened up on formations of bicycle troops that came into view around the bend of the road. Some Japanese troops crossed the field toward the machine-gun post, shouting in English, "Don't shoot. We are Americans." They expected to find Dutchmen defending Java and thought that the ruse would work with them. Fujita answered them—with profanity and a burst of fire. Meanwhile the battery was preventing an advance along the road. When the Japanese brought up artillery to oppose the American guns, Japanese troops began to flank the battery. The Texans noticed that the Dutch lines on their flanks had been withdrawn. The order to retreat was given and the unit withdrew without casualty.

One of the American officers told a story that, while one of the batteries was waiting for the action to begin, an American officer took several of his men back to a town behind the lines to get some refreshments for the men on the line. They went into a bar for beer and cold drinks to take back with them and found the bar filled with Dutch officers and men drinking at their leisure. When the American officer inquired about the Dutch troop dispositions, he was told that the Dutch troops were being returned to barracks. As the officer turned to leave with his men, he addressed the group in general: "We're going back to the guns on the line now. Who's going with us?" Most of the Dutchmen pretended not to hear or not to understand;

a few looked ashamed, but no one got up to join the Americans. The officer again addressed the group but this time in all the insulting terms he could muster, and the response was the same. As a last attempt he taunted them: "Well, I wouldn't turn over my wife and children to the Japs without a fight." Still no one got up to go out to the guns with him.

Another case of this Allied cooperation occurred when a jeep was sent back from one of the batteries to bring supplies from the trucks in the motor pool of the battery behind the lines. The men were challenged by a Dutch sentry who told them that the Dutch forces had surrendered and that they must now surrender and give their arms to him. Pretending to surrender, the men caught the sentry off guard and slugged him. Because there was no hope of removing their trucks, they sprayed the trucks with bullets from the pair of .50-caliber machine guns (salvaged from a wrecked B-17) mounted on the jeep. If they couldn't have the trucks, at least the Japanese would not have them undamaged.

Opposed by both the Japanese and the Dutch, the 131st Field Artillery was forced to surrender piecemeal, in most cases to the Dutch. In the prison camps they joined Dutch and British troops. The British, being strangers in Java like the Americans, had fought for the defense of the island and earned the ingratitude of the Dutch, who feared that the Japanese would make the surrender terms more severe if there was any opposition.

At last I learned how the Dutchmen who had upbraided me for speaking German, who had boasted of fighting to the last man, and who had accused American sailors of running away from the Philippines would fight. I must admit, however, that the Dutch navy fought bravely though without skill, and the air force did its utmost until the planes were withdrawn from tactical tasks for evacuation. On the latter point I am especially bitter, because the lack of proper air reconnaissance was one of the reasons for the loss of the *Pope*.

The Dutch women visited the camps on the days permitted by the Japanese and brought food and cigarettes. It was not strange that they gave these gifts to the American and British troops and not to their own men. In fact it was some time before the Dutch women would speak to their men civilly.

Some of the *Houston*'s survivors were in one of the camps where the Texans were imprisoned. (The *Houston* had been sunk earlier on the same day that the *Pope* was sunk.) After several months in Java in various camps, a large group of prisoners were sent to Singapore, where they were outfitted with winter clothing and eventually shipped to Japan. The party that arrived in our camp on December 7, 1942, was from this group.

After a week in camp, the new prisoners (more than a year afterward we were still referring to this group as the "new" prisoners) were introduced to the shipyard. Most of them worked in the boiler shop; the remainder were split among the various other groups. About twenty Americans and Britishers joined my drilling party. By this time most of the scrap iron was cleared away and the ground was leveled so that the steel plates could be drilled.

The new blood in the dockyard helped to relieve the monotony, and the new faces and new stories, especially the good news of war developments, gave the Makassar prisoners a new interest in life. It was only after the new group had picked up our morale that we realized how apathetic we had been growing.

The weather was becoming increasingly colder, but the Japanese still failed to provide winter clothing for the prisoners. Some shoddy work clothes had been given to the men, but most were too small and the material was so flimsy that little or no warmth was obtained from them. Some men tried to make clothing from blankets until the Japanese found out what they were doing.

Improvements were being made to the camp. The officers' room was the first to get a ceiling; then in turn the other rooms had ceilings installed, albeit slowly. We still had no doors on the rooms—the breeze in the corridor blew into the rooms—so the Japanese issued straw sacking to hang over the doorways. The effect of this arrangement was that when the wind blew into the room, it blew in bits of straw.

Just before Christmas the Japanese issued army winter uniforms, but the prisoners were told that they could not wear them until after the New Year, and then only in the camp, not to the dockyard. This regulation was immediately disregarded, without any severe consequences.

The temperature seldom dropped to freezing, but the meager diet and lack of winter clothing made comparatively mild winter temperatures seem severe. The cold winter rain was the chief cause of illness in the camp; the men would get soaked through to the skin at work, return to camp at the end of the day, and have no warm clothes to change into. The next morning they would return to the yard wearing damp clothes. In time we filled the sick bay with pneumonia cases.

When we returned from the shipyard on Christmas Eve, we were surprised to find that the barracks had been decorated with crepe paper and tinsel by the prisoners who had remained in camp that day. The evening meal was the usual bowl of rice, but it was served with a special stew of curry and pork, just enough to give the stew a tantalizing flavor. An apple was included as an extra treat. After dinner we sang carols to create a real feeling of Christmas. The Dutch sang some of their own Christmas hymns; they had a talent for singing.

Oostdijk, one of the Dutch sergeants, came over to wish me a Merry Christmas. As he shook my hand he left a pack of cigarettes in it. Sometime in November I had given him my only Japanese money, a fifty-sen note, worth about a dime, to get me cigarettes. For weeks he had put me off, saying that the Japanese who was supplying the cigarettes was sick. I had just about given up hope of getting anything back. The cigarettes were Sakuras (cherry), the best Japanese brand. After getting by on butts and any scraps of tobacco I could roll into a smoke, this was indeed opulence. I was grateful to Oostdijk for getting the cigarettes for me, and I was touched that he waited until Christmas Eve to deliver not just a pack of cigarettes but a pack of the best cigarettes available.

We were informed that, in response to our requests, a Catholic priest and a Protestant minister would come from Nagasaki to hold Christmas services for the prisoners on Christmas morning before we went to the dockyard. The camp commander was a Christian, which accounted for the ready compliance with our desires for religious services; he also supplied the decorations for the camp to make Christmas a social occasion. The fact that, as a Christian, he did not do more to improve conditions in camp we attributed to his rank of *chui*, first lieutenant, in the Japanese army. Apparently the rank carried no more authority in the Japanese army than the corresponding rank in our own. Our general opinion was that the man was sincere and well meaning but was in the unenviable position of reconciling Christian tenets with the Japanese war effort.

It seemed to me that the Christian Japanese felt a greater compulsion to show themselves true Christians in a country with a definite minority than Christians in so-called Christian countries. The Japanese YMCA, for instance, supplied us with a library from their limited supply of English books and later sent gifts of tangerines to the camp.

Allen told an amusing story in this connection. One of the sentries on the ship transporting the prisoners from Java to Singapore approached him and, pointing to himself, said "Christos." Then he pointed to Allen, who indicated that he too was a Christian. The sentry took a Bible from his pocket and asked to see Allen's. Happily, Allen was carrying a Bible. The sentry repeated this procedure with several other prisoners nearby, and by chance they all had Bibles with them. The sentry then left, apparently convinced that all good Christians regardless of nationality always carried Bibles.

The next morning the mass was held in the courtyard near the officers' room. This courtyard was equipped for use as a wash place, except for running water. The Protestant services were held in the other courtyard near the galley, which was now completed and in operation. I attended mass and was impressed to see the number of men who had given up an hour of much needed sleep to stand in the cold. Most of the men received holy communion as they knelt on the rocky ground. The Japanese priest delivered a sermon in Japanese, and we were given copies printed in English. The substance of the sermon was that Japan was trying to create a new order in the world and thereby bring about peace and that we should cooperate in this effort in whatever way we could.

The sermon spoiled the whole effect of the ceremony for me. I felt that it was out of order for a Catholic priest, in what is assumed to be a church without nationality, to broach this subject on Christmas Day to prisoners from enemy nations. That he was not required to do this was evident from the fact that the Protestant minister, also Japanese, confined himself to remarks concerning the significance of Christmas and urging the prisoners to keep up their spirits so that they might spend some future Christmas back with their families.

The following week went quickly enough because we were buoyed by anticipation of the four-day holiday that the Japanese were planning in observance of the New Year. On the eve of the holiday there was little work done in the dockyard, because most of the Japanese were planning to leave work as soon as possible to get an early start to visit their families outside of Nagasaki. Many came to work in good clothes so that they would not miss the ferry by having to change after work.

The prisoners were put to work cleaning up the dockyard so that the New Year could be started with a fresh slate. There was a definite holiday spirit, and most of the prisoners had little trouble bumming cigarettes from their honchos. During our first few months in the dockyard, when there was no cigarette issue in the camp, the Japanese workers were good about giving cigarettes to the prisoners who worked with them. Some of the prisoners would occasionally trade soap and various personal belongings, sometimes watches and rings, to obtain cigarettes; the cigarettes would, in turn, be traded in camp for food.

Back in camp the Japanese guard set in motion the plans for their holiday banquets by having the galley staff (prisoners) prepare special dishes and bake buns and cookies. Barrels of sake (rice wine) were broken out from the storeroom and taken to the Japanese rooms. The prisoners benefited from the Japanese festival spirit by receiving slightly larger rations for a few of the meals. Because the Japanese were having such large meals, there were almost always leftovers. Groups of prisoners would wait in the passageway near the Japanese soldiers' rooms, which were now under the same roof with ours, to get the extra fish and rice by offering to take the "empty" serving buckets back to the galley. Often there was such a scramble for the spoils that the Japanese would chase the prisoners away and forbid them to collect in the corridor. Some of the prisoners would wait for hours to get something extra to eat.

For the Japanese it was a festive time; food and wine were plentiful and the war was going in their favor. One of the sentries, who was slightly inebriated, entered one of the American army rooms and delivered a speech in English saying, "To hell with the war, we're all friends." He followed this with handshakes and the distribution of cigarettes. A little later an equally inebriated comrade came to lead him back to the Japanese room , which was a little way down the corridor, presumably for another drink.

My own observance of the New Year was somewhat less festive. I spent my time reading, making a pair of cloth "booties," and sleeping. It was cold even in the room, and when my fingers were too stiff to sew, I would read, keeping my hands in my pockets between turning pages. When I tired of this, I pulled the blankets over me and slept. In this manner I managed to finish reading *Altogether,* a collection of W. Somerset Maugham's short stories and novelettes, and completed my booties, which turned out to be a trifle small but were otherwise serviceable. Sometimes I played bridge, but only when I felt particularly warm, for it was cold holding the cards.

During this cold weather, we always looked forward to the arrival of the tea bucket. The hot tea helped make us feel full in the absense of food. We called it tea (*o cha,* the honorable tea, as the Japanese called it), but in most cases it was merely hot water. Sometimes there were green leaves floating in the bucket, giving the liquid an acrid taste and a slight discoloration. We considered these manifestations as attempts to lend substance to the fiction.

For most of the prisoners the four days away from the dockyard were too much at one stretch because there was so little to do for amusement. Most of the reading material consisted of books that a few of the prisoners had brought to Japan as part of their personal gear. The inactivity made the cold and hunger keener. At least in the dockyard the time went faster for most of the men, and the manual labor, although tiring, had the virtue of giving warmth.

I would have preferred to stay in camp, for my job in the yard made the days pass slowly, and I had a hard time keeping warm. I was forbidden to speak to the men during working hours except to transmit instructions from the Japanese. Whenever I tried to pass the time of day in conversation, the honcho would tell me to move on and not talk so much.

The drilling section was outdoors so I got the full effect of the weather, as did the rest of the party. I had no intention of trying my hand at drilling to keep warm or make the time pass; once I started, the Japanese would want me to do it all the time. If I had been able to sit down occasionally, it would not have been such a strain, but this too was forbidden.

As a result I spent most of the day trying to kill time and achieved only meager results. I tried solving mathematical problems in my head, but this had certain hazards: if I became too preoccupied, I might fail to notice the overhead crane approaching with a load of steel plates. Even if the cable was strong enough, there was always a chance that the load would be at just the right height to knock off my hat with my head in it. Or a sentry might come along and want to know what my job was and try to increase my interest with a rifle butt. At five o'clock I usually felt as though I had completed a long day of physical labor. I looked forward to the end of the holidays with about as much enthusiasm as I used to look forward to returning to the naval academy after Christmas leave in New York when I was a midshipman. As a prisoner of war, most of my recollections of the academy for some reason centered around the mess hall.

On January 4, 1943, McCreary, a machinist's mate from the *Perch,* died of pneumonia with contributing causes of malnutrition and improper clothing and housing. This was the first death in my group, and it was a shock to most of the men. "Big Mac" was well liked, and some of the men had been shipmates with him for five to six years. Our greatest concern was the speed with which he succumbed. He had been sick only three days, and the doctor had not considered him sick enough to send to sick bay, which was crowded with pneumonia cases, mostly Dutch and British. All the deaths in camp up to this time were from these nationalities.

Mac had received only aspirin, because only the most serious cases were given medicine from the minute supply available. The doctors had to purchase the medicine secretly through friendly Japanese in the dockyard because the Japanese army would not supply it to the camp.

The day after McCreary's death, I was permitted to stay in camp with a number of the American sailors who were to be pallbearers for the funeral in Nagasaki. There were to be two funerals; the other was for a Dutchman who had died a few hours after McCreary.

We left camp about an hour after the regular work party had gone to the dockyard. The pallbearers carried the plain wooden coffins on their shoulders to the ferry landing at the dockyard. The Dutch coffin led, draped in a small Dutch flag; McCreary's coffin had no flag because there was no American flag in the camp. At the ferry landing we embarked in a diesel-powered boat about the size of the Japanese fishing boats we used to see around Hawaii. The coffins were left topside while we crowded into the small cabin out of the wind.

The water was just rough enough to make the trip uncomfortable in a small craft. The boat's motion and the stuffiness of the cabin eventually drove most of us topside despite the cold. On the way to Nagasaki we passed the Mitsubishi shipyard. It seemed larger than ours (Kawainami), and the name was more familiar to us. The ships fitting out at the yard were larger than the types we were building, and there were also a number of naval ships being built.

After the Mitsubishi yard passed from view, we concentrated our attention on the city, which extended up several valleys from the business and waterfront area. The valleys were separated by mountains that rose abruptly to heights of about two thousand feet. The main part of the city was to our right as we headed to the north end of the bay where a small stream permitted our boat to proceed into the city. This shortened the trip to the crematorium. Both sides of the stream were walled with stone, and the boat stopped at a landing on the west bank. Several small boats similar to ours were tied up near the landing, and Japanese laborers were unloading fish and vegetables from them.

Our arrival with the coffins did not arouse more than polite curiosity among the Japanese civilians on the street above the landing. Because this was not a busy part of town, we did not encounter many people. We passed a few small shops and dwellings along the way. Above the doors of the houses were oranges and small sheaves of rice. These, Budding explained, were New Year's offerings for good luck in the coming year. There was practically no motor traffic on the streets, and the few vehicles we saw were using charcoal burners. A few horse-drawn wagons were in evidence, and the horses looked well cared for. In fact, they looked healthier than most of the people we saw.

The road skirted an enclosed park or temple grounds and then left the stream bank and began to climb through a more rural district. We passed a tiny garden patch near the road and were surprised to see green vegetables growing at this season of the year. Although the spot was protected, the garden made us realize that the cold we constantly complained about was not entirely a matter of temperature.

The grade of the road made it necessary to stop frequently to rest the bearers and allow them to shift the coffins to the opposite shoulder. We passed a wooded section where the leaves were still on the trees, which made us realize how completely lacking in trees the areas around the camp and dockyard were. Although there were trees on the island, few were in sight of the camp.

As we rounded a bend in the road, the crematorium came into view. It was a large wooden building set in neatly landscaped grounds at the end of the road. The building was typical of the traditional Japanese architecture with its high, gracefully sweeping tile roof.

The coffins were placed on stands just inside the entrance. While we were waiting, we witnessed a funeral ceremony conducted by a Shinto priest. He chanted rapidly in a monotone, pausing occasionally for breath and then beginning again in a slightly higher key. At intervals he would strike a small brass bell, probably to indicate certain points in his ceremony, for his chanting must have been unintelligible to the Japanese themselves.

After the ceremony, which I think was intended to include our dead as well as the Japanese, most of our funeral party returned to the boat for the trip back to camp. Budding, Goodwine (McCreary's best friend), Sergeant Saito, and I waited in the lounge provided by the establishment for the families of the deceased. The sergeant supplied us with cigarettes at frequent intervals.

Sergeant Saito was very tall and, though he wore typical Japanese glasses and had Japanese features, didn't look Japanese. He was better educated than most of the Japanese I had encountered, and he spoke passable English. There was something subdued and scholarly about him that made his uniform and military saber inappropriate. To my knowledge he never showed anything but a kind attitude to the prisoners. Budding, who had considerable contact with him in camp, thought highly of him.

This admiration must have been mutual, because Saito felt free to discuss certain things with Budding that most Japanese would not have confided to a prisoner of war. When Budding learned that Saito had been stationed on the Siberian border in Manchuria, he asked him about the so-called border clashes about which we had received such shadowy reports before the war. Saito had laughed and replied, "When twenty-five thousand men are killed, you don't call it a border clash."

Later we were called into the furnace room to witness the placing of the coffins in the furnace. The room had white tile walls and a row of furnace doors. The coffins were placed on steel carts, which were wheeled into the furnace compartments. First the brick-lined fire doors were closed, then the outer iron doors.

After a short wait the attendant informed Budding that the cremation was finished and brought out earthenware pots for the ashes. The attendant opened the furnace doors and pulled out the carts. Oversized chopsticks were given to us so we could pick out the bones from the embers of the coffins and place them in the urns. I was hesitant at first, but when Budding and Goodwine stoically began to pick up the bones I joined them. After we had placed most of the bones in the urns, the attendant brushed off the pieces of wood and tilted the steel trays on the carts to pour the ashes into the urns. We placed the urns in individual wooden boxes and covered them with silk brocade provided by the crematorium. Although I was repulsed by the sight of the bones and ashes, I was convinced that cremation had its advantages.

With Budding and Goodwine carrying the urns, we started back down the road. It was easier going downhill and we made good time. We crossed a bridge just above the landing, which led us toward the main part of town. A few blocks from the bridge we waited for a trolley car to take us to the Catholic church, where we hoped to have a mass said for the dead men or, at least, proper funeral services.

We had a long wait before a trolley car stopped; a number of crowded ones passed without slowing down. Finally we pushed our way into a car and joined the strap hangers. The passengers did not seem to notice that we were not Japanese; perhaps the army overcoats gave us a Japanese appearance. I had a beard, which would have made my features less discernible. The conductor, an undernourished youth with a ratty look, nudged me for my fare. Saito spoke up and indicated Budding, Goodwine, and me as being in his party. I did not see Saito pay, so I concluded that service personnel had free transportation on the trolleys.

The car was smaller than the usual stateside trolley, and the ceiling was low. Because the windows were well below my eye level, the impression of the ride was that of a series of roadside ditches interrupted by a mass of bobbing heads at each stop. After about twenty minutes, Saito gave a shout and we got out at the next stop. I looked around for a church but saw none. Then Saito told us we had to walk awhile. We were in a residential area of small private dwellings that lined both sides of the street. The street was roughly paved, more like a country road, and there were few sidewalks. Most of the intersections were shopping centers with stores on at least three of the corners.

We finally caught a view of the church and were impressed by its size and location. The red brick structure with two steeples was like a part of the Western world transplanted. I was surprised to see such a large and elaborate building, but Budding reminded me that for centuries Nagasaki had been the center of Christianity in Japan and had been visited by St. Francis Xavier in the sixteenth century. The Dutch as well as the Spanish and Portuguese had had contact with the Japanese during this period. When the Japanese decided to limit European trade and contact, Nagasaki was one of the few places designated as open to foreign trade.

Situated on top of a steep hill, the church dominated the buildings of the surrounding sections. The sun was setting and the church was bathed in the golden light of the last rays as the valley below grew indistinct in the twilight. To one side of the church were the priest's house and a school for children. From the latter we could hear a choir singing hymns in Latin.

We waited outside the church while Saito spoke to the priest. The grounds were well kept. On the hillside toward the valley we noticed an orange tree and tried to think of ways to get some of the fruit. Saito returned and told us that the priest would say mass the next day and would open the church now so that we could go inside with the ashes and say a few prayers.

The priest opened the door at the side of the church and indicated for us to remove our shoes before entering the building. The floor was wooden and highly polished; to wear shoes would have been sacrilegious. The church was almost completely dark inside, so the priest turned on electric lights and lit candles. With the ashes in front of the altar, the priest said prayers in Latin and conducted a brief funeral service. We knelt on the floor because there were no pews or prie-dieux. When the prayers were over, the priest repeated that a mass would be said for the deceased the next day and that the ashes would be kept at the church until they were wanted.

Our trip down the hill and the return to the trolley station were hurried. Budding told Goodwine and me that Saito was afraid we would miss the ferry back to the island. The trolley carried us to within a block of the ferry landing in the main part of town, but we found that we had just missed the ferry and would have to wait more than an hour before the next one.

To help pass the time, Saito bought us a copy of the *Nippon Times,* a newspaper printed in English presumably for the nonenemy Europeans residing in Japan. This was a treat but not a wholly unexpected one, for Budding had brought back papers from previous funeral trips. We waited our turns to read the paper; I could barely control my impatience while Budding finished. Perhaps realizing my state, he threw me scraps of news from time to time.

Meanwhile Saito bought us tangerines from a fruit stand outside the waiting room. Our bows and *arigato gozaimas*'s ("thanks very much," a more polite form than a mere *arigato*) did not fully express our appreciation for these acts of kindness.

At last the ferry arrived and we embarked for the trip back. We had the boat almost to ourselves. The few passengers looked like dockyard workers en route to the yard for a night shift.

At about the midpoint of our trip, the lights in the ferry were extinguished while we passed a stretch of water that led out to the open sea, probably an antisubmarine precaution. Before long the lights of our dockyard were in view and the flashes of the arc welding created a bizarre effect. By this time we were all hungry, and the bowl of rice and soup that would be waiting at the camp seemed especially inviting.

Back in camp the other officers sat around and questioned Budding and me while we ate. Everyone wanted to read the paper at the same time but managed to avoid any dissension. They wanted to know what we had seen on the way and what sort of a trip we had, but the news from the paper was the most important thing.

The occasional paper brought in from the funeral trips was our chief source of authentic news. In the yard the men heard rumors from their honchos and occasionally were able to get an English language paper (either the *Nippon Times* or the *Osaka Mainichi*). Most of the rumors came straight from the *benjo* (latrine), where the men gathered to pass the time, get an illicit smoke, and make up rumors. The news concerning the European war seemed particularly reliable, and German reverses, though occasionally minimized, were never censored.

The Japanese news, on the other hand, was definitely slanted, and extravagant claims of American losses were never balanced by even moderate Japanese losses. A typical report would read: "The Japanese Wild Eagles engaged American bomber and fighter units over Rabaul, shooting down fifteen of the enemy planes; the remainder fled severely damaged and it is doubted that they reached their base. Our own losses: one plane slightly damaged and one plane not yet returned to base."

We generally halved all Japanese claims and as a result failed to realize completely the seriousness of our position in the Solomons. Of course we were filled with the sublime confidence that no matter what happened, we would win. The only question was when.

8

The daily work in the dockyard was monotonous. In my group I had clashes with the honcho because of his tendency to strike the prisoners whenever he was displeased with their efforts. An innovation was the presentation of prizes: a small piece of alleged butter was given to each prisoner who drilled three hundred holes, a reasonable amount for beginners. I warned the men to avoid meeting these requirements and forgo the butter because the requirement would be jacked up as soon as most of the prisoners were able to do the required amount.

Some of the people in my party were not impressed by my reasoning and were soon drilling five hundred holes for the same piece of "butter." Eventually the required amount reached about fifteen hundred holes, and the prisoners were complying. The annoying part about these awards was the fact that they were distributed during the lunch period and cut into our time off. As honcho I always received a piece of butter; this was purely a matter of "face," because I could read the reluctance on the Japanese honcho's face in giving me, a nonproducer, a piece of "butter." Whatever the stuff was, it tasted good melted over the lunch rice.

The food situation was getting progressively worse. In the dockyard was a galley where food was prepared for Japanese workers who wished to purchase their lunch instead of bringing it with them. The galley could be seen from the *benjo*, which was directly opposite it about twenty yards distant. When I was in the *benjo* I noticed a tense crowd of prisoners watching the galley. A pair of women emerged from the galley carrying a barrel of slop, which they dumped into another barrel outside the galley. The latter barrel I knew was a

169

garbage pail; I had seen it filled with refuse whenever I went to the galley to draw the tea for my party at noontime. As soon as the women dumped the refuse there was a mad rush from the *benjo*. The prisoners dipped their empty lunch tins into the slop and hurried back to the *benjo* to eat it. I told the men that they should be ashamed of themselves for eating garbage and that they were inviting dysentery. They replied that they were hungry and that the slop was just leftovers from lunch.

I was happy to see that none of the Americans were in this hungry group. Perhaps it was not fair of me to censure these men; they were doing manual labor and would therefore be hungrier than I. But a man must draw a line somewhere, and that was where I drew it.

About two weeks after the end of our New Year's holiday, on January 18, 1943, to be exact, another death occurred in my group. Kirk, a water tender from the *Pope*, died of pneumonia and malnutrition. Kirk had been in my drilling party; his job had been easy enough, sweeping up steel shavings and dumping them into a dump bucket, but he contracted pneumonia working out in the cold. I remembered well the day he came to me and said he was sick. I got permission to take him to the sick bay, where we found he had a temperature of 104 degrees. By this time he was shivering. He was given tea to warm him up, and I left a jacket for him to wear.

At length he was returned to camp and put in the sick bay there. For a few days he seemed to be doing all right. I visited him and two other men in my party who were in sick bay at the time, Hyde and Stevenson, who also had pneumonia. I had gotten some pepper from Yamamichi, the interpreter for my party, to help make the food more palatable and overcome the sick men's loss of appetite. This helped only a bit.

One day Yamamichi brought some tangerines I had requested for Kirk, who had been feeling low. When I took the fruit to the sick bay, I was told that Kirk had died that afternoon. I gave the tangerines to Hyde and Stevenson and returned to my room wondering hopelessly how many more men we would lose. I had lost two and had two more seriously ill. Hyde was delirious and kept asking Stevenson when the ship was getting under way. Stevenson was frail looking, and I feared that he would not get well.

With Kirk's death I again had the opportunity to go to Nagasaki, but this was a high price to pay. I held a funeral service for Kirk in the American navy room. I don't suppose it made any difference for a Catholic to conduct services for a Protestant. Churches might take a dim view of such proceedings, but because they had temporized on greater issues I supposed they could swallow this irregularity. All I knew was that I had lost another man from my original twenty-four (Connor and Rafalovich in the new group kept my strength at twenty-four), and I had two more probables. An Englishman had died at the time of Kirk's death, so we had another double funeral.

This time the services after the cremation were held in a Protestant church near the center of Nagasaki. It was much smaller than the Catholic church but it had pews. The minister said the service in English and expressed his condolences as we left the church. The boat that had brought us to Nagasaki waited for us, so the whole party including pallbearers attended the services. We arrived back in camp shortly after dark.

My shoes by this time were completely worn out. I had had them resoled by the camp cobbler, but this time the uppers were giving way. The Japanese were replacing worn-out shoes with rubber-soled *tabi*. These sneakerlike canvas shoes had a separate compartment for the big toe, much like the thumb in a mitten; instead of laces, metal tabs fitted through loops on the back of the shoe to make the closure. Because of the peculiar shape of the shoe, the wearer left a footprint like that of an elongated hoof of a cow. For most of us it was uncomfortable to wear a shoe with the big toe separated from the other toes, especially because our socks were not split the same way.

The design of some Japanese shoes was determined by conditions. Because of the general lack of paved roads in Japan except in and around the large cities, and the abundance of mud in rainy weather, and the fact that farmers liberally fertilized their fields with "night soil," a type of footwear evolved known as geta. It consists of a thin piece of wood slightly greater than the width and length of the foot; to the bottom of this piece are attached two blocks of wood, one under the ball of the foot and the other under the heel. These blocks, which extend the width of the geta, elevate the wearer two to three inches above the ground.

To keep the geta on the foot, a strap, secured at each side of the platform and between the big toe and the second toe, extends across the top of the foot. This connection of the strap to the wood, between the toes, keeps the geta on the foot. Because the Japanese start wearing this footgear at a young age, they become inured to the discomfort.

The *tabi* were designed to be worn with the geta in cold weather. The rubber-soled *tabi* seemed to be a logical development when rubber came to be used commercially, so that the *tabi* could be worn without the geta in dry weather or where steadier footing was required. The split toe of the rubber-soled *tabi* made it possible to wear geta with them when necessary. That the Japanese wore these split-toed shoes on Bataan to cause the Americans to think that the tracks were those of carabao (water buffalo) gives the Japanese credit for a ruse they had not intended.

The limited stock of unsplit-toed shoes that the Japanese had in the camp had been exhausted by the time my shoes wore out, and the variety now in stock went up to only size ten. Knowing that all the larger-footed individuals without shoes were kept in camp (we were known as *kutsu nashi,* or no shoes), I asked for size eleven. I tried to conceal my disappointment when I was told I'd have to stay in camp until larger sizes arrived.

The next two months I spent in camp more or less at my leisure. I reread H. G. Wells's *Outline of History* and read several novels and most of Shakespeare's plays. When I tired of reading, I slept.

There were a few minor drawbacks to being in camp. There was not much company, because the people who were allowed to stay in camp, other than the shoeless, were too sick to be interested in chitchat. One day, however, Commander Chubb lost his voice. Though this would not have been enough to keep a worker home from the yard, Chubb persuaded the Japanese doctor, whose apparent purpose in camp was to make sure only those at death's door were placed on the sick list, that as a honcho he had to shout instructions to the men; without his voice he would be utterly useless in the dockyard. (When Major Horrigan was placed on the sick list with the same complaint, we dubbed the ailment *shosa's* disease, *shosa* being the rank corresponding to major and lieutenant commander.)

Chubb and Horrigan were good company, but whenever I tried to carry on a conversation I would end up whispering. Horrigan taught me to play cribbage, an excellent way to pass the time when we were tired of reading. On sunny days we would take a bench into the courtyard and find a place in the sun and out of the wind to play cribbage. One day a sentry saw us playing cards and chased us inside. The Japanese seemed to abhor the idea of anyone amusing himself while others were working, especially if that anyone happened to be a prisoner of war.

One day Budding came into the room and said that there were some Japanese newspaper men in the camp, and the camp commandant wanted an officer of each nationality to attend a press conference. Doctor Syred represented the British point of view; Doctor Wijzviss, Lieutenant Frank, and Lieutenant Budding the Dutch; and I the American. We went to the newly completed administration building to meet with the camp commandant and his relief, an older officer apparently recalled from retirement, and the representatives of the Japanese press, including photographers.

We were motioned to be seated, and the camp commandant told us through Budding to feel free to say what we wanted. While the reporters took notes, Budding gave them our names and nationalities. A round of questions and answers followed. Syred mentioned the lack of medical supplies. I was asked if I thought we were being well treated. I replied that the food was insufficient and that the clothing and housing were inadequate for the climate. As proof of this I reminded them that the number of deaths since we had arrived in Japan was more than fifty and that all of these men had left the Dutch East Indies in good health.

As an example of the poor sanitary conditions in camp, I pointed out that the *benjo* was located just outside the galley where in warm weather the flies would contaminate the food and probably cause an epidemic of dysentery. My reference to the *benjo* seemed to amuse the Japanese; apparently they considered the location satisfactory.

Then each of us was asked who would win the war. Syred, Frank, and I said that we thought the Allies would win. Budding gave a diplomatic answer: "I don't think we'll lose." Wijzviss answered, "I really don't know. One can't tell what's in the future." This answer seemed to satisfy the Japanese; I'm sure they gave it a prominent display in their newspapers.

We paused while pictures were taken, then one of the reporters said he had a question for the American officer. Addressing me in what I felt was an insulting manner, he asked, "How do you account for the fact that there are so many American prisoners of war and no Japanese prisoners?" (The Japanese believed that no Japanese soldier ever surrendered.) I answered, "Maybe the Japanese run too fast." At first they looked pleased at this answer. Then some of them began to talk in Japanese among themselves, and I was subjected to both interested and angry glances.

The camp commandant announced abruptly that the interview was at an end. As we were leaving, some of the reporters asked me my rank and branch of service. I have always wondered just how my remarks were reported in the newspaper.

On the way back to my room I felt a certain elation about having gotten the best of the exchange. I was somewhat afraid that there might be repercussions for being too outspoken, but the camp commander kept the promise he implied when he told us to speak freely.

There was a rumor that Red Cross supplies would soon arrive in camp. In time they did arrive, about forty individual parcels to divide among thirteen hundred men, giving each man roughly half a single article in the parcel. Some men received as their share half a bar of soap. Sacks of sugar and cartons of cocoa were included in the shipment. Although the amount was pitifully inadequate, the fact that any Red Cross supplies had arrived improved morale tremendously, and there was always the hope that more parcels were on the way.

Because these first supplies were from the British Red Cross, most of the British enlisted men felt that the parcels were meant primarily for the British prisoners of war. They had no objection to the Yanks sharing with them, but they were vehemently against the Dutch participating. The British officers wisely decided that unless all nationalities shared, it would have an adverse effect upon relations in the camp.

When the time came to divide the parcels, we had the small thrill of drawing for precedence in picking our items. Blain and I were paired for this lottery; when our turn came we chose a canned apple pudding—all the canned meats had already been claimed. We hoarded this for about a week before we ate it. Dividing the sugar and cocoa equitably required precise mathematics; even so, some sugar and cocoa were left over, so it was decided to donate the extras to the people in the sick bay.

With the distribution of these meager supplies, trade in the camp was revived, and there was a temporary departure from the cigarette-rice medium of exchange. To some it might seem strange that supposedly hungry men would trade food for cigarettes. Until I entered prison camp I was a nonsmoker. I took up the habit out of boredom and continued it for the relaxation and the modicum of enjoyment it gave me.

Only on rare occasions did I trade food for cigarettes, but I could understand some of the others doing it fairly often. Cigarettes have a tendency to kill one's appetite. It was often hard to tell whether the gnawing feeling was for tobacco or food. A few prisoners gave up tobacco so that they could trade cigarettes for food, but the abstention increased their appetites so much that the extra food they received for their cigarettes failed to make up for their greater desire for food. They usually reverted to smoking. There was no regular issue of cigarettes by the Japanese. The only cigarettes in camp were obtained in the dockyard or had been brought from Makassar.

One day the Japanese decided to pay the officers in accordance with international law. Apparently it was easier to get money than it was clothing or medical supplies. I received the pay of a *chui* (lieutenant, junior grade), a handsome eighty-five yen a month (equivalent to about twenty-one dollars).

January was the first month we were paid, and I received forty yen in cash; the remainder was split between my mess bills (we were charged a flat fifteen yen for food) and my war savings. All prisoners who were working had bank accounts opened for them, and part of their pay was deposited each month. Actual bankbooks were used to record these deposits, and at the proper intervals interest was computed and recorded.

One reason for the bank accounts was to limit the amount of money in circulation; prisoners spending their money in the dockyard would contribute to inflation. I think there was another reason as well, although I don't like to give the Japanese credit for it. The Japanese wanted to make sure that the prisoners would return to their defeated countries with some cash in their pockets, good solid Japanese yen. The amount of cash we received was later cut to twenty yen, but that was still ample for what we could buy.

While I was in the camp *kutsu nashi,* Blain was going to the yard every day. There he used our combined fortunes to buy as many cigarettes as possible and to buy any available food or condiments. All these commodities were brought into the yard by Japanese workers and usually sold at a price that made it worth their while to take the trouble.

Some Japanese brought in cigarettes and food and sold them for cost out of compassion for the prisoners. Occasionally it was possible to have a newspaper brought in. Each night when Blain came into the room, I would wait expectantly while he broke out the items acquired in the day's transactions. We soon collected a sizable stock of cigarettes and then began to concentrate on food.

Because most food was rationed, the articles we were able to get were not especially filling or even nutritious, but they helped lend variety and color to our meals. We tried fish paste; dried shrimp, which were minute; dried eggs, about which we were a little dubious; very thin tomato catsup, probably watered; pickled garlic; and peaches in syrup, the most expensive item but also the best. The fish paste seemed to be the best buy, fifty sen a jar (about twelve cents). It went well with the bread we were getting for the noon meal as a change from rice, so we bought the paste whenever we could.

The bread was baked in the form of hamburger buns; the normal ration was three, but sick men received only two—an incentive to get well, no doubt. The buns were an excellent medium of exchange and soon acquired a standard value of ten Japanese cigarettes or half a bowl of rice. Because the buns were not uniform in size, the smallest became known as "trade" buns.

There was a tendency to trade bowls of rice that were less full than the normal bowl, and cigarettes that were no longer "so round, so firm, so fully packed" found their way into the market. One soon learned to judge one's "business associates," and specifications as to the size and condition of the articles of trade often became necessary.

Soon after the officers received their pay, arrangements were made to pay the enlisted men. Budding, at Horrigan's request, redoubled his efforts to talk the Japanese into providing the camp with a regular cigarette issue, to be paid for by the prisoners from their pay. He was unsuccessful in getting cigarettes from Nagasaki for the whole camp, but a sergeant of the guard promised to get cigarettes for the officers. From this arrangement we received sixty cigarettes apiece. As a result there was a phenomenal concentration of wealth in our room. Soon thereafter, cigarettes were made available for the whole camp on an equal basis.

We were also able to buy cake, which astonished us when we first learned of it. The cake tasted like a jelly roll, but instead of a roll it consisted of a top and a bottom piece with jam in between. It was much smaller than a jelly roll and was sliced into small pieces. About a dozen pieces represented one man's ration. Because the cigarettes were issued at the same time as the cake, there was brisk trading. When it was learned that these items would be available regularly, trading "in futures" became a recognized practice.

This trading was the downfall of a number of prisoners. In time people went into "bankruptcy." The "bankrupts" could be divided into two classes: the inept and the dishonest. In the former category were those who consistently made poor bargains and would not learn from experience; the latter group consisted of those who made agreements with little or no intention of keeping them.

When a man could not keep his creditors satisfied, he was brought to his officer, who commenced "bankruptcy" proceedings. First, the man's name and number were announced to the camp at muster so that no one would unwittingly do business with him. The officer would then hold a conference with the man and his creditors to determine the extent of the debts.

It was startling how far people could get into debt in a relatively short time. One bankrupt owed more than fifty buns, thirty bowls of rice, his next five cigarette issues, and his next three Red Cross issues.

Bankrupts were made to pay off their debts a little at a time until all were paid. When this was not feasible, the officer would ask the creditors to scale down their demands and accept a loss. This was not fair to the creditors, but it was necessary to keep the bankrupt from starving.

Sometimes the bankrupt, a weak character anyway, was talked into one-sided deals. This would be revealed when the officer asked the creditors what they had given the bankrupt. Then the debts would be scaled down to normal trade prices. There was always some dissatisfaction, but the main consideration was that the debtor—in discharging his debts—did not endanger his health. I am not sure that the same would hold in normal life.

I was proud that in my group of naval enlisted men there was not a single bankruptcy, whereas there were several in each of the other groups represented in camp. I attributed this to several facts: the group was small and therefore had a better esprit de corps; all the men except one were petty officers; and the men made sure that any potential bankrupt in the group stopped trading, and they handled his debts until he was out of the "red."

For a while the officers received preferential treatment regarding the cake and cigarette issues. Because the officers had more money than the enlisted men, they were allowed to purchase slightly more than the men. This caused a certain amount of dissension, which was natural. I know that if there had been a group of very senior officers in the camp receiving a larger issue than the other officers, it would have been a cause for dissension among the junior officers. About a month after the canteen was started, this inequality was removed in a typically Japanese way. Instead of giving the men more cigarettes and cakes, they merely gave the officers less of each.

Discipline in the camp was generally good. A prisoner could break as many Japanese rules as he wished without censure from his fellow prisoners as long as his infractions did not affect the rest of the camp. If a prisoner committed an offense against another prisoner or the prisoners as a group, he was brought to his officer for punishment. These offenses might be theft, failure to obey the orders of the room chief, or failure to keep himself and his effects clean. For a serious case a court-martial would be held; there were only a few of these. Usually the case was settled by one officer who would give the man a reprimand or assign him extra duty in his room. Aggravated cases were deprived of cigarette issues.

Major Horrigan asked the Japanese if they would permit us to put a man in confinement for certain offenses. The Japanese were agreeable but would not guarantee that the man would not receive corporal punishment as well. They felt that all cases should be turned over to them anyway. Although there was great reluctance to turn over any prisoner to the Japanese for punishment, it was necessary in several instances.

In time of war most people realize that the final arbiter of the international situation is force. In peacetime and in the normal life of a city or country, there is a tendency to forget that force is still present. Most people obey laws because they feel it's the right thing to do, but some obey laws because policemen enforce them. So even in everyday life, force is a final arbiter. If people cannot be approached on moral grounds to follow a certain mode of conduct, they must be forced for the common good.

As prisoners of war, we could approach the other prisoners on only a moral basis, for we did not have the power to enforce punishment. The prisoners who were turned over to the Japanese for confinement were those who failed to respond to the punishment they had received for their first few offenses.

I recall a bankrupt who, when he could no longer obtain extra food through dubious deals, resorted to stealing from the rice issue for his room. When it was his turn to fetch the box of rice from the galley, he would fill his lunch tin with rice before he reached the room and thus secure for himself an extra ration at the expense of his roommates. He was caught in the act and given various extra duties as punishment. A few days later he was caught stealing rice again and was turned over to the Japanese for confinement in the brig. After a week he was released. That very night he was found stealing food from the galley and again was turned over to the Japanese.

The Japanese thought it was a good joke. Obviously the man was completely demoralized. It might be argued that if the Japanese had issued sufficient food he would not have succumbed to the temptation. But because everyone had to get along with the same amount of food, the same argument could be applied to everyone. It was therefore necessary to take strong steps to protect the rest of the camp from the few delinquents whose activities, if unchecked, would seriously affect the morale of the camp.

In most cases the men responded well to correction and there was seldom any resentment against the officers for the punishments they inflicted. Although there was no attempt to enforce military courtesies, such as saluting, there was always a brisk exchange of salutes and "good mornings" at the morning formation for the dockyard.

One reason for this was the fact that the officers in charge of parties frequently had to get the men out of trouble with the Japanese in the dockyard. Another reason was that because the men had to salute all Japanese sentries, they felt that they should at least salute their own officers.

The real answer for this show of military courtesy was the mutual respect that had grown between the officers and men with close contact over a period of time. My group of naval enlisted men usually settled their own differences, and there were only a few occasions when I was called to intervene.

Vanneste, a chief water tender, was chief of the room in which all of my original group lived. He was a little heavy handed in his management of the room (half American and half British), but his type was necessary when there were so many divergent points of view. On holidays he made the men scrub the tables, benches, and woodwork and air their bedding when they would have preferred to spend the entire day sleeping or playing cards.

I always felt that he irritated the men just enough to keep them from becoming too introspective. Some of the men came to me on occasion and hinted that they did not expect Vanneste to get back to the States alive. When I spoke about Vanneste to these men after liberation, they had nothing but praise for him and were sheepish about having ever felt otherwise.

As all good things must come to an end, so did my period as *kutsu nashi*. The Japanese promises that they would supply shoes for all men at last came to be realized, and I was issued a pair of leather shoes with hobnail soles and soft pigskin tops with the smooth side in. They were comfortable, but they hardly reconciled me with the fact that I would have to return to the dockyard. I had the consolation of having spent two restful months in camp. I had developed beriberi, but that was from lack of food, not lack of exercise. To counteract the edema in my legs caused by the disease, Doctor Syred had given me injections of vitamin B. The swelling disappeared overnight.

Before returning to the dockyard, I shaved off a luxuriant beard that I had cultivated from the day of our arrival in Japan. After having it for six months, I felt naked without it. The beard had helped keep me warm through the winter. It had never seemed to be an entirely hygienic appendage, and I had the feeling of never being particularly clean, which I probably was not. But then the camp's limited facilities made it a problem to keep myself and my clothing clean. In Makassar I had been accustomed to taking several showers a day; in fact, in that warm climate it was almost a necessity. Washing clothing there was seldom a task.

In Japan it was difficult to get sufficient water, and when water was available it was almost agony to wash clothes in cold weather. In the cold water one's knuckles would swell, and the cold would slowly flow from the hands to the rest of the body. Daily ablutions came to mean a perfunctory washing of the hands and face. When there was a chance to get warm water, I would strip in our cold room and give myself a sponge bath, and then spend the rest of the day trying to get warm. One evening just before I was to return to the yard, it was announced that we would be permitted to take a hot bath at the public baths in Boys' Town—the prisoners' name for the barracks located between our camp and the dockyard (the inhabitants of the barracks were mostly boys who worked in the yard). With a towel and a piece of soap, I joined the group falling in to go to the baths.

We ran most of the way to Boys' Town because this was an extra detail for the sentries and they were anxious to get it over with. The bathhouse had two adjacent dressing rooms and two adjacent bathing tanks about four feet deep. A wizened old woman sat at a desk overlooking both dressing rooms. During normal bathing hours she probably took tickets from the bathers. She was not at all abashed by our disrobing in her presence; in fact she took a benign interest in the proceedings.

The white-tiled bathrooms and tanks seemed deluxe, although a glance at the water in the tanks told us that many dirty bodies had used it before us. Undismayed we scooped out water with the wooden buckets provided and soaped down. After a rinse we climbed into the tank to soak up the heat, and God knows what else. After a few minutes the sentries told us to get dressed. We rushed to dry ourselves and get our clothes on before we lost a precious degree of heat. The water had been hot, and when we climbed out we all had a ruddy color that belied our state of health. The heat we had absorbed lasted a surprisingly long time. For the first time that winter I was warm and had a definite feeling of well-being.

Upon my return to the yard, the various Japanese connected with the drilling party asked what disease I had had and seemed disappointed when I answered *kutsu nashi*. The prisoners in the party seemed to have gotten along well in my absence. The honcho had given them little trouble, and I got the idea that my presence was a source of irritation to him, but this was only fair because I felt the same way about him.

The space allotted to the drilling party had been increased, and a shed with several electric grindstones had been installed. Five of the party were assigned to sharpen the drills, and although they did it expertly, they invariably ground more of the drills than necessary so that the other prisoners would not get the idea that they were trying to help the Japanese.

A steel shed had also been constructed for stowing the electric drills. It was the practice of the drill grinders to sneak a smoke there. One of the others would lock them in so that a naval sentry or policeman making the rounds would see a locked door and feel no need to investigate. When I tried this, the honcho beat on the side of the shed with a club to make me uncomfortable enough to leave. Thereafter I made sure that he didn't see me go into the shed.

A team of doctors and hospital corpsmen arrived in the camp. Lieutenant Commander Moe, Lieutenant (jg) Eppley, and all the corpsmen were naval personnel from Guam. The other doctor in the group was Lieutenant Stening, from the Australian cruiser *Perth,* which had been sunk in company with the *Houston.* The entire group had been at Zentsuji, a propaganda camp in Shikoku, and had been transferred to Moji, in the northern part of Kyushu, to take care of prisoners of war who had arrived from the Philippines more dead than alive. The medical team had done so well in Moji that they were sent to our camp to try to improve health conditions here.

The doctors had brought pictures of nearly all the officers in Zentsuji. Bill Spears and Red Bassett, from the *Pope,* looked thinner, but I was relieved to learn that they and the rest of the officers from the *Pope* and the *Perch* as well as the British officers who had left Makassar with them were alive and well.

I learned that Captain Blinn and Captain Hurt had had rough handling in Ofuna, the interrogation camp. All the personnel sent up from Makassar had been sent to Ofuna first, then to Zentsuji when the Japanese thought that they had gotten as much information as they could out of them. The more senior officers received special attention and were kept in Ofuna longer, because the Japanese expected them to know more about our war plans.

Jake Vandergrift, from the *Perch,* was questioned by a group of Japanese officers regarding the submarine's sonar gear. At first he pretended not to know what they were talking about. Then they showed him pictures of an American submarine, pointing out the piece of equipment and indicating that they knew that it was used for underwater detection of ships. He told them that it was used to listen for surface ships. When they asked him what was inside the domelike piece on top, Jake told them he did not know. "But you were in charge of this equipment aboard ship, surely you must know," they said.

Trying another tactic they asked, "What did you do when the equipment needed repair?" Jake avoided this question by saying that when the gear did not work, the submarine tender personnel removed it and installed a new unit. "But didn't you even try to find out about this equipment? As officer in charge, didn't you have to study it?" Jake replied that he was required to study the equipment but had never gotten around to it because he liked to go ashore in Manila and was not interested in his job anyway. At this the officer in charge of the interrogation stood up, shook his finger at Jake, and shouted, "Get out. You are a disgrace to the American navy." The next day Jake was on his way to Zentsuji.

Other officers did not have their ignorance so readily accepted and were subjected to the third degree. A few arrived in Zentsuji badly shaken.

The doctors told us of the capture of Guam. It had never been fortified by the United States because Congress felt, in the days of peace, that this would be an insult to the Japanese and might even be considered aggression. As a result of this farsighted policy, the only military force on Guam consisted of the hundred or so marines of the island police force and the naval personnel for the administration of the island, which was under naval jurisdiction.

The *Penguin*, a minesweeper, was the only naval vessel stationed there. After the Pearl Harbor attack, Guam was bombed by planes from Saipan, also supposedly unfortified. A pair of Chamorros from Rota, a neighboring Japanese island, were captured landing on the north end of Guam. They were taken to the governor, Captain McMillin, and told him that the Japanese were planning to attack the island. The next day the Japanese transports arrived and the landing was begun. An attempt was made to oppose the landings, but with such a small force and no artillery, the only effect was to annoy the Japanese. The Japanese landed a whole division of troops.

Because there was little doubt that the Japanese knew our exact strength on the island, it can only be concluded that they were taking the opportunity to put raw troops into action where the losses would be negligible. The military personnel of the island, including four nurses, were taken to Japan shortly after the fall of the island. The nurses were sent home on the first exchange ship. Except for a few Peeping Toms they were not bothered by the Japanese. Governor McMillin was sent to Formosa to join the rest of the governors of Allied possessions in the Far East. The others were sent to Zentsuji.

The prisoners at Zentsuji were allowed to write letters and make radio broadcasts. Japanese newspapers printed in English were distributed daily, and food and clothing were sufficient. Red Cross parcels were given to each prisoner, a parcel at a time, and cigarettes were plentiful. Some of the prisoners had already received personal parcels as well as letters from their families. When we heard this, we wanted to know how to go to Zentsuji. That such a camp existed and that prisoners were receiving mail from home lifted our spirits considerably. We all hoped that it would merely be a matter of time before we would enjoy the same advantages.

Health conditions in the camp began to improve. The medical team was not solely responsible—the winter was ending and a large amount of Red Cross medical supplies had arrived in camp—but they deserved the major share of the credit.

All through the winter, construction work had been going on in the camp. The hill on the north side gradually receded with the constant blasting and digging; the shoreline moved out into the bay as cartload after cartload was dumped at the water's edge. Almost as fast as the land was created, buildings were erected on it. The original barracks building was completed, making a square B out of the crude F. The administration building (sentries' quarters topside) was finished, and a large two-story barracks was taking shape seaward of our barracks.

It was evident that the Japanese were planning to bring more prisoners to our camp as soon as circumstances permitted. Interpreters in the dockyard told us so but there was always some delay. After a while we learned that our submarines were making it difficult for the Japanese to move ships between Japan and the conquered areas to the south. Some ships carrying prisoners had been sunk by our submarines. To the Japanese industrialists it was a bothersome detail, just a bottleneck in the supply line of slave labor.

I was beginning to find my dockyard job more and more unpleasant. Aside from the monotony, I was having daily scrapes with the honcho, who insisted on striking the prisoners whenever anything went wrong. Finally the interpreter to whom I complained decided that I was hard to get along with and had me transferred to the foundry.

The foundry was outside the dockyard proper. Although it was a sooty and dusty place to work, it was considered a fairly good job, because the yard police and naval sentries did not patrol it as heavily as the rest of the yard. Besides, black market contacts were easy to make there.

I was assigned to the group in the cast steel section of the foundry. A cast iron section, where another group worked, and a pattern shop made up the rest of the foundry. My section consisted of two bays about a hundred yards long and twenty-five yards wide. In this space were two electric furnaces, several baking and annealing ovens, sand mills, and a motley collection of paraphernalia indispensable to the production of steel castings.

The prisoners in my group worked at a number of jobs ranging from making molds to pushing wheelbarrows. The first week in my new surroundings was instructive. I had never been in a large foundry before, and each detail in the making of a casting was of interest. In time I became used to the loud, insistent hum of the electric furnace, but the pouring of the molten metal from the furnace to the ladles and from the ladles to the molds continued to fascinate me.

The advantages of the foundry over my former job were manifold. The new honcho was a gentleman. He bought cigarettes for me regularly. Although he once borrowed ten yen from me, he repaid it promptly on payday. Most of the enlisted men liked their jobs in the foundry and considered their honchos not too oppressive. Another advantage was that the hot castings ensured a means of warming one's lunch and, in cold weather, oneself. There was even a roof overhead. A number of Japanese women and girls worked in the foundry, and they used to strip to the waist to wash up before going home in the evening. Our interest was little more than academic, however, on the rations we were receiving.

One of the Dutchmen in the party had an arrangement with a Japanese worker to bring in a copy of either the *Osaka Mainichi* or the *Nippon Times*. The *Nippon Times* used a format similar to that of the *New York Times,* with almost identical print. The sheets of paper were smaller, however, and the entire newspaper consisted of only one double sheet (four pages). Except for an occasional ad for Suntory whiskey, there was little advertising. In the boxes at the top of the first page (where the *New York Times* has "All the News That's Fit to Print" and the weather), the *Nippon Times* ran slogans such as "Asia for the Asiatics" and "Remember the Days *Before* Pearl Harbor." Most of the Japanese I spoke to on a friendly basis could remember the days before Pearl Harbor all too clearly, when they could buy a decent pair of shoes or a suit of clothes at a reasonable price. Their memories were sharper after the second year of the war. After two years their shoes and woolen clothing were beginning to wear out, and there were no replacements to be had.

Despite the rabid slogans, the news in the papers was fairly accurate. This was especially true of the European news. The Japanese were not convinced that the European war was also their war, so German losses in Russia were reported in a detached manner. News of the Japanese war fronts, however, were full of propaganda.

Through all the frills, the general outline of the war's course was still discernible. There was a tendency to leave the basic facts untouched but to minimize or omit Japanese losses and to increase or overemphasize enemy losses. Thus the reader was able to learn that a battle had taken place in a certain region; by disregarding claims but by noticing where the next battle took place in that region, the reader could tell whether the Japanese were retreating or advancing. For example, the Japanese newspapers claimed great victories during the Solomon Islands campaign, but the scenes of successive battles shifted north, and finally the Solomons were not mentioned in the news except to report that Japanese "Wild Eagles" had bombed American installations there.

Each morning the same Dutchman in our party would get the newspaper from the Japanese worker. At fifty sen a copy, ten times the purchase price, the Japanese must have considered it a good business. I would borrow the paper from the Dutchman and go to a quiet spot, out of view of all except possibly the driver of the overhead crane, behind some conveniently located billet molds. Here I would read the paper quickly and memorize the salient points. After returning the paper to its owner, I would make the rounds of my groups and, while pretending to direct the men's labors, I would tell them the news. The men used to look forward to this daily broadcast and so did I. To me it was a means of passing several hours, and it made me feel useful and perhaps a little important.

After the arrival of the medical party from Zentsuji, we were able to induce the authorities at our camp to provide us with the *Nippon Times,* because that paper had been issued to the prisoners at Zentsuji. The papers usually reached us a day or two late; the office staff would invariably forget to distribute them to us. A delay of two days was, of course, not vital.

The *Nippon Times* provided us with many unintended laughs. The stories from correspondents at the front or at advance bases were given a dateline as follows: "From X Base, XX Date." With a striking lack of originality the central figure of the article was a Lieutenant X or a Sergeant X (we never encountered a Madame X). The actions of these characters generally defied the laws of nature and human behavior, with surprising results. There was Pilot X who returned from a mission, made his report, and fell dead. Nothing improbable there. However, upon examining the man's body it was discovered that he had been dead for more than an hour. This may have been the first and only instance of the use of zombies in modern warfare.

Then there was Seaman X who was aboard a Japanese warship under air attack. A bomb hit had set fire to a shell at one of the antiaircraft guns. Seaman X grabbed the shell and jumped overboard with it, thus saving the ship at the sacrifice of his own life. The article did not attempt to explain why it would not have been simpler though not as spectacular, of course, to merely drop the shell over the side.

By no means exhausting the stock of *Nippon Times* supermen was the case of Petty Officer X who was wounded in the leg when his ship was seriously damaged in action. When the officer tried to go below to open storerooms to which he alone had the keys, he found that his leg hindered him. He stopped a shipmate and said, "My leg—cut it off; it bothers me." The article, as I recall, did not say whether the leg was cut off or what good it would have done to cut it off anyway. Obviously the man was out of his head, and that goes for the correspondent who wrote the piece, too.

We were able to read the *Nippon Times* through the Sicily campaign. Then, as we were waiting to see when and where the landings would be made in Italy, the newspapers were stopped. This was an arbitrary decision made by our camp authorities, for the papers were delivered to the camp daily for a while thereafter.

Fortunately we still had a source of newspapers in the dockyard, and the next papers we read told all about the treacherous Italians who knew when to quit. Tojo stated that the fall of Italy was of no importance; in fact, with Italy out of the war Germany would be stronger because she would not have to send supplies to Italy. What made this remark interesting was a statement made by Tojo a month or so before to the effect that if one member of the Axis fell, the others would fall with it.

As prime minister, Tojo had a lot to say, and most of it was printed in the newspapers. In this way we got to find out that Japanese politicians were just as ignorant as some of our own and every bit as forgetful of previous statements.

The reason the camp officials offered for stopping the newspapers was that the war news would excite the prisoners too much and that we would not be able to work well. There was a measure of truth in this, but the real reason was that Asians need to save face. The popular and slightly vulgar camp expression was: "Save face and lose ass." Invariably the Japanese lost more face when they tried to save it.

From the time that the papers were stopped, the Japanese pursued a policy of keeping all news from the prisoners, who were forbidden to discuss the war. We responded by smuggling the papers in from the dockyard and arranging to circulate the news within the camp.

As warm weather approached, the dockyard and the camp seemed less grim. The sunshine and warmth were therapeutic. The shrine on the hill behind our camp became a mass of cherry blossoms. The Japanese workers brought blossoms to work with them and told us proudly that the flowers were *sakura* (cherry). In camp the warmer weather produced a change in our diet. We began to get early vegetables as a relief from *daikon* (Japanese radish). It is ironic that when the Japanese nationals interned in the United States objected to the Japanese foods provided to them, they were able to buy milk, eggs, and meat from local grocers. We had not seen milk or eggs in the six months we had so far spent in Japan.

The three senior officers were allowed to stay in the camp as a concession to the vernal season and their rank. Major Horrigan was given the task of raising tomatoes and potatoes, a job he performed conscientiously and that gave him much satisfaction. Lieutenant Commander Chubb was given rabbits to breed; this detail came to an end when the buck became impotent on the meager rations provided by the Japanese. Lieutenant Commander Visser did not attempt anything constructive himself. When he was not giving unsought advice, he was feeling Horrigan's tomatoes to see if they were ripe. The rest of the officers who were still going to the dockyard felt that as soon as enough jobs could be "found" in the camp, we would all quit the dockyard. Gradually more officers stayed in the camp, but it was not until the middle of 1944 that all the officers were allowed to remain here.

The summer of 1943 was the best time we had in Camp Fukuoka

No. 2. The long winter with its many deaths was over; the food was improving and cigarettes were being issued regularly and in reasonable quantities. At last the camp seemed organized, and constant improvement seemed a reasonable expectation. We were even allowed to buy beer on several occasions. Because a number of prisoners were willing to sell their rations of beer, it was possible to acquire a fair amount, and there were a number of happy drunks about the camp. No one got too drunk, for fear that the Japanese would no longer allow us to have beer. Because the bathing facilities of the camp were still nonexistent, it was not difficult to persuade the camp authorities to permit us to swim in the bay that bordered one side of our camp. Although the swims were pleasant, they were a poor substitute for hot water and soap.

Meanwhile, a number of the more talented prisoners began to organize string quartets and other entertainment. From the Japanese YMCA we received two phonographs with popular and classical records, several violins, a mandolin, and an accordion. These were supplemented by guitars and ukeleles made in the dockyard and smuggled into camp. The Japanese to the very end believed that these instruments had been brought up from NEI.

The Dutch provided the best bands and singers, but the British were better at skits and novelty numbers. The Americans contributed nothing to the camp entertainment except comedy in the person of "Corky" Corcoran, a Texas National Guardsman. He used to give lectures on Texas to British and American audiences. He always used two interpreters, one for the British and one for the Americans.

To complicate things, the prisoners were not permitted to have musical entertainment in the rooms without first getting permission from the Japanese, and then they were required to hang a "music chit," a shingle with Japanese characters, outside the room. In addition, only the people assigned to a particular room were allowed to witness the entertainment in the room.

For some reason the Japanese took great pleasure in enforcing the latter rule. One day a Dutch room was holding a concert, and the audience was at least double the number of men assigned to the room. One of the Japanese petty officers, Morai, who was particularly nasty, passed the room and noticed many prisoners. Eager to make a large haul, he closed the doors of the room to prevent anyone from leaving, and called for a sentry. Meanwhile the people inside who did not belong in the room began to crawl into the storage spaces under the lower bunks on each side of the room (the windows were barred). These spaces, which were fitted with sliding doors, connected directly with similar spaces in the adjacent rooms. By the time Morai and his sentry entered the music room, they found only the correct number of people. Unaware of the storage spaces, they were completely baffled and grudgingly permitted the concert to continue.

Another change that accompanied the arrival of spring was the appointment of certain officers to act as *shuban* (duty officer). Each officer on the list took the duty for a week at a time and had one of his own petty officers *(shuban kashikan)* assist him. He would make the rounds with the Japanese *shuban* at morning and evening muster and prepare the muster sheet, determining the number of workers going to the dockyard.

The duty officer was responsible for the cleanliness of the camp and any other detail the Japanese happened to assign him. Although being *shuban* meant getting up before reveille and turning in after taps, it was a change from the dockyard. The Japanese had instituted the detail in order to lighten their own work, especially that of totaling the number of dockyard workers. It was a constant source of amusement to watch the dockyard policemen count the workers in each party and then try to obtain the total the *shuban* gave them. They would count the parties as many as five times, and each policeman would take a turn at the abacus to attempt to add the figures. When finally the figures agreed, smiles would wreathe the faces of the policemen, and the senior man would give the order to march off. The Japanese soldiers and petty officers, who had a military man's typically low opinion of civilians, used to laugh at the policemen's efforts, except when it was raining; then they became annoyed. I doubt if they could have done as well themselves.

Spring also brought heavy rains, and many a day we returned from the dockyard soaking wet and with our shoes covered with mud. That evening in camp the prisoners would hang their dripping work clothes from every conceivable place indoors, giving the barracks the appearance of a slum. We finally got the Japanese to issue rain clothes, but the men were forbidden to wear them to the dockyard.

I should have known that my detail in the foundry was too quiet to last. Our original Japanese honcho was also boss of the foundry. For some reason it was considered necessary to have a special honcho for the prisoners. In fact we got two honchos, Kato and Okayama.

Kato was a grotesque little man with a nasty disposition; he was about thirty-five years old but seemed older physically and much younger mentally. Because of the constant annoying attention he gave our group, we called him "The Fly." Okayama was more personable but, like most Japanese, he was not averse to laying his hands on the prisoners when he thought the occasion warranted it. Because he wore glasses, we gave him the obvious name of "Glasses."

The foundry was a large place, and the prisoners were split into small groups. Try as they might, our new honchos did not succeed in being everywhere at once, and we got used to them as we had gotten used to so many things in the past year.

The best way to make time pass in the dockyard was to have an interesting job that did not require much exertion, but there were not many jobs of this sort. A pleasant but risky way was to find a quiet spot, almost inaccessible, and sleep. One of the prisoners working in the boiler shop found just such a place but made the error of sleeping until 7 P.M. Because we knocked off at 5 P.M., the Japanese knew that one man was missing at the muster before we returned to camp. That evening in camp the Japanese held three or four more musters, getting more upset with each one. Meanwhile the sleeper awoke and reported to the naval sentries in the dockyard. The sentries were happy to see him and showed their pleasure by beating him on the spot. When the prisoner was returned to camp, the soldiers of the guard beat him again. Then he was put in the brig for two weeks.

In the foundry I discovered a safer way to pass the time, and the whole group was able to participate. Whenever the camp boat, which was used to fetch supplies from Nagasaki, passed the foundry, one of my men would report to me. I then went around to each man in the group and asked him what time he thought the boat would pass the foundry on the return trip, recording the time next to his name in my notebook. The honchos seeing me go to each man and make a note probably thought I was being attentive, checking something they had forgotten. The man with the closest time would receive a cigarette from everyone else in the party. Despite the fact that my watch was used to decide the winning time, I never managed to win the prize, but I used to kill a lot of time without getting into trouble.

Sometimes trouble was hard to avoid. Usually the harder one tried to avoid it, the more inevitable it became. One warm October afternoon, Wielinga, the Dutchman who had the newspaper contact, was reported for sleeping on the job. Because his job necessitated sitting, he had probably just dozed off. When I arrived on the scene, Wielinga had already denied sleeping, so all I could do was tell the sentry to whom the matter was reported that Wielinga had not been asleep.

An interpreter was called and the whole matter was gone over several times. Finally the sentry put down his rifle and picked up a piece of steel about two inches in diameter and two and a half feet long. I turned to the interpreter and protested, "He's not going to hit him with that, is he? He'll kill the man." "No," the Japanese reassured me, "he's going to hit you. Turn around and hold up your hands." All I could think of as I waited for the blow was the certainty of getting my back broken if he aimed too high.

It was a relief to feel the first blow across my buttocks and a surprise to note how painless it was. The piece of steel was too heavy to be swung fast, and all I received was a push from it. After the second blow, I was told to shove off. From a distance I watched Wielinga receive three strokes. Meanwhile I was furious because of the humiliation of being punished in front of all the foundry workers. There was also the frustration that was always present in our prisoner-of-war life, the inability to strike back. A prisoner could strike back if he wished, but the chances were that he would get a bayonet in his belly.

Once a prisoner did strike back, but it was against a civilian and not a sentry. One of the Indonesians in the riveting gang was struck by his honcho. The prisoner, who had been an amateur boxer, reacted with a right to the Japanese man's jaw. When the Japanese picked himself up, he found that his jaw was broken and his inclination to molest prisoners gone. Because of the loss of face involved in pursuing this episode, he did not report it. Meanwhile the prisoner had a sprained thumb and was unable to rivet for several days. An accident report was sent in, and the subsequent investigation revealed the whole story. The prisoner was given a court-martial and sentenced to two years in a criminal prison. We all considered this a death sentence because of the terrible reputation of Japanese prisons.

In the spring of 1945, when the sentence was nearing completion, we were not surprised when Budding, the Dutch interpreter, accompanied the camp's sergeant major to Fukuoka, a city in northern Kyushu, to fetch the man's ashes. We were all feeling sad about the man, and the Dutch were planning to hold funeral services for him.

When we saw Budding upon his return to camp, he was cheerful; the ashes were those of another man. The sergeant major, whom we heartily detested, was reprimanded for not checking the identity inside the box. The Japanese officer who had been sent down from Fukuoka to retrieve the ashes said that our man was well and happy. He was doing leatherwork and had no desire to return to our camp. This seemed too good to be true, but I had the final proof when I spoke to the man on Okinawa after liberation.

9

One of the hardships of life as a prisoner of war was the lack of mail from home. As we learned later, sometimes what we perceived as a lack was actually a delay, which was caused by Japanese as well as our own bureaucrats. The Japanese had failed to send in our names from Makassar, and the postcards we had been permitted to send in Japan were a long time in reaching their destination. For reasons still unknown, American authorities would not allow letters to be sent to anyone not officially declared a prisoner of war.

It was not until October 1943 when I made a recording for a radio broadcast that my family learned that I was alive. The British refused to make recordings because of service regulations designed chiefly to prevent the use of such recordings on German propaganda broadcasts. I felt that the effect of Japanese propaganda in the United States would be nil, and further I had never been instructed not to make a broadcast.

Although the subject matter of my broadcast was restricted, a certain amount of freedom was permitted. Aside from personal comments, I was allowed to say that the *Pope* had been sunk in the Java Sea, that all the crew except one man had been rescued, and that certain officers, whom I named, were still in the NEI when I left for Japan. Because I wanted to include a long list of names in my message, I had my enlisted men report the names of the men who had died in the camp. In that way we hoped to cover everyone so that people back in the States could correlate the information from all the messages.

My radio recording, I learned upon my return home, was broadcast exactly as I had made it. Not only was it my family's first indication that I was alive, it was also the basis for changing the status of

Donovan, Antrim, and the rest of the officers in Makassar from "missing" to "prisoner of war." By putting two and two together, our authorities should have been able to declare all of the *Pope* and *Perch* crews prisoners of war.

The eventual arrival of mail in camp caused mixed emotions. Those who received letters were eyed enviously by those who hadn't. The news was not always good. There were deaths in families and wedding announcements from former fiancées. The news that was hardest for a man to take was hearing that his wife had another man's baby. Why relatives at home felt it necessary to break news of that sort to a man who had been away from home for almost two years is incomprehensible.

Personal parcels that arrived in the camp often suffered the ravages of transit and of the Japanese inspectors. Major Horrigan, who was among the first to receive a parcel, shared his edible items, such as dehydrated soups, with the rest of the officers. My parcel arrived a few months late—at the same time that parcels for Lieutenant Michie and for Robinson, one of my enlisted men, arrived. We were called over to the office, where some smirking Japanese petty officers indicated our parcels to us—three paper light shades filled haphazardly with the articles from the parcels. There were no signs of the original cartons or wrappings.

When we returned to our room, we found that all three parcels had been mixed up and then divided again. It was obvious that the Japanese had helped themselves to whatever they wanted and left the rest for us. We decided to pool the three parcels, divide them into three piles, and draw lots for choice. This took care of such anomalies as one man receiving all the razors and the other all the razor blades. Everything was covered with fine dust from crushed tooth powder packages.

Although half a loaf is better than no loaf at all, I could not help wishing that my family had not bothered to send a parcel, although there were others who made out even worse. One man received a lone pack out of a carton of cigarettes. Many of the Dutch and British received no personal parcels.

Although personal parcels helped the morale of a few prisoners in the camp, Red Cross parcels gave everyone a lift. Our first Red

Cross supplies were British, from England, Canada, and South Africa, but later we received only American parcels and clothing. There were no Dutch Red Cross parcels for the simple reason that the Dutch had never joined the International Red Cross. As a nation with a traditional policy of neutrality, it did not feel that contributions to a Red Cross fund would be a profitable investment. It might be argued that because Holland and the East Indies were overrun by the enemy, it was impossible for the Dutch to support such an agency. On the other hand, Dutch investments and gold deposits in the United States were substantial. I thought it was a matter of attitude and not resources.

With concessions to such items as the pound of butter in the Canadian parcel and the bacon in the English parcel, most prisoners considered the Amercan parcel the best for variety and quantity. The outstanding feature of the American parcel was the five or six packs of cigarettes that were used to fill in empty spaces around tins and packages. Powdered coffee and powdered milk were also highly prized.

The rest of the parcel consisted of cans of corned beef and various types of luncheon meat, canned butter, cheese, sugar, dried fruit, and chocolate. These parcels were paid for by the U.S. government; the Red Cross bore the expenses of shipping and distributing the parcels.

In Japan, with its lack of luxuries and fancy goods (anything except fish and rice and a few vegetables constituted fancy food), it was to be expected that there would be a certain amount of theft and misappropriation of Red Cross supplies. I think that the Red Cross should have had more neutral representatives to supervise the distribution of supplies in Japan. The Japanese of course were not too cooperative and adopted the attitude that once the supplies were turned over to them for distribution, they could do as they pleased. Several times we were chided for our lack of appreciation toward the Japanese for "giving" us the Red Cross parcels.

Nevertheless, we did receive most of the supplies that came into the camp, although never as fast as we would have liked. The Japanese were always saving something for an emergency, and they would issue one tin of meat to four men as a weekly Red Cross ration. On the one occasion when we each received a complete food parcel, we were like children opening Christmas stockings. The difference was that after the first surge of elation, there was spirited trading wherein every item in the parcel was given a market price in terms of cigarettes.

There was thievery among the prisoners. I can understand how theft was once punished by death, for it can create a feeling of unrest and distrust in a community, especially a small one where each individual has only a few possessions. One man had practically his entire parcel stolen the day after he received it, and he was driven to tears by the vexation and frustration of the situation. The thief was never discovered, so the roommates of the man made up a parcel for him out of their own.

At times things became so monotonous that it was difficult to tell one day or one month from another. Looking back it is difficult to tell one year from another. Special events stand out and refresh our memories. For instance in the fall of 1943 the bathhouse in camp was completed. This was an event to remember because of its effect on the welfare and comfort of the prisoners.

The bathhouse was a wooden structure faced with cement inside and out. The floor was cemented and had two raised dressing areas on either side of the door. A cement tank, built up from the floor, extended out from the wall opposite the entrance. The tank was about forty feet by twenty feet and about two and a half feet deep. A steam pipe carried steam directly into the water.

The normal procedure in taking a bath was to soap down, rinse off outside the tank, and then climb into the tank to soak. In cold weather one could soak up enough heat in the bath to last most of the night. Despite the convenience of the bath, there were a number of people who did not take full advantage of it. Occasionally it was necessary to supervise the bathing of some of the more resistent men.

Sometimes there was not enough fresh water to allow baths every day. Water shortages aboard ship are not unusual, but on land they seemed strange. Saltwater from the bay was an unsatisfactory substitute. Here too we had difficulty; at low tide the pump could not lift the water to the bathhouse. Despite the inadequacies of the bath, it was considered the best thing about the camp. It gave warmth and a feeling of well-being that were never equaled by the meals or the blankets.

The approach of winter was noted in the evening and early morning chill. There was not the glorious fall to which one is accustomed in the northern part of the United States. On our little island there were few deciduous trees; indeed, there were few trees of any type. They had been used long ago for lumber or fuel.

Before we realized it, Christmas was upon us again—the Christmas that we had been certain we would spend at home. This year the Japanese gave us a holiday on Christmas Day and provided materials with which to decorate the rooms. We were allowed to have a special Christmas program (held in the bathhouse) and extra food for our meals that day, to be made up from subsequent rations.

Most of us enjoyed the day. A few were sick from overeating or from the unaccustomed richness of the food. But in prison camp one can derive a certain satisfaction from that, for it happened so seldom. We even had steak that day—whale meat, but still steak. Fresh whale meat can be very appetizing; the not-so-fresh whalemeat we received was still edible but a little strong.

With the New Year the Japanese soldiers repeated their large meals and drinking bouts. After only a few drinks, most of them were drunk. They did not bother the prisoners while drunk, because those who had not passed out were too busy falling down stairs or being sick.

Although we did not have four days this time to celebrate the New Year, the Japanese in the dockyard acted as though they did. They knocked off work two days in advance and spent most of the time cleaning up their work areas so that they could start the New Year with everything comparatively clean and in order. We fitted into these schemes well and wasted time along with the Japanese. After the holiday, most of them were nursing hangovers, so little work was accomplished for a day or two.

On January 24, 1944, an event in the dockyard gave immense satisfaction to all the prisoners. The Japanese had been constructing a huge dock large enough to build four Liberty-sized ships at a time. In order to speed up completion of the dock, the director of the dockyard ordered certain weights removed from the seaward end of the dock, against the advice of the engineers constructing the dock.

Although the dock was not finished, construction had been started on two ships several months before. When the ships reached the point where they could be floated, a caisson was built to divide one dock in two. The dock was flooded and the ships were floated and moved to the seaward half of the dock. The caisson was put in place and the dock was pumped dry again. In effect there were now two docks, one at the seaward end with the two ships resting on the keel blocks with the sea being held out by the cofferdam, and the other dock at the land end. The caisson was between them. It was not serving any purpose at the moment, but as soon as the dock was finished the caisson would make it possible to remove the two partially completed ships without interrupting work on two additional ships being constructed in the other half of the dock.

When the weights near the cofferdam were lifted, water began to leak into the dock. The cofferdam quickly collapsed. The nearly completed ships were again floated, this time unintentionally, and they rushed forward with the push of water toward the caisson. The wave hit the caisson first and bounded back, slowing down the ships, which nevertheless crashed into the caisson. It held on the first impact but gave way after repeated hits by the surging waves and ships. The water poured into the second half of the dock with such force that the frameworks of the two ships being built there were carried forward and thrown on the stairways at the head of the dock.

Soon there were timbers, stagings, and bodies floating in the water. Matthews, one of my *Pope* men, pulled out a Dutchman and then went into the water to rescue a Japanese worker. Several other prisoners helped to rescue workers caught by the flooding of the dock. There were no casualties among the prisoners, but an estimated one hundred Japanese workers were killed. The Japanese authorities admitted losing only twenty. The damage to the ships and the dock was extensive. We estimated that the accident set production back six months. For several weeks thereafter, divers searched for bodies among the wreckage, and a Shinto priest came to chase the devils away from the dock.

Matthews and the other prisoners who had helped rescue people during the disaster were duly rewarded for risking injury and possibly pneumonia. Matthews received three packs of Japanese cigarettes (thirty cigarettes), two small jars of red pepper, and a bottle of tomato catsup. The others who had saved only one man apiece received the same reward less the catsup. Because the men had done their deeds without thought of reward, the Japanese should have rewarded them generously. If they lacked the means of providing a suitable reward, a commendation would have been proper. To give too little is often worse than giving nothing at all.

Bennett and Egan, two of the British officers, were aboard one of the floating ships when the cofferdam collapsed. They had gone aboard to kill time and have a smoke belowdecks. When they came on deck they found the pillars on the dockside flashing by like telegraph poles seen from a speeding train. The abrupt stop threw them to the deck, but their main worry was to get back to their parties before anyone noticed them missing.

There were other occasions when the Japanese made sabotage on the part of the prisoners unnecessary. One day a gang of prisoners assigned to caulking were slow in getting their job done, namely, caulking a long seam in the ship's bottom. Because the ship was to be launched the next day, the Japanese honcho was prodding them to finish the job.

Meanwhile an "inspector" (often these men were of high school age) came along with a can of paint and daubed the seam to indicate that it had been caulked. The prisoners did not bother to finish the seam but gave an appearance of activity until it was time to knock off.

The next day as the dock was flooded gradually, the Japanese dignitaries stood smiling before the makeshift altar bearing the symbolic offerings of fish, rice, and fruit, and the ship's sponsor awaited the moment to release the white doves when the ship became waterborne.

The level of the water in the dock continued to rise but without producing the expected effect on the ship. When the water reached a level several feet above the point at which the ship should have floated, an excited voice yelled from on board that the water was flooding the ship.

After the dock was pumped dry, the steady stream of water along the uncaulked seam revealed the source of the trouble. The Japanese honcho tried to blame the prisoners, but they pointed to the inspector's paint marks. Although the matter ended there, that honcho always remained unfriendly toward the prisoners.

Meanwhile the war continued. More and more Japanese workers were called into the service. Young boys seen on the job every day suddenly appeared in recruits' uniforms to make their farewells according to a ritual from which the Japanese seldom departed. The recruit arrived with his flag, upon which his friends would write slogans. One of the more important honchos would assemble the workers of the recruit's group. Flags were handed to all the members of the party (and collected again after the ceremony). The honcho would then address the group, directing most of his remarks to the recruit. The recruit would then reply, showing pride in the role he would play in saving Japan and confusion in his unaccustomed role as an orator.

At the conclusion of the recruit's speech, the honcho again took over and led the banzai cheer. Then there were a lot of individual farewells with interminable bouts of bowing. These ceremonies usually took place during lunchtime so that no company time would be lost. The prisoners looking on usually chimed in on the banzais with "Self-blast, you bastard!" (*Self-blast* was the term used in Japanese newspapers to explain the failure of any Japanese ship, plane, or individual to return to base. The term was used before kamikazes, who actually did "self-blast," came into vogue.)

One day in the foundry we had the rare but dubious honor of witnessing Japanese entertainment for the benefit of the Japanese foundry workers. The show apparently still had its original acts. We decided this not because of the age of the jokes—we couldn't understand what was said—but because in one of the acts of sleight of hand, three flags were produced out of a fan: Japanese, German, and Italian, almost a year after Badoglio's surrender. The company consisted of only a man and a woman who sang, juggled, and did skits along with their feats of magic. The performance was well received by the Japanese and the prisoners, all of whom preferred this sort of thing to work.

On several occasions all the Japanese were called off the job to listen to speeches urging them to increase their efforts to produce more ships. The effect of these speeches was to spur the workers on to greater labors for the half hour immediately thereafter. The prisoners were usually expected to hold on somewhat longer.

The Japanese decided that prisoners of war should work harder than the Japanese themselves and were disappointed that we didn't. Along with this attitude was a misconception as to the recipient of the prisoners' allegiance. With such a state of mind among the Japanese authorities in the dockyard, it was not surprising that the prisoner honchos were lectured on "high Japanese culture." The president of the dockyard lectured us on this subject in his office on two occasions, and we were equally amused both times.

During one of these visits we learned a novel cure for tuberculosis: the patient should go to a mountain and live by himself, eating sparingly and thinking deeply. At least I think that's what the interpreter said. We also found out about an illustrious Japanese of antiquity who had the ability to outstare Korean lions. While the lions were busy staring back, he killed them with his bow and arrow. The story of Ghengis Khan's amphibious operation against Japan was kicked around with little regard for the facts. And we were shown a samurai sword reputed to be very old and that no doubt was.

The second lecture was a more social occasion. We were served coffee ("from the southern regions of plenty") with cream and sugar while we were told how Japan was forced into the war by the Allied powers, and how necessary it was for Japan to establish a new order in Asia. We also learned that all thefts in Japan were attributable to the Koreans and that it was unsafe to leave any articles of value unwatched while we were working, because there were so many Koreans in the yard.

The industrial might of Japan was pointed out to us, but no suitable answer was given to the question of why so many American and British tools and machines were used in the yard. We asked increasingly embarrassing questions one after another. It was not surprising that that was the last of the lectures.

As spring approached again, speculations were made as to when and where the second front would be made. In the officers' room we started a pool on the invasion. Visser entered the pool; his guess as to when the invasion would be made was typical: "Never." Most of the others picked late spring or early summer. Then we all waited for the news. Rumors were started in the *benjo*.

My birthday, May 13, arrived, but there was no invasion. In prison, camp birthdays had special significance. I received a birthday gift that gave immediate and tangible pleasure. Oostdijk and Andrews came to my room with a present of cigarettes from the foundry group, and Andrews delivered my birthday greetings:

Accept this token Michel San
From the foundry working party
Upon your *toshi ni ju rok* [age 26]
May you live long and hearty.
We toast your health for a hundred years
Sorry it's tea not beer
With the hope you'll spend your 27th
With your folks at home—not here.

The whole thing came as a surprise to me; I could not figure out how they knew it was my birthday. Oostdijk reminded me that several months before we had talked of birthdays, and he had remembered mine because it was near his wife's. The little celebration made me feel happy and sad at the same time.

June marked the end of work in the dockyard for the officers. For a year and a half we had nagged the Japanese to allow us to stay in camp, and at last they gave in. We expected to be able to relax completely and spend time following our own fancies. But we should have remembered that the Japanese abhorred a nonworking prisoner of war. First we were given the job of untwisting small lengths of wire cable and straightening the individual strands. As the piles of wire slowly grew, our already slight interest diminished rapidly.

Because the Japanese could not think of a good use for the wires and were getting tired of trying to keep us on the job, they began to devise new tasks for us. One was the startling suggestion that we make a basketball court on the open space on the southeast side of the camp (toward the bay). A number of us were enthusiastic about leveling the ground for the court, and we worked hard at it. The court was also used for volleyball. But after watching the prisoners enjoy themselves playing games on their days off from the dockyard, the Japanese had a change of heart and decided there would be no more sports. A new project was put into effect. The sport place was to become the assembly ground, and the former assembly place was to become a garden. We began to dig up the ground, which had developed a cementlike surface after a year and a half of pounding by thousands of boots. Because we were continually digging up stones, we decided to make a border of them rather than have to haul them away. Then we had to fill in the holes with soil to bring our garden back up to ground level.

Meanwhile some enlisted men were kept in camp from the dockyard to start work on an air raid shelter. It was to occupy the area formerly allotted to Major Horrigan for his potato patch. (We dug up the potatoes before the excavation was begun.) Someone advanced the opinion that the Japanese were waiting for us to finish our garden before they would have it dug up for another shelter. That's exactly what happened.

The Japanese told us that we would never have to use the air raid shelters because American planes would be shot down by the Japanese "Wild Eagles" before reaching Japan. Work went on, however, and we offered what suggestions we could to make the shelters as secure as possible. The shelters had definite limitations. A depth of only three feet could be reached before water seeped through the filled-in ground. Wooden frames and planking formed a tunnel around which earth was piled. The thickness of the layer of soil on the roof could not exceed two feet, because the weight would crack the planks.

To make sure that every officer was kept busy, the Japanese sergeant major detailed us to jobs, so many to the garden detail, a couple to supervise the building of the shelters, and a couple to gather grass for the livestock, which included the few remaining rabbits, the chickens that Chubb had taken on to compensate for the diminished activity among the rabbits, and some new arrivals—goats.

The Japanese sergeant major was a particularly obnoxious type who insisted that the officers salute him. When we refused he sent the interpreter (Japanese) around to wheedle compliance out of us.

After a week or so of no salutes (we were required to salute officers only), we were ordered to salute all Japanese sentries. It might be thought that our stubbornness caused us to salute all sentries instead of merely the sergeant major, but knowing the Japanese we knew we had little to lose. Once we gave in to the petty officer, the other soldiers would require our salutes too.

Because of this saluting problem, I received my second beating. Except for an occasional face slapping or a random rifle butt to my butt, I had enjoyed comparative freedom from Japanese hazing—until I failed to salute one of the sentries whom I had passed one evening. Reuben Slone was caught by the same sentry, and we were asked to explain via Budding the reason for our failure to salute.

I lamely offered the excuse that many times my salute had not been returned. The Japanese agreed that this occasionally happened but never with him. Slone had nothing better to offer, so we were given the choice of standing in front of the house at attention for an undisclosed length of time or of taking two blows across the buttocks. The latter seemed the lesser (or certainly the speedier) of two evils, so Slone and I agreed to take the beating. If we waited in front of the guardhouse at attention, we might get a beating anyway.

The sentry took a club about the size of a long pick handle from the house. I could hear the club whish as it was swung through the air, and when it connected I was lifted slightly forward with a burning sensation in the seat of my trousers. I didn't think I could stand another blow, but before I could make up my mind a second fire was burning. After Reuben received his share, the Japanese asked us through Budding if we intended to salute in the future. We agreed that this would be wise. The next day, and for the next two weeks, we had very black and blue rear ends.

The beating I received was sufficient to make a deep impression on me, yet I had seen men receive many times the number of blows I had received and take it without flinching. I still don't see how they did it. Some had a knack for getting into trouble, and they went through the routine every week or so.

One of the most brutal beatings occurred in our camp when the Japanese discovered the gang of Indonesians who had been stealing cigarettes and cookies from the canteen. The thefts had gone unnoticed for several months because the Japanese had been helping themselves freely. A surprise inspection, instigated by the informer Ernst, an Indonesian with a reform school background, uncovered a cache of cigarettes and cookies.

The individuals involved were quickly rounded up, and the men were slapped and clubbed and kicked until they screamed for mercy. Those who had been lucky enough to faint had a bucket of water dashed in their faces. The culprits were kept in camp for several weeks and as punishment were given the job of cleaning out a filthy drain, through which they had to crawl. Upon their release Ernst was beaten each night by unknown assailants until the Japanese threatened to punish the whole camp unless he was left unmolested.

This threat of mass punishment reminded me of the time the Japanese had the occupants of ten rooms, about five hundred men, standing at attention after evening muster because someone who was unwilling to disclose his identity had broken or stolen something. All the men were to remain there, all night if necessary, until someone confessed.

After a half hour of this, Matthews, one of my enlisted men, called Budding, who was standing in front of the group with the camp commander, and said, "I didn't do it, but tell him if he wants to start beating on someone to start on me. I'm tired and I want to get to bed."

Budding translated this to the Japanese officer, who then had Matthews step out of ranks and accompany him outside the building. Matthews returned with smiles and a couple of packs of cigarettes and went to bed; the others had to spend another hour in ranks. Those unpredictable Japanese!

The officers' fare one day took a wondrous change due to the untimely demise of one of Chubb's rabbits at the jaws of Kino, the camp mascot, a dog of uncertain ancestry but of occasionally useful traits. We told the Japanese that the rabbit had died so that they would not want the carcass, but asked permission to have it made into a stew for us. Because we were apparently foolish enough to eat an animal that died of some unknown disease, they humored us and even allowed some excellent carrots and potatoes to be added.

The arrangements for getting the stew cooked were made by Jenkins, who was good at that sort of thing and who had a persistence that the Japanese seldom overcame. Besides, Jenkins was a good friend of Yamata's, the civilian cook (exmerchant marine and therefore considerably more broad-minded than most Japanese). The stew that was produced was marvelous, and we all wanted Chubb to arrange to have a rabbit meet an accidental death each week.

It was necessary to collect grass and other greens for the rabbits and goats because there was not enough grass growing in camp to support the animals. Usually two officers accompanied by a sentry would form the party. I always enjoyed these trips because they were opportunities to get out of camp and see the other parts of the island.

The best areas for collecting grass and leaves were in the hills behind the camp in the opposite direction of the dockyard. The narrow, winding paths that climbed the hills were interesting. In ten minutes along one of these paths, the camp and the dockyard would disappear from sight. Quaint cottages would come into view as the turns were rounded. Every bit of land capable of being used formed vegetable gardens. The steep sides of the paths would be buttressed by moss-covered stones and planted with small trees and shrubs to create a woodland scene and at the same time provide privacy.

There were many small houses along the way but one met them one at a time; the twist of the path and the difference in elevation gave each house a feeling of pleasant isolation. We pulled up the grass at the sides of the paths, and whenever we spied an onion or potato patch we would ease our way over to it so that we could collect some food for ourselves along with the grass.

In early spring we often found yellow jonquils, which we brought back to brighten up our room. If we were lucky and had the right guard with us, we would try to make our way to a spot where an orange tree grew and bring back some of the fruit.

It was always a thrill to reach the top of the rise and see the ocean stretching to the horizon. It gave us a feeling of freedom. From our camp and the dockyard it was not possible to see the ocean, only the narrow bay and the hills of Kyushu. If the guard did not suggest that we stop and have a smoke, we would ask him for permission, often bumming a cigarette from him for good measure.

The trip back to the camp was always less pleasant than the trip out. The baskets were full and fairly heavy, and we would discover that we had tired ourselves much more than we realized while pulling the grass.

With the invasion of northern France, morale in the camp bounded upward. We knew from the newspapers that the overall strategy of the Allies called for the defeat of Germany first, and we were jubilant that the one step likely to bring about an early defeat of Hitler had been undertaken. (I think that the Japanese always resented the fact that they were considered a secondary foe to be contained for the time being and then dealt with at our convenience.)

Marshaling our hopes for Germany's demise—the Germans would quit before the borders of Germany were reached to prevent further damage to the country; the peoples of the occupied countries would rise up en masse and hamstring the German defense with sabotage and outright battle—there were few of us who did not conclude that we would be spending Christmas 1944 at home or, at worst, on the way home: the Americans would reach the West Coast in time, but the British, having a longer trip home, might miss the holidays by a week or so.

The news from the Pacific was also good. We were advancing steadily and had lost no ground except in China and Burma. Because of my lack of familiarity with the names of places in these areas and also the type of reports the Japanese papers carried on the fighting there, I never had a clear picture of what was going on. At the same time, because I did not think that the war with Japan would be decided on the continent of Asia, perhaps unconsciously I refused to take an interest. But we had never had anything as exciting as the invasion of Europe to talk about.

With so much good news, we found it necessary to warn the less discreet prisoners not to let the Japanese know that we had the news, and further not to become too cocky with the Japanese on the strength of the advance in Europe. Yasutaki, the sergeant major, was especially anxious to keep news from the prisoners and used to sneak around trying to catch prisoners discussing news. Because he could not speak English, it is difficult to see how he expected to know what we were talking about. (I did not mention Dutch because not one Japanese in a million would even attempt that language. A number of Japanese did pick up Malay from the Indonesians.)

Yasutaki, or Boko-go, as we usually called him, was remedying his lack of English by learning one important word a day. (*Boko-go* was the word he used for the air raid shelter; because he used it so often, we decided to call him that, not knowing his proper name at the time. The other Japanese were highly amused to learn of this nickname.) Boko-go would approach a group of prisoners and ask fluently, "News-*ka?*" (The *ka* at the end of a word indicated a question.) When he thought he had discovered an attempt to mislead him, he would come out with, "Oooh, camouflage." When he knew we had misled him and he couldn't prove it, he would say "cun-ning" in a voice that indicated disapproval and chagrin. His other strategic phrase was "smoking-*ka?*"

Although Boko-go was short on vocabulary and brains, he was long on obnoxiousness, and he soon became hated in the camp. It was not the kind of hate that would make you want to kill him but just to give him a good kick where it would do the most good.

Major Rinaman, an army doctor, and Captain Farley, an army dentist, arrived in the camp straight from the Philippines and were our first contact with American personnel from Bataan. They were accompanied by several of their hospital corpsmen, who had all been outfitted with navy dress blues. I thought at first they were sailors. Later when I was talking to one of my own men about the new arrivals, I mentioned that I thought it strange that the soldiers were wearing navy uniforms. He answered in a dispirited voice, "I guess they let anyone wear the uniform these days." It was not long afterward that some of my men swapped Japanese-issue clothes to get the dress blues.

Major Rinaman was a big man with a mustache and a hearty manner. As we soon found out, he had a strong sense of duty and a sincere desire to improve the health conditions in the camp. In attempting to do his job, he was hindered by Doctor Wijzviss and the Japanese. Wijzviss had been the senior doctor up to this time, and he refused to step down gracefully for Rinaman, who was a grade senior.

The Dutch doctor's relations with the Japanese medical officer precluded a simple ousting of Wijzviss. As a junior doctor, he would have to take his turn in the dockyard sick bay and would also cease being the boss of the camp sick bay.

There weren't five people in camp who liked Wijzviss; some of the Dutch officers were civil to him, but no one else spoke to him unless it was absolutely necessary. Some of the Indonesians who considered him responsible for the deaths of friends and relatives in the camp vowed that he would never reach Java again. The only effect all this had on Wijzviss was to make him more complacent and dictatorial.

Although Rinaman had had an interview with the Japanese medical officer, he was not put to work as a doctor. Instead he was told, "We will tell you when we need you." It was only after the camp commander found out that Rinaman was not working that the matter came to a head. Then Rinaman was placed in charge of the sick bay. Nevertheless Wijzviss managed to maintain his close cooperation with the Japanese medical officer.

Because of Rinaman's failure to get along with the Japanese medical officer, who tried to maintain a high dockyard quota even though it meant sending sick men to work, and who limited the amounts of medicine to be issued regardless of need, Rinaman was later relegated to a secondary position.

Major Rinaman utilized his period of disfavor by borrowing the Japanese microscope to examine stool specimens for dysentery amoeba and parasites. Wijzviss had never felt the need to do this in all the time he had been in the camp. After running a test on everyone in the camp, Rinaman had enough data to scare the Japanese into issuing more medicine to treat dysentery cases. Although there were few active cases, nearly everyone had amoebic cysts, a dormant state of the amoeba.

When he was not doing medical work, Major Rinaman experimented with ways to make the food more nourishing and palatable. None of his suggestions was adopted because they all insinuated that the Japanese sergeant in charge of the galley served food that was less than perfect. Another project met with greater success: the Japanese permitted Rinaman to produce salt by boiling water from the bay in an open iron tub. (For some reason salt was almost as scarce as sugar.) The salt was distributed to the camp to make up for the lack of it in the camp diet.

Captain Farley was physically and temperamentally almost the opposite of Major Rinaman. He had a smaller and slighter build but was of above average height, and he was inclined to be reserved. Prematurely gray hair gave him a distinguished but not too elderly look. When he was forced to cut his hair short, however, he looked just as ordinary as the rest of us. Being the only dentist in camp, he was independent of Wijzviss and, for that matter, of the Japanese in terms of professional duties.

Because there was no Japanese dentist in camp, Farley received all the Japanese cases. This work, which was on a voluntary basis, was a source of pleasure and cigarettes for him. The cigarettes were gifts for doing the work, and the pleasure came from being able to administer pain to the nasty types without them knowing that it was intentional.

Farley's busiest time was always in the evening when the men returned from the dockyard. With crude implements he was able to get surprising results. Because there had been no dentist in the camp before, there were many cavities to be filled and teeth to be pulled. With temporary fillings (material was not available for permanent fillings), he was able to save a lot of teeth. Previously, Wijzviss used to pull teeth because he did not have the means to treat them.

Despite Farley's full schedule, there seemed to be less trouble with teeth than would have been expected. Some people thought the lack of sugar and sweets in our diet helped. Neither did we have to worry about getting a piece of steak caught between our teeth. Or it may have been the remarkable Japanese tooth powder, which removed tea stains from cups. (Farley warned us to use it sparingly because it was so abrasive.) It was also an excellent substitute for baking powder.

The Japanese apparently had more of this powder than any other item in the country. Whenever we asked for an issue of soap we were turned down but given tooth powder to keep us happy. We soon had more tooth powder than we knew what to do with, so it had absolutely no trade value. Some of the more imaginative but less scrupulous prisoners mixed the tooth powder with powdered milk and traded off the mixture as all milk. With no means of enforcing a pure food and drug law, all trading in loose powdered milk was discontinued, or the buyer required that the can be opened in his presence.

About halfway through the summer of 1944, we began to hear rumors that more prisoners were coming to our camp, so although we were not surprised to see prisoners disembarking from a ferry boat at a landing near the camp one morning, we were excited and curious to find out who the new arrivals were. Even at a distance we could recognize the broad-brimmed felt hats of the Australian army; the shouted commands in the distinctive accent removed all doubt.

Although they looked smart as they marched up to the gate of the camp, we could see that many of the men appeared ill as the column passed close by us. There were three officers in the group and nearly two hundred men. Most of the men showed signs of fatigue from carrying their packs from the landing.

Even before the last man in the column passed through the gate, we learned a lot from the group. They had been taken prisoner with the fall of Singapore and after a while had been moved to Thailand (Siam) to build the Burma-Thailand Railroad. Later they were returned to Singapore in preparation for their journey to Japan. They were seventy days en route to Japan, which was the chief cause of their poor condition.

Because most of the men had lice and many had bedbugs in their packs, we prevailed upon the Japanese to allow us to arrange a hot bath for the men and a good steaming for their belongings. It was a pitiful sight to see the rags and bits of junk the men had brought with them because they had nothing better. Most of the gear went into a bonfire when the men learned that they would get a clothing issue as soon as room assignments were made. Part of the clothing issue was Japanese and the rest, including the shoes, was Red Cross. The Australians were billeted in the new barracks, which had been used only as a storehouse. Their rooms were free from bedbugs (all the rooms in the old barracks had become infested), and we hoped that our precautions would keep them from another infestation.

The Japanese established a quarantine for the "new" prisoners. Up to this time the prisoners of the first group had continued to refer to the prisoners who had arrived from Singapore in December 1942 as the "new" men; if the Australians had not arrived, we would still have been calling them that. The quarantine may have been to prevent the spread of any diseases they brought with them, for they had left an area where cholera was endemic. It was also to prevent the spread of information between groups.

We had beaten the Japanese to the punch, however, by having the officers in for a cup of tea while the Japanese made up their minds just what to do with the new men. Frank Rutherford, a captain, was the senior officer; John McIntosh was a warrant officer; and Father Kennedy was the first and only chaplain of Fukuoka No. 2. Frank and Mac looked handsome, although somewhat overdressed, with their long, wavy hair. Padre did not ever have to worry about haircuts. We told the officers to give us their soap, books, and anything else they wanted to keep from the Japanese who would be inspecting their packs.

When Boko-go came in later searching for the Australian officers, he was angry because we had been talking to them. They were placed in a room by themselves and were thoroughly bored by the time the quarantine ended.

Later when the Australian officers were permitted to move in with us, they told us about their life in Thailand. The camps were usually makeshift because the prisoners were moved frequently with the advance of the railroad. During the rainy season the mud in the "streets" of the camps would be up to their knees, and the latrines would overflow, almost ensuring that everyone would contract dysentery in one form or another. When cholera broke out in a camp, half the prisoners would die before the epidemic spent itself. As if these two diseases were not enough, there was the ever-present threat of malaria and the Japanese. It was not surprising that so many of the men were in poor condition.

For a change, the Japanese in the camp took cognizance of their state of health and promised them two weeks' rest before sending them to work in the dockyard, and they gave the men a slightly larger ration than the rest of the camp. Major Rinaman ran blood sedimentation tests on the Australians to get a definite indication of their state of health. I helped him for a while but never did succeed in becoming expert in drawing blood into the pipette and getting my finger over the top before the blood ran down the tube again. Too strong a suction often resulted in a taste of blood, a not too pleasant sensation.

As cold weather approached, we began to spend less time working in the gardens. It was too cold to enjoy being in the open air, and we were a lazy lot anyway. This laziness we always attributed to a lack of nourishing food. Because a fair number of good books were now arriving in the camp, thanks to the Red Cross, most of us were anxious to spend our time reading. Van Marle, the librarian, had worked out a system to make the new books available to the officers in the daytime when the men were in the dockyard, and had arranged to redistribute the books to the men in the evening. The system worked well, and the books were given maximum circulation.

During the approach of cold weather, the Japanese petty officers tried to keep us working out of doors, but they did not like the cold any more than we did. To ensure that we did not spend too much time sleeping, they would make surprise visits to our room, although their intent was often defeated by a special regulation that required the first man to see the Japanese enter the room to shout *kyut-s'ke* (or anything sounding like it) to call everyone to attention. (We were forbidden to give the order in English.) This would awaken anyone who had dozed off; our conditioned reflexes took care of the rest.

With gardening as a form of exercise, we needed something to keep us in condition. The Japanese were always willing to think of a way to keep us healthy as long as it did not involve issuing more food or medicine. *Taiso*, the Japanese form of Swedish drill, was scheduled for fifteen minutes each morning and afternoon. Jenkins led the drill; he had had this job earlier, before all the officers were allowed to stay in the camp; he had thought of it as a means of getting out of the dockyard.

Everyone would be awake at ten in the morning without fail, for this was the time for the midmorning smoke period (for those who had the means). During this break, the officers and all the camp working details gathered in the galley courtyard, or in the corridor nearby in rainy weather, to smoke. We had to have ashtrays, even outdoors. After the smoke we usually arranged to get a bucket of tea for our room. When we could get it, we used India tea or Japanese black tea; otherwise we accepted the regular Japanese tea for its warmth alone.

When we were tired of reading, it was not difficult to start discussions. The subject matter was varied. Life in Texas was popular. The differences in British and American pronunciations and spellings were always good for heated arguments. The differences were never accepted as such; one had to be proved more logical than another. One day Slone and Bennett were arguing loudly about economics and speaking glibly about laws that were hardly known to them. The rest of us added remarks at random, helping to confuse the issue further. At one point we all started laughing at some preposterous statement and could hardly stop. We did stop when the Japanese petty officer in charge of the sick bay came in shouting. His office was not far from our room, and our laughter must have disturbed him.

Although the arguments and the sudden interruption were forgotten by nightfall, at evening muster the petty officer showed that he was still annoyed at us and mounted a table outside our room to give us a lecture. We found out that he thought the cause of our laughter was ridicule of the Japanese. He continued talking long after he had anything to say and worked himself into a frenzy. His speech became more rapid and less intelligible. (It was not for nothing that we had nicknamed him "Donald Duck.") When Budding gave up trying to translate, the Japanese shouted at him to continue. Budding then gave us a discourse in Dutch, which none of the Japanese understood, saying the man was "mad, completely mad"; Budding matched the man's ranting with a stream of Dutch curses.

Some of us started snickering, and "Donald Duck" began to stamp and dance on the table. He aimed a kick at Jenkins's nose and hit Bennett on the head with a flashlight. The rear rank was shaking with laughter and the front rank was trying to keep straight faces to avoid provoking further violence. Finally the Japanese got off the table and slapped a few faces indiscriminately. We were required to stand at attention until the end of muster, about twenty minutes. Bennett was the only one who thought the performance could have been more amusing.

As in previous years, Christmas rolled around and we were still in captivity. Things were looking better, though. Our advances in the Philippines indicated that that campaign would soon be drawing to a close. For some reason Germany was still holding out; reports of the bombing raids and the numbers of planes involved made us wonder how there could be anything left to bomb.

There was no question that we would definitely be home by next Christmas. There was a little concern, however, about our chances of surviving until then. Rations were being cut, and most men were losing weight steadily. An attack of diarrhea, usually due to some form of dysentery, would cause a man to lose weight rapidly, and there was little likelihood of him putting it back on. I averaged about one of these attacks a month. During the attack I would lend out about half of my ration for a week so that I could get it back when I felt better and could benefit from the food.

The other question about survival was how the Japanese would treat us in the event of an invasion, or defeat without invasion. There was always the possibility that some fanatic would decide to kill all the prisoners as a last, futile gesture.

But these morbid thoughts did not stay with us long. We knew that on Christmas Day at least we would get more food than we could comfortably eat. The "extras," as usual, were part of our regular rations that had been held back so that we could have something special for the holiday, and there would be a Red Cross issue that the Japanese would distribute as if they were the donors.

Because the Japanese were anxious to have us decorate the camp so that pictures could be taken of the "happy, well-treated prisoners of Nippon," we did not have much trouble getting colored paper and tinsel for decorations. Jenkins had been preparing entertainment for nearly a month, and we were all looking forward to an outstanding performance.

Indeed it was; even Boko-go enjoyed it. We had Scottish comedians, kilts and all; a convincing impersonation of a French chanteuse; and a number of other excellent acts. These brief interludes when we could forget about being prisoners always boosted our morale, and the effects often lasted as long as a week, or as long as the Red Cross issue held out.

As the war situation continued to deteriorate for Japan, the Japanese in the camp became more news conscious and redoubled their efforts to prevent the prisoners from learning what was going on.

Nevertheless we continued getting news regularly. It was more difficult now to get newspapers printed in English. There had been some
trouble in the dockyard about papers, and several Japanese had been
reprimanded.

It was not difficult to get a paper printed in Japanese, and we had
these coming into the camp daily. They were translated by two Chinese boys from Singapore. The distribution of the news had to be
done with extreme care because of a number of informers in the
camp. We knew the names of some of them, but there were others
we had not suspected.

In early December 1944 we received more new men in the
camp—American civilians who had been captured on Wake Island.
Some were young and clean cut; others had obviously been re-
cruited from waterfront dives to work on Wake Island construction
jobs. One of the latter was DeLay, a shifty-eyed, weak-mouthed individual whose standards of personal cleanliness were about as high
as his sense of loyalty.

When the group arrived in camp, Major Horrigan went around
to the room assigned them, introduced himself, and gave them a few
pointers on the camp. He told them not to work any harder than
was necessary and to stay out of trouble; he also warned them about
certain Japanese in the camp.

Less than a week later, Horrigan was called to the interpreter's office for questioning. He was accused of inciting the prisoners to disobedience and planning sabotage. When Horrigan denied these
charges, the interpreter read off excerpts from Horrigan's talk to the
Wake Island group. After a stern warning, Horrigan was dismissed.

A little investigation revealed that DeLay had a reputation for in-
forming and that he had been observed taking notes during Horrigan's talk. We were not surprised later to observe DeLay furtively approaching the Japanese interpreter's office.

There was no immediate action that we could take against DeLay
except to warn the camp that he was an informer and to deny him
any information that he could repeat to the Japanese. This was a neg-
ative approach, but we had learned with Ernst, an Indonesian informer, that a more direct approach had its limitations. (Certain prisoners had sneaked up on him in the dark so that they would not be

recognized and had given him a pounding. The Japanese had threatened to punish the entire camp by a food reduction and by withdrawal of smoking privileges if Ernst or any other of their informers were molested.)

There were no immediate effects from DeLay's disclosures, but we tightened up our news setup as much as possible. We reduced the number of people involved to a minimum and tried to keep the names of key personnel secret. No allusion was ever to be made to the source of the news, and if the Japanese should ask questions about getting news, the answers were to be as evasive as possible, attributing any information received to vague rumors heard in the dockyard. All hands were warned not to discuss news within earshot of any of the known informers, and if in doubt about a prisoner's allegiance, to assume that he was not to be trusted. This resulted in a number of people being viewed with suspicion from time to time.

This approach was considered the safest procedure, because an outright denial of having heard any news at all would be easily undermined, and once the Japanese caught a man in an outright lie it would be a simple matter to pressure him into telling everything he knew.

In March 1945 the Japanese started another news "purge." Several men were picked up for trading in the dockyard and were placed in *eiso* (the cells) to be available for questioning and beating, whichever happened to be on the program for the day. Horrigan was sent for again, and this time he was placed in the *eiso*. This was a shock, because Horrigan had always been treated with respect by most of the Japanese in camp. The villains were without doubt Morai, the corporal, and the Japanese interpreter, who had always shown a dislike for Horrigan. Horrigan was accused of operating the newspaper "syndicate" as well as organizing opposition to the orders of the Japanese.

The sentry who locked up Horrigan, as we later found out from Horrigan, was apologetic about the whole thing. He used to tell Horrigan in advance whether his rations were to be cut that day. Horrigan would inform our room orderly when he brought out his ration, and we would plan accordingly. If Horrigan was to get only two meals a day, we would see to it that the rice was well packed in the bowl so that a ration and a half could be sent in without arousing suspicion, and we would make sure that his soup bowl contained mostly solid food. The first day we surprised him by filling his canteen with coffee (milk and sugar added). Horrigan would also pass word out via the orderly as to the nature of his questioning and would try to give us an idea of how much he thought the Japanese knew.

One of the Wake Island men, Read, was in the cells at the same time as Horrigan, supposedly for stealing a Japanese worker's lunch. A little old hunchbacked man, Read thought up all kinds of games to pass away the time. He also could throw a fit at will, which occasionally came in handy to take the Japanese by surprise when they tried to give him a rough time.

Deleman, one of my men, was in the cells for trading in the dockyard. Strouse, another of my men, soon joined him on the same charge. Because the Japanese already had them for this charge, they tried to charge them with bringing newspapers into the camp. They were beaten regularly and were denied food and water for a week. Once they made Strouse drink seawater from a fire bucket when he asked for water. The purpose of this maltreatment was to force them to give evidence against Horrigan, but the Japanese did not succeed in shaking the men's stories.

While Deleman was in the cells, he lost a finger because the Japanese refused him medical care for an injury he had received in the dockyard. I saw Strouse immediately after his release; his eyes were black, his face was swollen, and his body was covered with black-and-blue marks. He said that he had denied any knowledge of the newspaper setup. I had this information relayed to Horrigan, who was still in the cells, so that he would not be tricked into admitting anything to the Japanese.

A few days later Horrigan was released without the Japanese having proven anything against him. He had not been beaten at any stage of the investigation, but he was under nervous tension all the time. He brushed it all off with his characteristic laugh.

Read, who had been kept in the cells after Horrigan's release, died two days later. The Japanese removed him from his cell a few hours before his death, and they ordered the POW doctors to sign a death certificate stating that he had died of natural causes. When the POW doctors persisted in attributing the death to starvation, the Japanese doctor finally signed the death certificate himself. After Read's death, the Japanese discontinued their news purges, or at least they stopped putting prisoners in the cells for a while.

The number of deaths in the camp had now come close to a hundred. With a few exceptions, all were attributable to the Japanese in one way or another. A few of the men had been killed in accidents at the dockyard, with its lack of safeguards. Among the Japanese workers there must have been at least one death a day. For each Japanese killed there were about twenty serious accidents. The small hospital opposite the foundry, where I used to work, was always crowded. One sad case was a Japanese girl about fourteen years old who lost an arm in a punching machine in the dockyard. A number of prisoners, chiefly drillers and caulkers, had lost sight in an eye from accidents. One prisoner lost a foot; many men broke limbs.

The lack of proper safety precautions in the dockyard was indicative of general conditions throughout Japanese factories. The high accident rate may have been due to the Asian attitude that life is cheaper than safety devices, or the combination of inexperienced personnel and the comparatively short industrial history of Japan. I saw a Japanese use a single strand of wire to lift a steel plate when he should have used a wire cable. The makeshift worked, so he probably thought his method was a good one. The same Japanese made a practice of taking power from a switchbox by hooking in on the power side of the fuses (the fuses had long since blown). He never did understand why the wooden switchbox caught fire from time to time.

One day when I was *shuban*, I was told to bring two Dutch prisoners to the main office for a commendation by the camp commander. Budding, who had been called to interpret, said that the men were being commended for extinguishing a fire in the dockyard. I asked him why they hadn't let the fire burn and do a little damage. I was annoyed that they had gone out of their way to help the Japanese. The answer was that they had set fire to a switchbox while getting a light for an illicit smoke. They had taken a piece of wire and made a resistance coil, similar to an electric lighter, and had placed the two ends across the power terminals in the switchbox long enough to heat the coils. In the process they struck an arc that set fire to the box.

After hurriedly putting out the fire, they hoped to leave the scene before anyone spotted them. One of the Japanese honchos saw them putting out the fire and, not knowing they had caused it in the first place, took their names and reported them for taking prompt action to prevent damage to the dockyard.

The camp commander read a citation, which Budding translated, and gave each of the men two packs of cigarettes for their service to Japan. The men looked sheepish throughout the ceremony, which the commander probably attributed to exceptional modesty.

Just after the news purges ceased, the sinking of the *Awa Maru* by an American submarine was reported in the Japanese papers. One evening shortly thereafter, as the men returned from the yard, all Americans were required to remain on the parade ground. When all officers and men were mustered, the camp interpreter read us an article from a Japanese newspaper, reading it first in Japanese and then in English. The story was that the American government had granted free passage for the *Awa Maru* to carry Red Cross supplies to POWs in Singapore and then return to Japan. On the return trip an American submarine had torpedoed the Japanese ship even though it supposedly had been burning the prescribed lights and following the agreed-upon course. The commander of the American sub stated in the article that the ship had been forty miles off course and had not been burning the proper lights.

The interpreter followed his translation with a tirade on American bestiality. He mentioned that he was not trying to "propagate" (his word) us but that "this monkey business, this animal thing" was a disgrace to the American people. He said that the Americans were all barbarians, then he repeated the story of the sinking, embellishing each detail.

At the conclusion of his speech he read off a list of American prisoners who were to report to the office; the rest were dismissed. The list included all the officers and an equal number of enlisted men. In the office we were given paper and pencils and told to write our opinions of the sinking of the *Awa Maru*. I wrote that there were two versions of the sinking, and that I naturally believed the American story rather than the Japanese version. I cited that the ship was reported forty miles off course and not burning the proper lights and therefore could have been another Japanese ship trying to sneak through the submarine blockade.

Most of the others wrote papers in a similar vein. A few stated that they thought a horrible mistake had been made and that the people concerned should be punished. (Actually, a mistake had been made, and the submarine skipper was later removed from his command. The sub had been off course and had not been expecting the *Awa Maru* in its area.) After the papers were collected, we were permitted to return to our rooms.

10

Toward the end of April, a few days after the *Awa Maru* incident, we were working in the garden when the interpreter came along in his fur-collared cape and wood geta, carrying a cane. His usually solemn and always ugly face had a serious expression.

When he reached the corner of the garden where we were working, he stopped and looked up at us. He gave Jenkins a growl for not saluting him; no one else had saluted except perhaps one of the Dutch officers. Then he saw Horrigan and shouted at him to come over. The interpreter's voice seemed to come from about two feet below his puny frame. Then surprisingly he called out to me. After I joined Horrigan the interpreter said, "Come to my office at twelve-thirty; I want to talk to you about some things." His deep voice and the slow, measured delivery gave the invitation a sinister cast.

As soon as he left, I asked Hoot (Horrigan's nickname) why the interpreter wanted to see us. "I hope it's not about the newspaper again" was all Hoot had to offer. Meanwhile the other officers began to ride us with such pleasantries as: "We'll see that your meals are sent over to the cells for you" and "Well, it's not so cold in the cells these nights."

We had an inkling that the meeting might concern what we had written about the sinking of the *Awa Maru*. Checking with the other American officers, we found that our opinions had been considered brutally frank without any diplomatic double-talk. Other officers had been more moderate in their statements. What I had intended to avoid in my statement was the likelihood that it would be used as a propaganda piece. Apparently I had succeeded quite well.

Horrigan and I reported to the interpreter's office at the appointed time, made the requisite number of bows, and stood at at-

224

tention before the desk. The interpreter's greeting was icy, and he confirmed our suspicions about the nature of the meeting with his first question: "Did you write these lies?" We pretended not to know what he was talking about, so he mentioned the name *Awa Maru*. "Oh, that," I said, trying to give the impression that we had obviously been called about something farthest from our minds. "Well, you asked us to give our opinions of the episode, and we did."

This was not exactly the right answer. He repeated his tirade about the bestiality of Americans in general and of the crew of the submarine alleged to have sunk the *Awa Maru* in particular. He recovered most of the ground gone over in his previous harangue. After about fifteen minutes the interpreter either disliked our attitude or found it difficult to continue looking up at us from so far below (I was six foot two and Horrigan was six foot four), for he ordered us to kneel before his desk.

From this position we continued answering the questions. I reiterated my opinions and Horrigan his, but our logic did not prevail. Horrigan was particularly amusing when he argued his case from his knees. He still had an inch on the interpreter, and he would reach out and tap the table in front of the Japanese to make his point. The whole affair was so grotesque that I had trouble suppressing a snicker now and then, but the discomfort of kneeling on the hard, cold concrete floor reminded me that I was more than a mere spectator.

After about fifteen minutes more, the interpreter lost patience, came around to our side of the desk, and stood before Horrigan. He glowered at him, then struck him in the face with his clenched fist. Knowing that I would receive the same attention in another minute, I tensed myself for the blow. When it came I nearly laughed; it was like being struck by a child, and not a particularly strong one. Then he said he'd have us hanged and placed in the *eiso*. With a sweeping gesture he dismissed us to contemplate our impending doom.

We were not worried about the interpreter carrying out his threat, because he was out of favor with the camp commandant. Also, it seemed unlikely that the Japanese would take such a drastic step at this stage of the war. The phrasing of the threat was so ridiculous that we could not take it seriously in any case. We were relieved, however, to be dismissed. During an "interview" that Jenkins had had a few weeks before, the interpreter had called in four of the tougher sentries and had let them work over Jenkins. Fortunately our case did not reach that stage.

The next day, April 23, 1945, while we were all waiting to start work in the garden (and while Horrigan and I were wondering if we would get another call to the office), we were informed that there would be no work in the garden that day. Budding came in a little while later with the news that most of the officers would be transferred to another camp. Just where this new camp was located was not mentioned. It turned out that all the officers would be leaving except Frank, who was needed for administration; Riedijk, who was needed for supply; Budding, who was still indispensable to the Japanese because their own interpreter could not speak Dutch; and all the doctors. The British and Dutch warrant officers were also to remain.

Piecing together what the Japanese around the camp said to various prisoners, and the news that had been translated from the latest Japanese newspaper from the dockyards, we concluded that with the fall of Iwo Jima and the invasion of Okinawa, the Japanese were expecting the next attack to be on Kyushu. Their reason for transferring most of the officers was that they feared an outbreak among the prisoners, led by the officers, in case of a landing in Kyushu. Actually any attempt at an uprising, unless the landing was made in the vicinity of our camp, would have been foolhardy and of no military significance. It occurred to me that the Japanese might slaughter all the prisoners to prevent recapture.

Regardless of the reasons for the move, it seemed like a good idea to me. I had been in Fukuoka No. 2 for two and a half years and was ready for a change. The fact that I would also be out of reach of the interpreter, even if he was only trying to scare us, made the move that much more desirable. Just where we might be heading was of some concern. A move into the interior would be all right, but another sea voyage, with American submarines mopping up Japanese shipping within sight of the islands, did not seem too attractive.

By midmorning we had definite word that we would leave early the next day, and we started packing immediately. There hadn't been so much excitement in the camp in months. It felt like the last day of school before summer vacation.

In the evening when the men returned from the dockyard, the usual bridge and cribbage games gave way to farewells. I said good-bye to my men and turned over "the command" to Vanneste. It was wrenching to leave. We had been together through so much.

Budding came from the Japanese office later in the evening to tell us that the galley would issue us food for a three-day journey—three buns for each meal (the extra weight of twenty-seven buns in our packs would be borne cheerfully). We would also be issued two tins of butter (about four ounces) per man, a can of corned beef for each group of three men, and five packs of American cigarettes per man, all from the Red Cross stock in camp.

In the course of the evening, many business deals had to be liquidated. There was one deal consummated that night that hadn't started out as a deal. Allen had come into camp back in December 1942 (which seemed like yesterday) with a fine leather briefcase. It had been turned in with other articles to a storeroom provided, and occasionally rifled, by the Japanese for our spare gear. There it was seen by the Japanese supply officer, who obtained "permission" from Allen to use the case. Later the supply officer was ordered to the Solomons and apparently took the briefcase with him, for when Allen went to the storeroom to get the case before leaving camp, it was not there.

This caused some consternation among the Japanese. They were about to lose face; the honor of an officer in the Japanese Imperial Army was involved. Excuses were made (the officer could have overlooked the matter in the confusion of packing and leaving camp), but to keep the record straight Allen was asked to set a price, in cigarettes, for the briefcase. This was acceptable to Allen, and he settled for one thousand Japanese cigarettes. He spent the evening trading them for American cigarettes to men staying in the camp. At the current rate of exchange, he got twenty-five packs, making him a man of considerable means.

The next morning we were up at four o'clock to start our journey. Rinaman, Syred, Farley, and the five warrant officers were the only ones left in the British-American room. They looked forlorn, and we were all sorry they were not coming with us. Farley promised to look out for the interests of my men.

It was still dark as we made our way to the far end of the camp, where the camp launch was tied up. Budding was up to see us off, and a few of the men from the galley detail came out to wave good-bye. Our guards for the trip were Boko-go (to our disgust) and Tahura, who could speak English. After the usual trouble with starting the boat's diesel engine, we were off for Nagasaki, across the bay.

Before we passed the north end of the camp, the motor died. We drifted to shore and made fast just off the parade ground. Tahura was dispatched to report the news to the camp commandant. Meanwhile Boko-go reviled the boatmen and the engine and turned to us with, "Tobacco *nai*" (no smoking).

Jenkins summed up the situation with, "We'll be in this bloody place another bloody day." It was a letdown to start off at five and still be at the camp an hour later. To return to camp after saying good-bye to everyone would be that much more of a letdown. We were all impatient at the delay, even if it was to hurry to another camp where we could sit and wait for the war to end.

After more waiting we saw a boat round the point just off the camp and head for us. It was now light and we could see Tahura aboard the boat, which had no doubt been borrowed from the dockyard. We transferred to the new boat and were soon on our way, hoping we'd seen Fukuoka No. 2 for the last time.

We passed the Kawainami shipyard without any pulls on our heartstrings. The sun was up now, and its brightness dispelled the morning chill. As we proceeded farther up the bay, traffic increased, mostly ferry boats packed to the gunwales with dockyard workers. Several large ships were in the harbor. Before we reached Nagasaki, we passed the Mitsubishi shipyard, which was bigger than "ours." There were what seemed to be cruiser hulls on the way, and several destroyers or minelayers were nearing completion at the fitting-out basin. A few minutes more and we were tied up at a wharf in Nagasaki.

Our guards rushed us off the boat, and we ran the three or four blocks to the railroad station. The few Japanese civilians we passed on the way displayed little curiosity. We arrived at the station, which smelled of fish, in time to see the train we were supposed to catch pulling out. Boko-go was annoyed and again told us not to smoke.

In a little while another train pulled in and we got aboard. Boko-go cleared one end of a car for us (Tahura explained that the previous train had seats reserved for us). Just before the train started, another group of prisoners arrived. They were from the camp in Nagasaki and had worked in the Mitsubishi yard. Among them was John Hickley, who had been with us in Makassar. He had been executive officer of the HMS *Encounter*, which had been with the *Pope* in that last action in the Java Sea. He and Gibson, an Australian, had come to Nagasaki in 1944 when their ship had been torpedoed within sight of the city. Neither of them could remember how he had gotten out of the hold before the ship sank. One of the doctors from the *Exeter* had been lost on the same ship.

From Hickley I learned that all the American officers in Makassar except Fisher had been transferred to Java. Yoshida, the Japanese who had beaten Fisher, apparently had arranged out of spite for Fisher to remain in Makassar. Most of the American enlisted men were still there too.

The train ride was like a holiday for me. After being on a small island for two and a half years, most of it spent in the dockyard or the camp, it was an adventure to be out in the world again. We passed terraced orange groves and rice paddies. The train skirted the bases of mountains and sometimes ran along the shores of bays. The stops were the most interesting part of the journey. The stations were crowded with travelers and their friends seeing them off. It seemed strange that so many people had so many places to go. Most of the men were dressed in the military-like civilian uniform, a war measure to conserve material and labor. The women were less somberly dressed, but only occasionally were bright colored kimonos seen.

The car we were in soon became crowded, but the Japanese passengers stayed clear of our section. I wondered if they thought it incongruous that all the prisoners had seats while many of the Japanese had to stand. Most of the civilians were quiet, and any curiosity they had about us was unobtrusive; perhaps the sight of the guards with us kept them from displaying more interest.

About noon we stopped at a station where we changed cars. More prisoners came aboard, so that now the whole car was filled with POWs and their guards. There were a number of Americans in the new group, but no one I knew. We noticed that the prisoners from other camps seemed to be on more friendly terms with their guards than we with ours. Some of the prisoners had complete individual Red Cross parcels with them, which made us disappointed with our issue. The conversation in the car was lively, with friends greeting one another after months, and sometimes years, apart. Except for our strange garb and the lack of liquor, it might have been a stag "special" going to a college football game.

A few stops later we passed a bombed-out station in a large town and pulled up at a smaller station that showed signs of recent repair of bombing damage. Here we disembarked and joined a large group of prisoners, mostly Americans but with a sprinkling of Dutch and British. A cordon of army sentries surrounded the area. After a short wait we were mustered and then marched off in small groups. Some of the prisoners—officers and men who had recently arrived in Japan from the Philippines—were in trucks. A glance revealed that they were too weak to walk. Some of them were just skin and bones, and all were pale.

We marched from the station toward what seemed to be a park. On the way we passed an area where wooden barracks-like buildings were being constructed. We guessed that they were for the bombed-out civilians. We passed between the columns of a huge concrete *torii* and headed down a wide, dusty road. Fields flanked the road on either side, and it was strange to see so much open space in Japan not under cultivation.

At last we came to groves of small pine trees where a number of prisoners were gathered. We were told to remain in the area and were allowed to fall out. I wandered about looking for naval officers and made the acquaintance of Commander Smith, a doctor, and Lieutenant Fraleigh, a dentist. They both seemed to be in poor physical condition and were busy opening tins from a Red Cross parcel as though they hadn't seen food in days. Our entire group from Fukuoka No. 2 seemed to be in much better physical shape than most of the other prisoners, many of whom crawled from group to group too weak to stand up. I pitied them, but I was proud of the fact that I (all of 148 pounds) was stronger and healthier than they were—and I felt ashamed.

Toward evening a large group of prisoners, mostly British, marched up. Allen and Slone recognized officers from their National Guard outfit (131st Field Artillery, Texas) whom they had left in Singapore. When the men fell out, I went over to an American naval officer who looked familiar although I was sure I had never made his acquaintance. He turned out to be Herb Levitt, who had served on the *Houston* (it also turned out that we had gone to DeWitt Clinton High School together in New York but had never met). He knew all the American officers from Fukuoka No. 2, having been with them in Java.

Everywhere prisoners were renewing old friendships and making new ones. Experiences and the latest news were exchanged. Although we were not exactly jovial, there was a decidedly cheerful atmosphere about the gathering, and optimism about an early end to the war ran high. The fact that officers were being withdrawn from all camps in Kyushu indicated that something was in the wind. We learned from one of the sentries that we were in the city of Fukuoka and that we would go aboard a ship that night. We surmised that we would be going across the Strait of Tsushima to Korea.

At dusk we fell in again and were marched on a road that ran along the shore of a bay. There was little activity on the road until we approached the dock area. I thought we would never reach our destination; the bag I was carrying seemed increasingly heavy and constantly slipped from my shoulder. We passed stables for cavalry horses and, later, extensive ammunition dumps with rows on rows of shells. The wharves and ships were not far from us now.

Soon we were in the midst of bustling activity. Working parties of soldiers were hurriedly hauling carts of supplies. It seemed as though we were in a besieged city. It was pleasant, though a bit fanciful, to think that a landing had already been made on Kyushu. We halted in the dock area, where we were again mustered and turned over to another group of army guards. Meanwhile another large group of prisoners arrived, swelling our number to about a thousand.

It was dark when we went aboard what someone said was the packet boat for Korea. One of the officers who came from a camp in the area said that the Japanese normally ran two boats a day, one in the morning and one in the evening, and that the boats made more than twenty knots. The group I was in went down two decks into a large compartment with raised platforms on either side and a third platform down the middle; this space took roughly a third the length of the ship. We were distributed on the side platforms, each man receiving enough space to lie down. The third platform was reserved for the guards. I was uneasy about our location. If we were torpedoed en route, it would be impossible to get out. It was no consolation that still more prisoners were berthed on the deck below us.

We settled ourselves in our new surroundings, but it was still too early to sleep, and most of us were not in the mood anyway. I saw a naval officer nearby and asked what ship he was from. I was surprised when he said the *Peary,* because I thought I knew all the officers from that ship. He said his name was Cal George. "Good God, we're classmates and I didn't even recognize you" was my reply. He relieved my embarrassment by asking my name. George had been injured in Cavite when the *Peary* had been bombed in the yard at the beginning of the war, and he had gone to an army hospital—to be captured when Manila fell. We had known each other vaguely at the naval academy but had seen each other frequently in Manila before the war.

Later when more prisoners were brought to our compartment, I saw Kenny Wheeler, whom I had neither seen nor heard of since the beginning of the war. I went up to his part of the platform, which happened to be on the same side as mine. We had a long talk and I told him all about Fisher, who was one of his best friends. They had gone through supply corps school together and had come out to the Asiatic Station on the same ship. I had met him through Fisher and we had gone out together frequently in Manila.

Wheeler had had little to eat that day, so I got some of my buns for him, which he shared with a friend. I joined them in eating some corned beef, from a tin that Kenny opened, to have with the buns.

The guards indicated by shouts and gestures that we were to turn in for the night, so I scurried back to my place to lie down. Just as everyone had fallen asleep, we were roused and told to get up and take all our gear with us. When we were topside, we found the city completely blacked out. We gathered that an air raid was in progress, but we could not hear any planes or explosions. We were led onto the pier and told to stay there until the raid was over.

Many of the prisoners went back to sleep on the bare ground. I was not tired enough for that and soon found myself in conversation with American army officers from one of the other camps. They had recently come from a camp near Kobe. From their camp they had been able to see the fires from the nightly bombing raids. On the way down they had seen areas that had been flattened by the raids, and they wondered how there could be anything left to bomb.

We compared notes on the camps we had been in and ended up talking about home. One of the men, Walt Farrell, was from MIT and had been called to duty in the Philippines. Another, James McEntee, who was with Standard Oil, was from Long Island; we found we had mutual friends and spent time talking about what a small world it was.

As the night grew cold, I kept wishing we could go back aboard ship into a stuffy compartment. It was almost dawn when we returned to the ship, but this time I found myself on the lowest deck. We must have been just above the bilges, because the compartment was narrowed to two platforms. At this point I was happy to have a place to lie down.

When I awoke we were still tied up, or at least there was no motion or vibration to the ship. There was a buzz of voices to the effect that food was about to be distributed. This was a pleasant surprise, for we had left camp with the understanding that we were carrying the only food we'd see on the trip. The ship's food was distributed in paper-thin wooden containers and consisted of cold boiled rice, seaweed, and a suggestion of fish. No one turned up his nose at this fare; our only requirement was that it be edible.

When at last we felt the vibration of the ship's screws, we knew we were under way. I was relieved that we were sailing by daylight, because the chances of a submarine attack seemed less likely. Later, someone who had managed to get topside, taking a sick man up for fresh air, reported that we had an aircraft escort, and I felt more reassured.

The voyage would have been a happy one but for the death of one of the prisoners. An American major who had been suffering from dysentery and beriberi died on board. In his condition he should not have been required to make the trip, and there were a number of men in similar condition. To think that a man could go through the hazards of combat unscathed, manage to keep alive for three years of prison life, and then die on an unnecessary journey was disheartening. I know his death made many of the sick men wonder if they would last the trip.

We arrived in Fusan late in the afternoon. We knew where we were because someone had recognized the place or had overheard one of the guards mention the name. After mustering on the pier we marched through town to a theater building, where we would spend the night. What I saw of Fusan on the way impressed me favorably. The streets were clean and the buildings were substantial. Business seemed to be going on as usual, and the war seemed far away.

The seats in the theater had been removed and the floor was covered with straw mats, a consideration I had not expected. A meal of rice was served in boxes. We were warned not to smoke because of the fire hazard. The time until the lights were put out was spent in swapping experiences with our new acquaintances.

Early the next morning about half of our entire group, including Wheeler and George, departed for a camp somewhere in Korea. The rest of us were told to get ready to leave in about an hour. It was a short march to the station, but it was slow going because a number of the men had to be carried. Five cars had been reserved for us on the train. They were about the same size as American railroad cars, in contrast to the subway-sized cars of most Japanese trains.

Although there was no club car or dining car, there was a seat for each man. We arranged ourselves in groups of four so that we could have the seats facing one another to facilitate bridge games and to be able to put up our feet on the opposite seat. I was with Allen, Tweedie, and Naylor. Tweedie was suffering from asthma again and spent most of the time trying to sleep; his attacks wore him out. Fraleigh and Smith were across the aisle from me. Fraleigh started talking about creole cooking and restaurants in New Orleans. He went into great detail about the preparation of various dishes and had me drooling. I couldn't decide whether he was a sadist or a masochist or both. Meanwhile I made notes on the dishes I would try when I got home.

After leaving Fusan the train traveled through rolling countryside that grew gradually more hilly. The fields and farmhouses along the way were neat and orderly, indicating an industrious, if not prosperous, peasantry. On railroad sidings we saw so many freight cars filled with grain and soybeans that we began to wonder whether there would be any food left where we were going.

I noticed that no roads paralleled the railroad. There were hardly any automobiles or trucks; most of the people we saw were on foot. Until the Japanese guards decided that we would have to pull down the shades at all the railroad stations, we saw Korean women in their long, full skirts and tight bodices, their straight black hair tightly drawn back into a bun; the men wore baggy trousers that seemed to be tied at the ankle. The predominant clothing color for both sexes was white, which gave the effect of sparkling cleanliness. Instead of the geta worn by the Japanese, the Koreans wore slippers.

At one stop a group of schoolchildren equipped with flags and lusty voices were giving some young men called into the army a send-off. (The Japanese allowed the Koreans to serve in the armed forces starting in late 1944 or early 1945.) These men entered the car forward of ours and waved from the windows as the train pulled out to the cheers and banzais of the rooting section. As our car passed, the cheers, which had started to slacken, picked up again. The children probably thought we were some of those pale city draftees, so we waved back not to disappoint them.

There seemed to be almost no woodlands on our route. I presumed that in a country this old, most of the forests had been cleared long ago, and the contemporary demand for timber and fuel prevented any large forests from developing. Or perhaps the railroad simply missed the woodlands.

We received three rice meals our first day on the train. The food seemed to improve with each meal. The rice was of a better quality than we had been used to, and pickles and fish supplanted the seaweed. The quantity did not increase appreciably, but then all we were doing was sitting and resting.

At night all the shades were drawn and only a weak light was left on at each end of the car. The problem of getting into a comfortable position for the night presented itself. Some of the men stretched out under the seats; although this gave maximum space, there was always the chance that someone would plant his feet unintentionally but firmly in your face, not to mention sharing the space with all those cigarette butts. Phil Egan found the ideal solution for himself; he climbed into the baggage rack, where his slight build and five-foot length was as comfortable as an average-sized man in a Pullman upper bunk. I spent the night in a series of catnaps, waking up at every stop and a few times in between.

At each station I heard the man checking the journal boxes—it took me a while to figure out what that noise was. Voices in no language I recognized shouted occasionally. At one point we crossed a fairly wide river; McEntee, who was sleeping about as well as I was, figured that we were near Seoul, according to the map in his notebook.

At one station someone tried to climb in through an open window, which we quickly closed. The other cars must have been so crowded that ours looked good enough to be worth a try through the window. We had noticed during the day that people were hanging onto the platforms of some of the trains that passed us.

By the time I dropped off to sleep it was morning and everyone else was up, making noises that were altogether too cheerful. It was cool before the sun came up. The passing terrain took on a new appearance. The low mountains of Korea were giving way to an open rolling plain. About midmorning, we passed through a fairly large town, and it was obvious that we were no longer in Korea. The first indications were the dress and appearance of the people. Instead of the neat, fresh-looking costumes of the Korean peasants, we saw the blue working clothes of Chinese coolies. The neat farms were replaced by sprawling slums. Factory chimneys marked each town on the horizon.

Our breakfast box of rice did not show up when we expected it. The pessimists immediately began saying "I knew this was too good to last." Finally a report was received that the Japanese officer escorting us had inspected the rice and, finding it sour, had condemned the whole lot. About noon we received our noon ration on time and a promise that we would get two rations at the evening meal. We'd believe this when we saw it.

Although we were required to pull down the shades whenever we stopped at a station, by peeking out when the sentries were not look-ing we got glimpses of the stations and the waiting crowds of pas-sengers. There was nothing to see that would explain the need for the shades being down, but by this time we had learned not to be surprised by the workings of the Asian, particularly the Japanese, mind. The scenery was not interesting except when approaching a town. Although some of the POWs idly watched the views, most of us sprawled out and dozed. I played a few rubbers of bridge; when that palled I settled down for a nap.

In late afternoon we passed over a bridge that was heavily guarded with pillboxes on both sides of the stream. We impulsively concluded that guerrillas were active in the area. Actually it may just have been a normal security measure. A road paralleled the railroad at this point, and there was a steady stream of traffic—mostly pedestrians and cyclists and an occasional ricksha. A mile or so farther we stopped at the station in a large town. We were allowed to leave the train to fill canteens from a water spigot at the end of the station.

I left the car to stretch my legs and fill my canteen. The station was on a small rise, and I was able to get a good view of the town. The buildings were Western in appearance, and the streets were wide. It might have been an American or European town. A droshky standing near the station was a reminder of bygone days of Russian influence in Manchuria. In the late afternoon sunshine it was a peaceful and pleasant sight.

Back in the car I learned that the impossible had actually hap-pened: two rations were being distributed to each man. And what rations! The rice was fried and very tasty. Among the "pickles" that went with each box was a small but thick slice of ham. Although mine was tough, it was the first piece of ham I had seen since 1942. There was no doubt in anyone's mind that we were on our way to the best camp in the whole "Greater East Asia Co-Prosperity Sphere." Every-one had a smile on his face, and for the first time that day the con-versation was gay and animated. Horrigan remarked, "If only I had a cigar now, everything would be just fine."

That night most of the prisoners went to sleep as if they had not slept most of the day. I dozed awhile but woke up at each stop to hear the trainman make his inspection of the journal boxes. I wondered how much farther we would travel. We had been told that it would be a three- or four-day trip, and this was the fourth night. Once we stopped for about half an hour within sight of a steel plant. The blazing of the blast furnaces was fascinating, but the thought that this might be our destination was depressing. Nearly everyone in the car was up, probably awakened by the absence of motion. When the train moved on I was relieved.

About an hour later we pulled into a large station. The shielded lights gave enough illumination for someone to recognize the place as Mukden. The sentries came through the car to make sure that everyone was awake and gave the order to disembark. We were told to wait on the platform; we had to take another train, which would arrive shortly.

The new train seemed to have been made up just for the remainder of our trip. The cars were almost luxurious compared to those of the other train, which were not bad for day coaches. After we embarked, the train pulled off onto a siding, where it remained until daybreak. For breakfast the sentries distributed small bags of biscuits, a sort of field ration, and told us we would be in camp before noon.

The actual distance to the camp was short, but the train stopped and backed up and was shunted from track to track so often that the trip consumed several hours. We passed a number of likely looking compounds en route and hoped that the camp would be one of them. A cold drizzle started coming down as we finally left the cars. The camp was about a quarter mile away and did not look cheerful in the rain. A high red brick wall surmounted by barbed wire enclosed a compound containing buildings of more red brick. Just inside the gate was a two-story administration building with a modern-looking entrance and a neat concrete driveway curving up to it.

Down to the right was another large building with a porch. The Japanese had tables set up there and were checking off the new draft against long muster lists. It seemed hours before I was checked off and allowed inside the building.

The entrance hall extended to the roof, and a staircase at each side led to the second floor. From the entrance hall we went into a long, wide room broken up by rows of wooden pillars supporting the second story. At the far end was another hall similar to the entrance. I could not imagine a logical use for the long room. The only furniture in it was the chairs and tables being used by the Japanese. It might have been used as an auditorium, but the pillars would obstruct the view and the acoustics would be poor. As a shelter from the rain, however, it was quite satisfactory.

After more waiting we were told to fall in according to nationality. Then we were told to fall in according to rank. Starting with the senior American officers, the Japanese began to issue numbers. It took me two hours to find out that I was now No. 1956. We received room assignments at the same time and were at last marched over to the barracks.

We passed two barracks on the way to our own, the third and last. They were identical two-story, gable-roofed brick buildings set in a row along one side of the compound. At the northeast corner of each barracks, a one-story addition containing the washroom and the latrine for that building extended to the next barracks. This made the spaces between the barracks courts enclosed on three sides, with the fourth side open to a parade ground that occupied the southwest corner of the compound.

Our new home was separated from the rest of the camp by a barbed wire fence. We were being quarantined to protect the health of the rest of the camp. My room, actually a bay off the hallway, was on the second floor of the barracks. A central corridor ran the length of the barracks; there were five bays on each side of the corridor.

Each pair of opposing bays formed a section, which was the unit for mustering, drawing food from the galley, and so forth. I found that my number entitled me to one of the top bunks. (A row of double-decker bunks lined each side of the bay, similar to the arrangement in Fukuoka No. 2.) At the end of each bay were two high windows with a stove between them.

I preferred having a top bunk because, in addition to the shelf that ran along the wall at the back of the bunk, I could use the rafters for hanging up clothing. This practice was not approved of by the Japanese, as I soon learned. As in Nagasaki, tables and benches were set up in each bay and the meals were served there. The first meal in our new camp was corn bread and a bowl of soybean soup. Although it left a little to be desired, most of us were willing to reserve judgment. We had seen some of the camp's inmates—they were the healthiest POWs we had ever seen.

Despite the quarantine regulation, we were able to talk to the other prisoners, most of whom were U.S. Army personnel. Roughly a fifth of the men were in the U.S. Navy; there were a few marines and some British soldiers. There were about nine officers—two or three British and the rest U.S. Army. They had come up from the Philippines in late 1942, about the same time that I had left Makassar for Japan. When they arrived in Mukden, the camp they now occupied had not been built, and they went to a makeshift camp located several miles to the northwest. Their first winter was a horror. About two hundred men died, probably due in part to the minus forty degree temperatures. After the first winter, conditions improved; the new camp was built and rations were increased. There were few deaths after the initial losses, and most of the prisoners began to put on weight.

Except for garden details and the usual camp jobs, most of the men worked at the MKK factory, a large plant near the camp. It had been American or British owned, but the owners were forced to sell to the Japanese when they began to incorporate Manchuria into the empire. It was apparently a pleasant enough place to work, because I seldom heard anyone complain about going to the factory as we had complained about going to the dockyard in Nagasaki. The workers were Chinese and the foremen Japanese, which should be a more satisfactory setup for the prisoners than working exclusively with Japanese.

There were several smaller camps in the area, but the prisoners had all come from the main camp. Occasionally a sick prisoner from another camp would be brought to the sick bay in our camp. The sick bay occupied a building the size of the barracks, an unusual concession to the welfare of the prisoners. Personnel would occasionally be exchanged among the camps.

After the evening meal, we had a chance to settle down and take stock of our new companions. Most of the officers in my bay were from the Philippines and had been in Japan for less than five months, a period that most of them had spent recovering from their sea voyage from the Philippines. They were all skin and bones, and at least two-thirds of them had beriberi and dysentery. Their experiences had affected them mentally as well as physically; they were distrustful and prone to squabbles.

Slone, Straughan, Allen, and I, who were in the same bay, all felt different from these other Americans. We felt sorry for them because they'd had such a tough time of it and because they were now still in such poor shape. But we found that, with only a few exceptions, we could not bring ourselves to like them right away. Several of them had come to Slone individually to warn him about trading with certain officers; by the time they were finished Slone had received a warning about nearly everyone in the bay.

When it came time to pick someone to ration out the food, Slone and Allen were chosen because the group from the Philippines trusted no one among themselves. In this atmosphere of suspicion there was a tendency for our Nagasaki group to continue to stick together.

There were eleven naval officers, two marine officers, and one marine warrant officer in the camp—all from the new group. One of the marines was "Bitch-bitch" Bennett, a classmate of mine from the naval academy. He had changed little, still full of caustic observations and gripes. He had a bad case of beriberi and spent most of the time in his bunk. I used to enjoy talking to him, because he usually made good sense and we never argued.

The other marine, who shall remain nameless, was more like the army types in our bay and not my idea of a marine at all. Compared to the outspoken, uncompromising Bennett, he was weak and colorless. He never did anything to me, but I couldn't stand him. Perhaps it was the incident of the buns. Some marine enlisted men had sent up a box of buns to be shared among the marine officers and warrant officer. The officer in question didn't bother to tell the others and finished off all the buns by himself. He made himself sick and thereby wasted a lot of good food. One of the young army aviators in the next bay pulled a similar trick with similar results. Some people just can't handle prosperity.

The senior line officer in the naval group was Dave Nash, a lieutenant who had been executive officer of the gunboat *Mindanao*.

Dave had gone through the same experiences as the others, but the only effect was to make him thinner—and more philosophical. He took over "command" of the naval group and immediately began to organize the records of the naval personnel in camp.

Before our group arrived, there had been no American naval officers in camp. The leadership of the men had been left to the chief petty officers, who had obviously done an excellent job. There was a wonderful spirit in the group. When we arrived one of the men was sent to Nash to find out what the officers needed. The next day they sent over clothing for the officers who needed it, cigarettes, soap, and bread. For nearly two months they sent over two buns a day for each officer. Some of the men had served with a few of the officers before, but the majority were strangers.

We had two doctors (Commander Smith and Lieutenant Langdon) and a dentist (Lieutenant Fraleigh). The other naval officers were Levitt, Mullins, McGrath, Russell, and Beale (all reserve ensigns) and Lieutenant Taylor. I had not known any of them before; except for Smith, Fraleigh, and Levitt, whom I had met on the trip to Mukden, they were still strangers.

When I got to know Dave Nash better, he told me some of the experiences of his trip from the Philippines to Japan. He had been evacuated from Manila (Bilibid Prison) late in 1944 when our carrier planes were making almost daily raids in the Manila area. He was in a draft of about sixteen hundred prisoners who were placed aboard the *Oryoko Maru* in Manila harbor. The prisoners were crowded into the holds of the ship, where there was not enough space for all to sit down; the heat and lack of proper ventilation added to the general discomfort. Meanwhile the Japanese loaded the rest of the ship with Japanese families being evacuated before the American push reached Luzon.

The ship stayed in the harbor overnight. In the holds, prisoners were suffocating from the crowded conditions; some were going mad from thirst. There were fights between crazed prisoners. Some men tried to drink the blood of prisoners who had died. "You would not believe such things could happen," Nash said. "You'd have to see them for yourself."

The next day the ship set out for Japan. The conditions below had not been improved except that the deaths meant that fewer people were breathing the air. Many of the prisoners never expected to survive the trip. Someone heard dive-bombers; then bombs exploded close by. The men cheered each explosion, but many called for the next bomb to explode in the hold and end their suffering.

The ship was badly damaged and had to be beached. Some of the prisoners were killed by the explosions, but the sentries topside would not let the prisoners out of the holds despite the dangerous condition of the ship. The dive-bombers returned to strafe the ship, and soon the prisoners were able to climb out of the holds. By this time most of the Japanese were already off the ship.

The ship was beached in Subic Bay, an American naval base before the war, located a few miles north of the entrance to Manila Bay. Nash and the rest of the prisoners who could leave the ship went over the side and swam to shore. The planes must have recognized them as Americans, for the strafing stopped almost immediately.

As the prisoners came ashore, the Japanese rounded them up and corralled them on the tennis courts on the base at Olongapo. Here at least they had air, but the tropical sun baked them. Not all the prisoners who were missing were dead in the ship; a few had taken off into the hills. Most, however, figured that the Japanese would not attempt to evacuate anyone else out of the Philippines and decided that they would not have more than a couple of months' wait before the Americans reached Manila.

The Japanese had other plans. Only the men too sick to travel were sent back to Bilibid; within a week, the rest were on their way to Japan in another ship. This one at least got clear of the Philippines. At Formosa, however, it was bombed, and repairs took a few days.

As the ship left the tropics, the prisoners began to feel the cold weather they had not experienced for more than three years. A number caught pneumonia. In combination with malnutrition and dysentery, it caused a few men to die in the holds every day. When the deaths were reported to the Japanese, their only response was to reduce the amount of food issued. The corpses were piled in the corners of the holds.

At last the ship arrived in Kyushu. Many of the prisoners congratulated themselves on surviving the trip, but there were still more to die. It didn't seem fair that a man should escape death so many times, then die in a prison camp.

Perhaps after the shattering experiences the men had gone through, it was not fair to judge them harshly for selfish and anti-social behavior. But there were people such as Dave Nash who held fast to their self-respect and who realized that being an officer carried a special responsibility with it.

Within a week the novelty of being in a new camp had worn off. Although all the faces were not those of friends, they were at any rate those of acquaintances. Our period of quarantine ended, and we were allowed to take a hot bath at the camp bathhouse. Arrangements were made to steam our clothing to rid them of lice. In Nagasaki my lice control had been effective; I was very annoyed to find that I had picked up some in Mukden. The single steaming did not do the job completely, but in a short while I was living alone again.

The food ration did not turn out to be as large as we had been led to expect. The same amount of food that had formerly been issued for about seven hundred men was now to suffice for more than a thousand. The "old" prisoners' stories about the large rations prior to our arrival met with little enthusiasm.

The end of the quarantine gave me an opportunity to meet some of the navy men. They were from nearly every naval activity in the Philippines: men from Patrol Wing 10 and from the PBY (Catalina) outfit that took such a beating at the beginning of the war; men from PT boats, submarines, and minesweepers; and men from the naval base at Cavite. Some of them had been in the naval battalion on Bataan—probably the most unorthodox group of infantrymen ever to go into combat—and some had been on the firing line on Corregidor when the Japanese made their assault. A few may have been back in the tunnels with the army.

The group was fortunate to have chief petty officers such as Joe Davis, Fred Feilzer, Sharkey Brown, Ward, and McCavanaugh. They proved themselves when the going was tough at Mukden. Without them the few army officers would not have been able to get the camp organized, for the senior army noncoms seemed to have been slow in taking hold until everything was set up.

I'd go over to the boiler house with Levitt to talk to Feilzer and Brown (their detail was the boiler house because they were chief water tenders). Often they would make "coffee" from burned soybeans, an acceptable substitute until the real thing came along. Sharkey could tell "sea tales" by the hour. With his white hair and pallid complexion, he looked like the Ancient Mariner. Fred preferred to talk about the camp and the latest news.

Fred was a handsome fellow, tall and well built; his nose had been "slightly" broken in prison camp but that had not spoiled his looks. Occasionally he would talk about his good-looking wife, who had taken a commission in the Coast Guard SPARS. Usually Sharkey or Fred would give us some cooked beans or a bun from their own rations, or sometimes it was something extra they had managed to get from the galley. They said that they always had more than enough to eat for themselves.

Because the new officers in the camp were assigned no duties by the Japanese, we tried to set up a program to pass some of the free time. I volunteered to represent my section of the barracks. There were not enough books in camp for each prisoner to draw a book from the library, so each section had to set up its own schedule. This was one of my jobs as a representative. A series of lectures was scheduled on subjects ranging from the Shanghai police force to tiger hunting in India. A duplicate bridge tournament was started, and classes in Spanish and Russian were organized.

Despite our attempts to keep our minds occupied, our constant thoughts were of food. The situation was eased somewhat by the generous action of the men who were in the camp before we arrived. They had been getting a regular Red Cross issue of food and cigarettes (from parcels that had been shipped into the camp months before). In the usual Japanese manner, the items had been doled out once a week—two or three men to a can of Spam one week, a pack of cigarettes the next. The men turned over to us all their Red Cross issues, because they felt that we needed the food more than they did.

The news setup in this camp was not as good as that in our camp at Nagasaki. The news we did get usually came a week or two late. Several people in camp could translate the Japanese newspapers brought in from the factory. The news was passed by word of mouth so there would be no danger of the Japanese picking up any written notes.

We were encouraged by the news of the occupation of Okinawa, but we were waiting for the fall of Germany to know how much longer we would be in prison. Most of us felt that with our forces closing in on Japan, she would not hold out long after Germany fell—just long enough to be able to claim in the future that Japan had surrendered only after all her allies had been defeated and the anti-Axis forces had concentrated their offensives on Japan.

About a month after our arrival in Mukden, a new group of prisoners arrived in camp—mostly officers of the rank of colonel and above. Prior to their arrival we were moved to another barracks, and they were billeted in our old barracks. They had spent most of their imprisonment on Formosa and had been shifted to a camp not far from Peiping (Peking) about nine months before joining us.

Among the naval officers were Capt. George McMillin, governor of Guam; Captain Hoeffel, the senior naval officer left in the Philippines at the surrender of Corregidor; Captains Davis, Roberts, and Lowman (all medical corps); Captain Wilterdink (supply corps); and Captain Pederson, a merchant skipper. There were two marine brigadiers and a host of British and American army brigadiers. General Wainwright and the most senior British and Dutch officers (including the civilian governors of Malaya and Java) were not in the group. Nevertheless, I had never seen such a concentration of seniority. Being prisoners of war must have been especially difficult for them; they were comparatively old men and must have felt the humiliation more keenly because of their rank.

Because we had already scheduled a happy hour (navy for "smoker") for the Sunday of the week that the senior officers arrived in camp, we invited them to join us so that we could introduce them to the men. Dave Nash had suggested that we have the get-together to meet all the men. The officers traded for cans of powdered coffee so that we could supply some liquid refreshment as a token of our thanks for the generosity the men had shown us.

The program consisted of musical numbers (the men provided this phase of the entertainment) and a review of the actions in which the *Houston* and the *Pope* had taken part. Levitt and I gave play-by-play descriptions of the respective actions. Only once were the proceedings interrupted by the Japanese, at which point we all burst into song to give the impression that it was musical entertainment.

Levitt described the last actions of the *Houston*. On the evening of February 26, 1942, a combined British, Dutch, and American naval force sailed from Surabaja to make a sweep in the Java Sea, hoping to encounter the Japanese invasion convoy that had been reported by air reconnaissance. The naval force consisted of the *Houston* (American) and the *Exeter* (British), heavy cruisers (8-inch guns); the *Java*, the *De Ruyter* (both Dutch), and the *Perth* (Australian), light cruisers (6- and 5.9-inch guns); the *Witte de With* and the *Kortenaer* (Dutch); the *Jupiter*, the *Electra*, and the *Encounter* (British); and the *Edwards*, the *Alden*, the *Ford*, and the *John Paul Jones* (American), all destroyers. The *Pope* was not in this group because of an engineering plant casualty. This was the most formidable Allied naval force thus far assembled in the Netherlands East Indies, and morale was high.

The force steamed all night and most of the next day before sighting the enemy. Contact was made on the afternoon of the twenty-seventh. The cruisers were in column *(De Ruyter, Exeter, Houston, Perth, and Java)*, with the three British destroyers in a screen ahead; the two Dutch destroyers were on the port flank, and the four American destroyers were astern of the cruisers.

Fire was opened at extreme range, which was later closed to about twenty thousand yards; the shells of the light cruisers were falling short even at this range. A better approach might have been to place the light cruisers between the heavy cruisers and the destroyers on the engaged side. This would have put the light cruisers in a position to support the destroyers against light Japanese forces and would have brought the light cruisers within firing range. Admiral Doorman may have elected not to do this because (1) he thought that any attempt to change the disposition would have resulted in a melee with the three different nationalities involved, or (2) it was too late, after action had been joined, to make any changes, or (3) he may have lacked the experience of handling a fleet of that size, which was no fault of his.

The Japanese sent in their destroyers for a torpedo attack. It was repulsed and the Japanese retired in a smoke screen. The gun duel between the cruisers continued while the destroyers reattacked. The light cruisers took the destroyers under fire and together with the Dutch and British destroyers again turned back the Japanese.

Then the *Exeter* received a hit from a Japanese heavy cruiser, putting six of her boilers out of commission, and she turned out of column. The *Houston,* not realizing that the *Exeter* had been hit, thought that a maneuver had been signaled, and she turned out of column too. The other cruisers followed suit. The *De Ruyter* steamed on until she noticed the confusion. She swung around to rejoin the other cruisers and signaled them to form up on her.

While this was going on, the *Kortenaer* received a torpedo hit and sank. The British destroyers made smoke to cover the cruisers while they reorganized. The Japanese continued their torpedo attacks while their cruisers continued their gunfire.

The British destroyers were ordered to make a torpedo attack, and they went back through their smoke to push home the attack. When they withdrew, the *Electra* failed to return and was presumed to have been sunk by Japanese gunfire. Meanwhile the *Exeter* was detached to return to port, and the *Witte de With* was detailed to accompany her. En route the *Exeter* engaged a Japanese light cruiser that had closed to take advantage of her damaged condition. After several hits by the *Exeter,* the Japanese ship turned away.

Doorman realized that he was not accomplishing his objective—to attack the transports bearing the invasion troops—and decided to break off the engagement with the covering force so that he could hunt for the convoy. The American destroyers were ordered to attack to cover this maneuver. They made two torpedo attacks, which turned the Japanese line, and then rejoined our forces making a smoke screen.

By this time it was almost dark, and the Allied force would have steamed away unmolested had it not been for the Japanese aircraft. The planes dogged our ships, dropping flares to silhouette them for the Japanese fleet. Later in the evening some cruisers were sighted and engaged. After a brief exchange of fire, contact was lost. Our force continued on its way toward the Java coast to intercept the transports. This was a logical move, because if the Japanese wanted to make a landing they would certainly have to reach the shore. On this sweep the *Jupiter* hit a mine and sank. The American four-stackers were getting low on fuel and were detached to return to Surabaja, the nearest port.

The Japanese planes continued to drop flares around the force. In the light of the flares the survivors of the *Kortenaer* were sighted in the water. The *Encounter,* which was also short of fuel, was detailed to pick up the survivors and return to Surabaja.

Just before midnight the Allied force sighted Japanese cruisers and opened fire. Shortly thereafter the *Java* and the *De Ruyter* received torpedo hits in rapid succession. The torpedoes may have come from the Japanese cruisers, or the ships may have run into a submarine trap, for the Japanese had had sufficient time to set up the trap. The two Dutch cruisers sank, leaving the *Houston* and the *Perth* alone to make their way to Tanjong Priok, the port of Batavia.

In the various engagements, our ships had sunk at least one Japanese cruiser and damaged several others. Two Japanese destroyers had been sunk and a number hit. Our losses on the whole were less than those of the Japanese, but we had no reserves and could not afford any losses at all. The whole affair was hopeless from the start, but none of our people seemed to have considered that.

Perhaps it was unwise to detach a destroyer to escort the *Exeter* to port and another to pick up survivors; it left the fighting units naked. But to Admiral Doorman it seemed the best move at the time. Whatever may be said or thought of the way Doorman handled his fleet, there can be no question of his courage. Although the Japanese outnumbered his forces almost two to one, he did not hesitate to continue his attack. He carried on the grand traditions of Admiral De Ruyter, after whom his flagship was named. The Netherlands East Indies needed many men like Doorman; unfortunately, he was not among the survivors.

The *Houston* and the *Perth* arrived in Tanjong Priok the morning of the twenty-eighth. They refueled, shifted ammunition, and cared for their wounded. That evening they left port to make their way through Sunda Strait to Australia. The *Evertsen,* a Dutch destroyer in port preparing for sea, later attempted to join them.

Near Banten Bay, on the northwest tip of Java, as the *Houston* and the *Perth* were heading into Sunda Strait, a Japanese force was sighted in the process of making a landing. The cruisers steamed in to attack the transports and were engaged by Japanese covering forces. Several transports were hit and were beached to avoid sinking. (This was admitted later in a roundabout way in the Japanese newspapers. The article described how the commanding general of the invasion troops was carried ashore on the backs of his staff officers to avoid getting wet. The transport was required to beach because of "unforeseen conditions.")

At the close range of the battle, the *Houston* and the *Perth* were soon hit. Japanese destroyers attacked with torpedoes, scoring hits on the *Perth,* which soon sank. The *Houston* continued the battle alone and received shell hits, which put her engineering plant out of commission and caused her to lose all power. The 5-inch battery and machine guns continued firing after the 8-inch mounts had lost power.

Helpless to maneuver, the *Houston* tried to beat off the attacks of the Japanese ships closing for the kill. Levitt estimated that five torpedoes hit the *Houston,* which by now had taken a heavy list to starboard. The Japanese destroyers were close enough to spray the decks with machine-gun fire. One of the *Houston*'s sailors shot out a Japanese searchlight with a Browning automatic rifle.

Captain Rooks, seeing that the ship was in danger of capsizing, gave the order to abandon ship. As he left the bridge to see his men get off, a Japanese shell exploding nearby killed him. Levitt, who was with him at the time, caught him as he fell.

About half the crew got off the *Houston* before she slid beneath the waves, taking with her her dead and those trapped below. With the *Perth* she had either sunk or seriously damaged thirteen ships. Some of the survivors were lucky enough to find the life rafts in the darkness; others clung to bits of floating wreckage. The stronger swimmers struck out for the shore. Most of the men had kapok life jackets, which enabled them to stay afloat in their exhausted and, in many cases, wounded condition.

Levitt reached the beach in fair shape and assembled a group of survivors who were willing to try to reach the Dutch lines. They took off inland, but their objective was an impossible one—there were no

Dutch lines. As Levitt put it, "They had probably melted in the hot Javanese sun."

After hiding in the hills for almost a day, they were discovered by natives, who offered to lead them around the Japanese but instead turned them over to a group of Japanese soldiers. They were taken to a town occupied by the Japanese and were locked up in the local jail.

Levitt was later taken before a Japanese officer for questioning, with a Japanese civilian acting as interpreter. When asked the name of his ship, Levitt replied proudly, "The USS *Houston*." The interpreter passed this on to the officer, who gave a long discourse in Japanese. The interpreter turned to Levitt and said, "We have heard of your ship." He then volunteered the information that the transport carrying the senior Japanese officers of the invasion force had been damaged by the *Houston*. After routine questioning, Levitt was returned to the jail.

A few weeks later, when the Japanese had full control of Java, Levitt and the rest of the prisoners were moved to another camp, where they met some of the men from the 131st Field Artillery (Texas). This group was later transferred to Singapore, where, after a brief stay, Levitt joined a draft going to Formosa. From there he was eventually sent to Japan.

The trip to Formosa was not a pleasant one. The lack of sufficient drinking water was the chief complaint. The situation was eased by the discovery that a pipe carrying fresh water passed through the hold in which the prisoners were kept. With the help of some of the men, Levitt made a hole in the pipe with a penknife and cut wooden plugs so that they could take water when they wanted it.

Herb met the captain of the *Evertsen* in prison camp and learned of his attempt to rejoin the *Houston* and the *Perth*. The Dutch destroyer was close enough to see the gunfire of the ships during the battle. As the *Evertsen* approached them, she was cut off by Japanese destroyers, which she engaged. After receiving serious damage, the Dutch ship was beached on an island in Sunda Strait.

In the sinking of the *Houston*, I lost several good friends. Kenny Kollmyer and "Bobo" Weiler were classmates of mine at the naval academy; "Tiny" Gingras, the chief engineer of the *Houston*, had been a shipmate on the *Salt Lake City;* and Cass Mayo had been my roommate aboard the *President Grant* on our way to the Philippines. It was a shame that they should have been sacrificed to defend Java when the Dutchmen ashore didn't think enough of their homes and families to put up a fight.

This is not a denunciation of all Dutchmen. The Dutch navy fought as bravely as any, and Dutch troops in the other islands of the Indies put up spirited resistance on several occasions. In Java, however, the will to fight had been broken, and there was no realization that, by attempting to hold the Japanese, an attempt to take Australia might be delayed or thwarted.

A number of things broke Java's spirit. The fall of Singapore was a tremendous blow to Dutch morale. The knowledge that there was a well-organized fifth column in Java and that many of the natives were awaiting the chance to rid themselves of their Dutch rulers produced an uneasiness that gave way to despair when the invasion force reached the Java coast. The Dutch thought that even if the island was occupied they would become internees and not prisoners of war and that eventually they would be able to lead more or less normal lives under the occupation. If there had been any way of telling how many men would die in the prison camps, the defense of Java might have been one of the bright spots in Dutch history.

The senior officers brought into camp the rumors of Germany's fall. We had heard news indicating that the German defense had been shattered, but we could not understand why we had no news of an actual surrender. I think that the Japanese withheld the news to soften the blow for their people and to take time to develop a new propaganda line: "Japan is stronger than ever because she now has only herself to defend."

The announcement, when it came, was an anticlimax. The Japanese had apparently made the decision to continue the war, feeling that they still had a strong position because the homeland was not yet invaded. After all, they had been offered only unconditional surrender. The Allies might be willing to offer a few terms to save the cost of an invasion. The Japanese figured that they would have little to lose if they awaited developments. The sentries in the camp acted much as they had before; if anything, they were a little more surly.

Most of the prisoners thought that the war would last perhaps six months more, that an actual landing in the Japanese islands would be necessary, and that we were lucky to be in Manchuria, where there was plenty of food, even though we didn't get much of it. There was also little likelihood of being bombed at this stage in the war.

There had been raids earlier in the war, and American bombs had hit the camp itself in the fall of 1944. The prisoners working in the factories were brought into camp for safety, and to make sure they didn't escape. There were no foxholes in the field within the compound then; the prisoners merely stretched out on the ground. Some lay on their backs to watch the B-29s as they circled over the city. Then the planes picked a target about half a mile from the camp, an ammunition factory. The aim was good and the factory was flattened. One plane, however, was slow in dropping her bombs, and two of them landed in the camp. One bomb removed a section of the brick wall around the compound and killed and wounded several prisoners and Japanese. The other bomb hit a latrine between the barracks and started a small fire.

Some of the prisoners received injuries that necessitated the amputation of arms and legs at the camp sick bay. To the credit of the camp doctors, including the Japanese doctor, most of the amputees recovered. The Japanese camp commander ordered all of the men who had been injured to write letters to the U.S. government to stop the bombings, saying that American bombs were killing prisoners of war. The men wrote the letters but they were not to the liking of the Japanese. One man wrote, "I lost an arm in an American bombing raid on Mukden; if this is what it takes to get me home, I have another arm left." The letters were never mailed.

At least two B-29s were shot down in the series of raids, and the crews were imprisoned in a stockade near the camp. Their food was supplied from the camp, and the prisoners who carried the food to them each day worked out a code so that they could communicate with the airmen. They made a false bottom for the wooden tub in which they carried the food so that they could sneak extra rations to the aviators. The conditions in which the airmen were forced to live were not suitable for hogs. No doubt the food carriers played a big part in keeping up their morale.

Foxholes were dug in the parade ground in the compound after the damage had been done, and the prisoners spent cold nights there on subsequent raids. With the arrival of our group from Japan and of the senior officers from China, it was necessary to dig more trenches. I joined the group of officers who volunteered to do the digging. Although the weather was warm at the time, we found that as soon as we dug about two feet below the surface, the earth was cold. With such long, cold winters and short summers, there must have been a layer of earth that was close to freezing the year around. The soil was dark and had few stones, which was probably why Manchuria could produce such exceptional crops without the aid of modern farming methods and machinery.

Because there was little to do in camp except read and play bridge, I welcomed the chance to leave the camp one day with a working party to cut grass at the camp cemetery. We left at about eight o'clock and hiked seven to eight miles to the burial grounds, not far from the location of the old camp. On the way we passed a number of small factories, all with brick walls and barbed wire to keep out burglars. Some of the walls had loopholes, as if the builders had envisaged an occasional siege. One group of buildings was surrounded by such high walls that we decided it was a prison for hardened criminals.

As we marched we passed fewer factories and instead saw clusters of small mud huts belonging to farmers. Most of the rolling fields along the road were under cultivation. What few trees we saw were at the sides of the road or along the banks of streams. The roads were unpaved and dusty but surprisingly wide, some so straight and wide that they may have been built primarily for military purposes. We passed not a single wagon or truck on the way.

The morning coolness soon wore off and we were grateful to hear the sentries call a halt to rest. We were allowed to smoke. Those who had brought canteens passed them around to their friends.

Farther on we passed through a hamlet with several small shops. Fruit and cakes were displayed amid swarms of flies. Occasionally a shop owner would make a halfhearted sweep of his arm to drive away the flies. Hungry as we were, the food did not look appetizing. Except for children and dirty-looking old men and women, there were few people in sight. Most of the young men and women were no doubt working in the fields.

After about two hours on the road we came to a small hill with a cemetery on top and two stone posts in the field below the hill. The graves of the prisoners of war were laid out in neat rows. White wooden crosses bearing the names of the men marked the graves. The three graves without crosses belonged to men who had tried to escape and had been executed. The Japanese had refused to allow crosses for them, for they had died with the unforgivable sin of trying to escape from the Japanese army.

We began our work of pulling weeds and cutting grass. A steady wind sweeping over the hill kept us cool, but the work was backbreaking because we were not used to it. At noon we stopped to eat our meal of soybean soup, which, for a change, had plenty of beans. We had brought the soup from camp in a wooden bucket and had taken turns carrying it. Each man brought along his own mess kit or canteen cup. As usual we all could have eaten double the portion. As we relaxed under a tree smoking cigarettes, the war seemed far away. One of the officers mentioned that the countryside reminded him of Kansas.

Down the hill, across the road from us, Chinese farmers were working in what seemed to be a patch of stringbeans. A donkey plodded in an endless circle to pump water by pulling a pole rigged to the pump. In the distance we could make out a large barn that would not have been out of place on a prosperous dairy farm in the States. Someone suggested that it might belong to one of the Russians who had settled here after the revolution. An officer familiar with the history of the area pointed out a monument several miles away that marked the battlefield of one of the bloody battles of the Russo-Japanese War. The Japanese had lost a large number of troops there and had erected an imposing monument in their honor.

After lunch we returned to our work. I was tired before I started and was glad when the word was passed two hours later to knock off and fall in to be counted. The trip back seemed much longer than the trip out. My legs ached and I felt drained of all energy. We reached camp at about four o'clock and I went straight to my bunk.

It was a week before I felt all right again. I had no idea that I was in such poor shape. Apparently I had been getting enough to eat as long as I did no work. Thereafter I was economical in my expenditure of energy. On sunny days I always spent an hour or two sunbathing in the afternoon.

In July I went to sick call one day with an upset stomach and found that I also had a fever. I was in the sick bay ward for about a week. This was not without its good points. After the first day I was able to eat again and could take advantage of the extra rations the galley always sent to the sick bay. Sharkey Brown was in the sick bay at the same time, and we used to play cribbage. Although I had a pleasant rest there, I was glad to get out when the week was up.

I took up Russian with Mihailov, an American army officer born in Siberia who had volunteered to teach me. A British colonel who had studied Russian in one of the Balkan countries before the war also joined the teaching staff (he even had a Berlitz book with him). We had reached the point where we could fluently say such useful phrases as "I put the book on the table" and "This pencil is long" when the Japanese ran us all up to the main office for holding classes without permission. The fact that we were learning Russian raised the question of our intent. After a brief reprimand we were warned not to hold classes again without permission. We bowed smartly and left the office.

If we had asked permission to hold classes, it would certainly have been refused. If we had held classes anyway, it would have been disobedience of a Japanese order and "heavy, heavy punishment."

Our monotony was broken somewhat by entertainment that was held in the hall where we had lined up to get our prisoner numbers. I was anxious to attend because I had been listening to the orchestra practice each evening and had not heard them finish a single number. The conductor, one of the British officers, would make them repeat each phrase until it sounded just right. Some of the instruments were homemade, but the Japanese had supplied an accordion and some inexpensive but serviceable violins.

Besides the orchestra, which played well, there were quartets, solos, a few skits, and community singing. The show lasted about three hours, which gave everyone in the camp a chance to get into the act.

After the surrender of Germany there was little news except for reports of bombing raids on Japanese cities. One day in August, however, came the report that the Russians had declared war on Japan and were attacking the Manchurian border. The report was confirmed by air raid warnings at night. We got to try out the foxholes we had dug. A day or two later the men who normally worked in the factories were told to stay in the camp. When further reports said that the Russians were advancing rapidly from the border, the Japanese began to pull in the prisoners from the satellite camps.

On August 14, 1945, rumors were flying about the camp. The men from the satellite camps were still coming back into our camp, and they brought their own rumors from reliable Chinese who worked beside them in the factory. Something was up, all right; we knew that the Russians had come into the war and had pushed across the Manchurian border. We didn't know how far they had advanced, because newspapers had stopped coming into the camp when the men stopped work at the factory. From the speed of the advance up to the time of the last report, we estimated that the Soviet forces must have arrived in the suburbs of Harbin, about three hundred miles northeast of Mukden.

No matter what happened, the war would not last much longer now. We assumed that all the prisoners were being put in one camp to facilitate administration and to limit the number of guards required. The speed of the Russian push was surprising to most of us. For years we had heard of the "crack" Kwantung army and the rugged border troops. Either the Japanese had reduced their garrisons or had stripped the army of its planes and artillery, or their morale was shot.

By afternoon an ugly rumor was making the rounds: there would be a forced march from camp for all men able to travel. The destination was the mountains near the Korean border, where we would be out of reach of the Russian forces striking along the railroad. The move didn't seem logical, which made some of us think it was typical of the Japanese.

About 4 P.M. the wildest rumor of all hit the camp: Americans who were not prisoners had arrived. I told my informer that I didn't believe it. "I didn't believe it either," he said, "but the men from the other camp said they saw them come through the gate. You might be able to see them yourself if you go up to the fence at the back of the sick bay."

On my way to the fence I thought of all the reasons why the report must have been the figment of someone's imagination, and a clumsy figment too. First of all, how did the fellow know they were Americans? He had said they weren't wearing uniforms that looked like any of our prewar stuff. All he had to go on was that they were big guys and "looked" like Americans. They weren't prisoners of war, because they still had their sidearms. Besides, if the Americans on one side of the fence could run around with pistols, why couldn't the Japanese tell the rest of us? Timor had been "retaken" too many times while I was in Makassar for me to be fooled by such a transparent story.

My logic had convinced me from the neck up, but the rest of me was slow in getting the word. I was practically running to get to the fence to see the Americans who weren't there. A knot of prisoners stood beside the sick bay talking together. "Where are the Americans with the sidearms?" I asked in a joking manner so that either way I would not appear stupid. "They're up there, but don't hang around the fence," came the answer. "The Japs just chased us away."

I walked past the end of the building and looked over the barbed wire fence. A few men stood near the wall just inside the gate. At that distance it was hard to say what their nationality was. Some were tall and obviously European, but more than that could not be said, at least not from my position. As for the sidearms, they might be pistol holders or they might be canteens. I was not convinced, but I was getting into a more receptive frame of mind.

I don't remember eating supper that night, but that was probably because the soup was so thin. I know that I would not have missed a meal unless I was too sick to eat. At any rate I was soon back up near the sick bay again; there was nothing to be seen now. I walked over to the other side of the camp toward the library and galley.

"Ski" Majewski, a sailor who worked in the bakery, beckoned to me. "What do you think?" he asked, slipping me a couple of buns. I told him I wasn't sure; I didn't want to get my hopes up only to be disappointed again. "Do you think they'll try to move us? We're mixing up a hell of a lot of dough in there. They said it's for the Japanese soldiers, but I think they're full of shit."

With the two buns Ski gave me in my pocket, which felt better than a couple of twenty dollar bills, and with a cigarette he gave me between my lips, I joined a noisy crowd of rumor mongers. Ski was a good kid to give me the buns and the cigarette. He hadn't known me before and would most likely never see me again after the war. There was nothing I could do for him in exchange except be friendly, and that required no effort.

The first group I accosted had just received some "hot" news: one of the prisoners whose job was to clean the Japanese quarters said he had gotten a close look at the "Americans" through the window of the commandant's office and had seen one of them leaning back in a chair and smoking a cigar. Another "American" in the room had lit a cigarette and thrown the extinguished match over his shoulder into the corner. Although these actions may not have been typical of Americans, they were certainly not actions any POWs would contemplate, let alone have a cigar to smoke. To top it all off, one of the "Americans" was shaking his finger at the commandant as though giving emphasis to a threat.

I left buoyed but still unconvinced. The next group I joined was discussing the sighting by several prisoners of parachutes in the air; the men assumed that the Japanese were holding a practice. But it was illogical for the Japanese to hold paratrooper practice with the Russians so close at hand, and the only way that Americans could arrive in Mukden was by parachute, so the incident seemed to bear out the rest of the rumors. But I was still skeptical, because I had heard nothing about the parachutes until after I had heard the other stories.

That evening we had *tenko* as usual, but when it was time to turn in, less than half of the prisoners went to bed. The lights in the bays were turned out, but several prisoners moved tables onto the staircase landing where they could play poker and bridge under the light. There was a lot of talking in the barracks, and when the sentry made his rounds he walked by without a fuss.

I couldn't sleep and decided to go to the latrine and have a cigarette. A sizable group of prisoners was standing in the washroom smoking and talking, rehashing the rumors of the day. While we were there a sentry of the perimeter guard stuck his head in the window and called out, "All men *tomodashi* (friends)." When we turned around he threw in a pack of cigarettes, and left. This was the most convincing evidence we'd had all day. Normally a sentry finding prisoners up, and smoking, after hours would start shouting and swinging.

After finishing my cigarette I went back to bed and slept. In the morning the word was passed for the prisoners of each nationality to assemble at different points in the camp. The American prisoners gathered in the area behind the galley where General Parker, the senior American officer, addressed us. We were told that an "armistice" had been declared and that we were to remain in the camp until further notice. The Japanese would maintain a guard about the camp but would not come into our area. Meanwhile we must do nothing to provoke the Japanese.

There was cheering; there should have been more, but everyone was convinced hours before that the war had ended. The question in everyone's mind was, when do we go home?

It was announced that the food ration would be increased immediately. This was expected, but it was reassuring to have it made official. The soup had gotten steadily weaker since our arrival in Mukden and the bread ration had been cut. Most of us were still thinking of food along with the prospect of returning home soon.

Captain McMillin called a meeting of the American naval officers to work out a plan of organization for our group in case we had to leave the camp on short notice. Because there was a good chance that the Chinese would start fighting among themselves as soon as the Japanese relinquished control, this seemed to be an excellent idea.

The B-29 pilots who had been kept in the stockade across the road from our camp were brought in on the day after the so-called armistice. We learned that they had been based in China. Questions about the Chinese war effort revealed that most of the lend-lease supplies to China were being hoarded for the expected civil war after the end of the Japanese war. That explained why we'd had no news of outstanding successes in China against the Japanese when most of the Japanese strength was engaged elsewhere.

Later in the day a B-24 flew over the camp and dropped leaflets printed in English and Chinese. The plane passed slowly at low altitude and waggled its wings. Everyone was out cheering. My eyes grew moist, and when I looked around I saw that most of the other prisoners had the same problem. There was a mad scramble for the leaflets, which announced the Japanese acceptance of surrender terms and advised the prisoners to stay in the camp until a liberation team arrived. What the message for the Chinese was I never learned.

Apparently the plane had been meant to drop the leaflets the same day that the parachute team had landed. The one-day delay could easily have meant death for the parachute team. The full story of their landing was soon around camp. They were an Office of Strategic Services (OSS) team from the China-Burma-India theater, and their mission was to get to the camp where General Wainwright was imprisoned. (The general was actually in a camp about ninety miles from us.)

The team had landed in a field not far from our camp, and the Chinese working in the field promptly ran away. The team set out in the direction of our camp, but before they had gotten very far a platoon of Japanese soldiers arrived and the platoon commander ordered the Americans to kneel down in the field. The Japanese-Hawaiian interpreter of the team kept walking and talking. If he had not done this, all of them would have been shot on the spot; at least that was the opinion of the other members of the team.

The interpreter had trouble convincing the Japanese that they were not saboteurs, but he created a doubt in the mind of the platoon commander and talked him into taking them before his superior officer. From there the going was comparatively easy. They even got the Japanese to send a truck to the field to pick up their supplies, which had been parachuted in a cylinder with them. (Their supplies included eight bottles of Haig & Haig; the booze and their radio set were undamaged.)

Once in our camp, the Americans set about convincing the camp commandant that the war was over. This was not easy, because he'd had no communications from Tokyo to prepare him, and the Japanese government had always followed the line that there would be no surrender. The commandant made some telephone calls and eventually received confirmation. Japanese communications must have been badly disrupted for such an important message to be delayed.

11

On August 16 Russian fighters buzzed the camp. After having seen only Japanese planes, it was strange to see Allied planes so close by. That evening we were called to assemble near the administration building, and the word was passed that the Russians had reached Mukden. In a few minutes Russian officers mounted a platform that had been hastily erected. With one of the POWs, an American army sergeant of Russian birth, acting as interpreter, the officers addressed the camp. The address, full of gestures and very dramatic, lost nothing in translation.

We were declared officially free in the name of the Soviet army, which had apparently rushed down from Siberia for just that purpose. General Parker expressed gratitude, on behalf of all of us, to the Russian Imperial Army for our liberation. The cheers were loud and frequent throughout the speeches. The Russians asked, "Where is General Wainwright?" and seemed annoyed that he was not in our camp. Apparently the Japanese had given them that impression.

Before the Russians left the platform, they were asked when we would be allowed to go into town. The answer was typically Asian: not just yet because you do not have proper clothing. The real reason was that the Russians did not want us to become involved in any of the disorder that would normally follow occupation of enemy territory. This would have been reason enough, had they been willing to admit the possibility of disorder.

We were told to return to our barracks to await a surrender ceremony. In a little while the Japanese guards were marched onto the field in front of the barracks. They filed past the line of prisoners, carrying their arms. Some of the prisoners jeered but most kept silent, feeling perhaps that jeers were inappropriate—we had been defeated by the Japanese in the early part of the war.

The guards were ordered to lay down their arms, and a group of American prisoners was called forth to pick up the rifles. The Japanese were marched back to the guardhouse flanked by Americans. There was cheering from the crowd at the crestfallen looks on the faces of the Japanese. Several Japanese soldiers marched off with the Japanese parade step (a high step similar to the goose step except that the knee is bent). Whether this was a salute to the victors or an indication of an unconquered spirit, I didn't know, but I found it touching.

The Russians did not leave the camp immediately after the "changing of the guard" but stayed to talk to the prisoners. Pairs of Russians were completely surrounded by ex-POWs exchanging questions and answers. Americans of Slavic extraction held the limelight acting as interpreters. The Russians made a good impression, much different from what we had expected. They were full of praise for the American lend-lease equipment and the general war effort.

The British were disliked by the Russians, who were cordial but otherwise made no attempt to conceal their feelings. This abashed the British, and any enthusiasm they may have had for the Russians dwindled quickly. No doubt Churchill's outspoken remarks at the time that Russia made its pact with Hitler and the abortive British expedition to aid Finland to repel the Russian attack were not forgotten in Russia and had probably been the subject of a propaganda campaign.

The camp was turned over to the U.S. Army for administration. Actually a conference of the senior officers of all nationalities was held daily to decide policy. The guard duties were assigned to each nationality in proportion to its number of men in the camp. Morning and evening musters were held on the field in front of the barracks, the foxholes for air raid protection having been filled in so that the field could be used for sports. For a change, everyone tried to present as smart an appearance as his "wardrobe" permitted.

Entertainment was planned for the next evening. Because there were no floodlights in the camp, it was decided to send a scavenging party to MKK, a factory near the camp in which the prisoners had worked. Fred Feilzer asked me if I wanted to go along. It sounded interesting, and there was nothing better to do.

At the gate we climbed into a Japanese camp truck along with four or five of our soldiers armed with Japanese rifles. The arms were brought in case we ran into trouble with the Chinese, who were looting any unprotected compounds and factories. We had an American flag on the truck, and as we drove the half mile or so to MKK, the Chinese along the way gave us cheers and smiles. Near the factory we saw two streams of Chinese rush by each other, one empty handed going toward the factory, the other headed away bearing office furniture, filing cabinets—anything that could be lifted. Fights broke out over questions of "ownership," but generally it was a well-ordered mob out for a quiet day of looting.

Our truck and the rifles gave our looting party an air of authority that the Chinese recognized at once. They kept clear of the truck, and our progress through the gates and up to the administration building was uninterrupted. We disembarked in front of the building, which was a low, wide structure with modern lines, and pushed our way through the mob and into the main office.

The last of the office furniture was being removed as we entered. The floor was ankle deep with the contents of the desks. Broken bottles, piles of paper, *bento* (lunch) boxes, and a mass of odds and ends covered the floor. The room was filled with Chinese men, women, and children scrambling for something to carry off. There didn't seem to be any rhyme or reason to what people were taking. Things of little or no value were eagerly grabbed. More than likely the really valuable articles were being ground under their feet.

We left the building to the Chinese and headed for another part of the factory where Feilzer thought we might find the floodlights. We passed through a large machine shop set up with costly lathes of American and Japanese manufacture. Several men were removing a large electric motor from its foundation. How they were going to carry it away and what they would use it for was a mystery to me. The floor of an office was strewn with American, British, and German technical magazines and books. Machines were being smashed just for the perverted joy of destroying something.

Feilzer led the way to the electrical shop, which was on the second floor and as yet undiscovered by the looters. We found the lights we wanted, then paused to go through the desks in the tidy office to see if anything of value had been left behind. I picked up some drawing instruments, pencils, and a small notebook. By this time some Chinese had joined us. They were deferential, and before taking anything they offered it to us first to see if we wanted it.

We made our way back to the truck and drove around to the electrical shop to pick up the lights. On the way back to the gate Feilzer suggested we stop by the galley. I recognized the place by the Chinese rushing away with sacks of flour on their backs. This was the only thing that made any sense to take. In a storeroom, we found cartons of bottled concentrated fruit flavoring with labels in English. We took several cases to make sure we got a good assortment.

I couldn't help but notice the apprehensive haste in which the Chinese rushed about. It seemed unlikely that the local police would take any action, but perhaps the Chinese feared that Russian troops would arrive on the scene and shoot the looters on sight.

When we returned to camp it was afternoon and most of the men were in the barracks eating. I took four bottles of the fruit concentrate to my section and put a bottle on each table, explaining that it was a concentrate and that just a little in a cup of water would be enough to make a pleasant fruit drink. I watched as some of the officers filled their cups with the undiluted liquid. When I told them they couldn't drink it that way, they laughed and pointed to the word *alcohol* on the label. I replied that it was a hell of a way to get drunk.

Although permission to leave the camp was still withheld, a few adventurous souls sneaked out at night to visit the city. With trigger-happy Russian troops about and with the unsettled conditions in the city, this was foolhardy at best.

Some of the men visited Chinese with whom they had worked in the factory. Judging from the condition in which these men returned to the camp, there had been celebrations in progress. One sailor made an unofficial trip to the factory and returned with several quarts of grain alcohol. Mixed with the fruit concentrate and ice water, it made a tasty but powerful drink. I felt that he had done the naval group a good turn in more ways than one; if they could get pleasantly drunk in camp, there was no need to risk sneaking out.

When the initial excitement of the liberation wore off, the days dragged. Even the thrill of having all one wanted to eat passed quickly. It wasn't long before I was getting picky about my food. We were still getting the same fare, but more of it and with some extras. I was gaining more than a pound a day. I could no longer sit down and read a book for more than a few minutes at a time, perhaps because of the break in routine and the impatience at having to wait around in camp knowing that the war was over.

Meanwhile the OSS team was making arrangements with the Russians to evacuate us. They had completed their special mission in freeing Wainwright but had the greater task of getting some three thousand prisoners out of a country in which communications had been disrupted by war and occupation. The Russians considered it too dangerous to move us out by rail; besides, they had military needs to fulfill. An arrangement was made to land B-24s at the airfield. The army wanted to bring in B-29s, but the runways were too lightly constructed.

Usually one B-24 would land each day, bringing in newspapers, magazines, movies, and incidental supplies; it would leave the next morning with twenty to thirty ex-POWs. This shuttle service was encouraging for some but disheartening for others. The highest priority was assigned to hospital cases; then very high rank and staff. After that, rank, health, and age were considered, but each trip was to be made up of all nationalities, in proportion, and enlisted men were to make up half of the list.

I had no complaint about the system, except for the staff members, but I did not care for the prospect of a winter or even an autumn in Manchuria. Attempts to increase the number of planes had indifferent success; the surrender ceremony in Tokyo and the attendant occupation of the islands limited the number of planes available to us. The only logical means for a rapid and large-scale evacuation of the ex-POWs was the railroad. Major Hennessy, the leader of the OSS team, continued his efforts with the Russians, but he could promise nothing.

In time we heard that an atom bomb had been dropped on Nagasaki. We were thankful that we had been shifted to Mukden, but we worried about the friends we had left there. Because the camp was not right in the city of Nagasaki, there was a good chance that they were safe. The other camp in the middle of the city could not possibly have escaped damage. Hoot Horrigan had read a brief description of the bomb in a magazine brought in by one of the B-24s. "This is Buck Rogers stuff," he told us. "They say that the part of the bomb that causes all the damage weighs only seven pounds. That I don't believe."

We were warned not to talk about the bomb to the Russians, because they did not have one and apparently were not going to. It was thought that if someone foolishly boasted to the Russians about the bomb, there would be hard feelings, and getting services from them would be more difficult. After all, they were the law in Manchuria and controlled everything.

The number of officers and men leaving the camp without permission each night increased steadily. When a navy man returned to camp, Captain McMillin had the man brought to "mast"; the review of his misconduct resulted in a few days of brig time as punishment. Our men felt that this was unjust, not because they thought the offense should go unpunished but because the army was not disciplining its cases. It was unfortunate that there was no agreement on a definite policy. My opinion was that the army was being too lax and might easily find itself faced with an unmanageable situation.

One morning, either because the number of AWOLs was getting out of hand or because the Russians had relented, or both, the word was passed that all hands were permitted to leave the camp to visit Mukden. Liberty was to expire at sunset. This was a poorly considered announcement, because no thought had been given to duty sections. As a result practically everyone went "ashore," including the galley detail. The evening meal was late, and there was no check on the number of men out of camp.

I left the camp, after the first rush, with Horrigan and Slone. At the gate were a number of "merchants" offering to buy whatever we had to sell. They had rolls of currency and were probably intending to convert it into something more durable before everyone else found out that there was nothing backing the money now that the Japanese had surrendered. These characters were persistent; when we said that we had nothing to sell, they must have sized us up as shrewd businessmen playing a cagey game. For a quarter of a mile we said we had nothing to sell while the traders tried to pull the shirts off our backs. What saved us was a group of ex-POWs coming out of the camp with arms full of "trade goods."

The road from the camp cut across a corn field and passed several small dwellings before joining the highway. The main road was macadam, so we no longer had to hop over puddles. Our first stop was the firehouse; from its tall brick tower we had an excellent view of the countryside. To the northwest we could make out the hangars of an airdrome; to the southwest, fairly close by, was Mukden. The rest of the circle was made up of rolling plain broken occasionally by a factory compound or farm buildings.

We descended from the tower and headed toward Mukden. The firehouse seemed to mark the end of the "urban" area, for up to that point the buildings that lined the road were cheek to jowl; beyond the firehouse the area abruptly took on a rural air.

Activity increased as we approached the city. First we passed groups of natives selling fruits, vegetables, eggs, and meats; they sat on straw mats with their stock before them. Eggs were in abundance, yet we had not seen any served in our camp; the same went for fruit. It was annoying to think that with so much available, the Japanese had been so stingy.

A steady stream of traffic flowed toward town. Heavy two-wheeled carts drawn by donkeys or oxen, pedal-driven rickshas, and horse-drawn droshkies formed the bulk of the stream, with only an occasional truck loaded with Russian troops. The Russian women looked rugged in uniform—they probably looked rugged anyway—but they seemed attractive after having seen nothing but Asian women for so long.

We passed a restaurant where the food was being prepared and served outdoors. The principal dish seemed to be noodles. A noodle-making machine set up in the yard was getting a good workout.

As we approached Mukden, the buildings were larger and the merchants conducted their business in shops instead of on mats on the roadside. Soon we saw the walls of the city before us. They looked like a continuation of the Great Wall. They were magnificent ruins, although some of the gateways were still in good condition. Outside the walls were several large groups of natives clustered as though they were watching a fight or a crap game. We went up to investigate and found that they were buying, selling, and swapping all kinds of goods. One young fellow was doing a brisk business in long woolen underwear, which he or one of his associates had no doubt looted from a factory or warehouse. Even in the heat of August, the Manchurians did not forget how cold winter could be.

We continued into the city and were surprised to find that the architecture was mostly Western in style and not very attractive. Few shops were open; most had boards over the windows. We heard that there had been a lot of rioting and looting, and we passed a couple of recently burned-out stores. The system seemed to be to start a fire, then, while everyone was rushing about putting out the fire, to start looting.

A movie theater was open and busy. On the sidewalks and in the street, natives were setting up displays of canned goods, fruits, and alcoholic beverages, including "Three Star Cognac"—a 100 octane product if I ever tasted one. Condensed milk and jams, all in cans with English labels, were available at about twenty yen a can. The price didn't bother me, high or low, because I had no money anyway.

We spent most of the afternoon walking about the city, finding it more tiring than interesting. Hoot suggested that we hire a droshky and ride back to camp. We all agreed; the matter of payment could be negotiated at the end of the ride. We started toward camp on a different road from the one we had come on. An American army officer named Mort from the camp was sitting in front of a building and obviously feeling no pain. He urged us to go upstairs for the "best lay in Mukden"; we declined politely. After checking to see that there was another ex-POW upstairs to see him home, we left the officer where we found him.

We passed a large factory compound where Russian troops were on sentry duty. Workers were coming out of the gate as we passed. It surprised us to find a factory still in operation; it may have been the power plant. By the length of our ride we should have reached the camp several times, but there was still no sign of it. We stopped to ask directions at a house where we saw some men. It turned out that they were Japanese, and they acted as if they expected us to put something over on them. We asked the direction back to camp and, figuring nothing ventured nothing gained, asked if they had any sake or beer. They had neither—at least not for sight-seeing ex-POWs— and we didn't press the point.

As we had suspected, we had gone beyond the camp. We doubled back until we reached the turnoff and ended up approaching the camp from the east. Surprisingly, Horrigan produced some currency to pay the driver. It wasn't enough—it never was—so we threw in a couple of packs of cigarettes.

There was a movie that night in the camp, and every night thereafter until we left Mukden. Before the feature we saw combat films and special GI films. I was extremely interested to see the action pictures of battles that had been only names in the Japanese newspapers.

The next day I stayed in camp, thinking I had seen enough of Mukden. I did go outside the gate to trade some old clothes for yen and to buy a dozen eggs. Allen had a can of condensed milk in the barracks, so I supplied the eggs for a delicious eggnog.

That night Herb Levitt came back into camp with a phonograph and a case of symphonic recordings. It seems that he had passed a Japanese record shop that had been looted and decided to take the phonograph and records before someone else did. He suggested that we go back the next day to look the shop over again and to get a meal in town.

The next morning we engaged a droshky as soon as we got outside the gate. The road was crowded with carts going into town. More shops were open than on my previous trip, and things in general seemed to be getting back to normal. We picked up Mort along the way; he seemed fully recovered from his earlier excursion but couldn't tell us how he got back to camp that night.

We rode through the native part of town into the European section. The change was astounding. The streets were wider and well kept. In the "downtown" section were tall, well-designed business buildings and modern-looking apartment houses. A few blocks from the main street were attractive suburban dwellings and a little farther on were imposing mansions. No doubt these had been built prior to the Japanese occupation of Manchuria and had been the residences of the European managers of the foreign-owned factories that had been built during the same period. Japanese were still living in some of the houses, but I noticed that Russian officers occupied a few of them.

On the way back to the record shop, we passed a platoon of Russian soldiers. They were all young boys—from fifteen to eighteen, I guessed. Their uniforms were in bad shape, as if they had not been changed since the start of the invasion of Manchuria. I wondered what kind of home life they had had, brought up in a country that had been at war for four years and hard-pressed most of the time. I wondered what kind of a future was before them.

We found the record shop; the street was comparatively deserted. Telling the driver to wait, we entered the shop. Broken records were strewn on the floor; the drawers of the counter were pulled out. The place had been well gone over, but there were still records on the shelves behind the counter.

We climbed the stairs to the upper floors. Some of the rooms were living quarters and some were used for business. The place had apparently been a camera shop as well, for there were many camera cases on the floor of one room— no cameras, however. Whatever furniture had been there had been removed, by the owners or the looters. We went back down to the store and picked out a few records of European music among the majority of Japanese records.

We left the shop and hurried to the droshky. We had been nervous for fear that Russian soldiers would come along while we were "exploring" and take a shot at us for looting or just for the hell of it.

We told the driver to take us to the Yamata Hotel, the largest hotel in the city, which was being used by the Russians as headquarters. At the hotel, which was a fine-looking five- or six-story building, we told the driver to wait while we went inside.

After the austerity of the prison camp, we were impressed by the entrance and lobby, although the hotel would probably not compare favorably with a second-rate hotel in the States. The rooms were well proportioned and furnished in good taste. The chairs and sofas in the lobby had seen much better days, but they represented a luxury to which we had been unaccustomed for more than three years. To the left of the lobby was a small ballroom with a parquet floor and a small stage. Beyond the ballroom was the dining room; all the tables had cloths on them, although they had obviously been used for several meals. We started to sit down, but a Chinese waiter indicated that meals were served only to the Russian officers living at the hotel. Levitt, who had visited the hotel the day before, told us that he would find us something to eat.

Levitt took us to a service stairway next to the dining room and led us below. We passed through the kitchens, where the Japanese cook gave us a surprised glance, and came to what was apparently a dining room for the hired help. Three Japanese men were seated at a table; they looked up as we sat down but made no attempt to ask us to leave. They all were wearing armbands with Japanese and Russian writing, and we assumed that they were acting as interpreters for the Russians.

The cook came over with a man who asked us in English what we wanted. When we asked for food he said there was none to be had. We asked for a glass of sake; this they couldn't deny because there were full glasses of it on the other table. They brought sake and began talking among themselves, probably wondering who we were and how soon we would leave.

While we were enjoying the sake and congratulating ourselves on being able to get a drink out of a Japanese, the English-speaking Japanese turned to us and asked who we were. Levitt answered that he and I were American naval officers and that Mort, who was wearing his army air force insignia, was an aviator. While the Japanese translated this to his friends, Levitt went on to explain that Mort and he had arrived in Mukden in a B-24 to liberate me and the other prisoners of war. This impressed the Japanese, and the cook brought out bread and butter and cold roast pork. We offered the Japanese some American cigarettes, which they smoked with relish and a good deal of conversation. The Japanese explained that they were interpreters for the Russians and as such took their meals at the hotel. He pointed out that we were eating Russian bread and butter, which was not usually served in Japan.

By this time we had gotten quite chummy, and more sake was brought to the table, this time in small bottles and superior to the sake we had been drinking. (The ordinary brand of sake comes in liter bottles and would compare to house wine. Our second round was, no doubt, of vintage quality.)

Then the Japanese began talking about aircraft and mentioned that he would like to see Mukden from the air. Levitt, who never missed a cue, asked him if he would like to take a ride in a B-24 over the city. The English-speaking Japanese translated this, and while they were discussing the prospect, the cook, who was good on cues himself, brought out three plates of curry and rice.

While we ate our meal, which was delicious (we had been used to rice in Japan but had gotten none in Manchuria), Levitt explained that we would have to check with the *shosa* (major) in charge of the plane because he himself was only a *cho-i* (ensign). This was understandable to the Japanese. Levitt also explained that the plane had been scheduled to leave Mukden the day before but had been delayed for repairs.

We had all entered into the spirit of the game. The Japanese asked if his friends could go along as well. We all nodded and told them how much room there was in a B-24. The Japanese then suggested that we all meet at the hotel the next day and have lunch together, on the Russians, before going to the airfield. This was agreed upon, and, because there was no more sake, we said good-bye to our friends.

I was embarrassed to have been a partner in leading the Japanese down the garden path. I consoled myself with the thought that the Japanese hadn't shown us a good time in prison camp and were just getting back some of their own punishment, but I did not have the "brass" to join the party planned for the next day. Levitt and Mort did, accompanied by a couple of other ex-POWs, and had a pleasant lunch. They explained that the plane was still not ready and required more work. The Japanese seemed satisfied with the explanation.

A day or so later I walked into town with Les Naylor to get away from the boredom of camp. We walked aimlessly about town and finally decided to hail a droshky to see the scenery in the foreign section of town. On the way we passed a couple of ex-POWs unloading a droshky parked in front of an apartment house. We stopped to see what was going on; when we found that they were unloading beer, we stayed to help.

For some reason they were not anxious to have our help. We found out why when I saw the attractive Russian girl who was leading the way to the apartment. It turned out that the two ex-POWs had moved in with two sisters and their parents. It was a very cozy arrangement. The two fellows gave us a couple of bottles of beer to see us on our way—with directions to the brewery.

We immediately opened the bottles. The beer was warm but we were thirsty. Although we were occasionally doubtful of our way, we were always reassured when we passed another droshky heading back well loaded with cases of beer. At a large railroad station at the edge of the foreign business section, Russian soldiers armed with tommy guns and carbines were herding Japanese troops and civilians into the streets. The Russians seemed to be using Mukden as a concentration center for Japanese in the area. After a sorting-out process, the Japanese were reloaded on the trains. We expected that most of them, especially the troops, would go to Siberia. The idea seemed to be to clear all Japanese out of Manchuria.

The Japanese women with their children were a sad sight. They carried their babies on their backs and led the children who were old enough to walk by the hand. Thus encumbered it was impossibe to carry more than one pack or bundle of possessions. The young, unmarried women were in a better position and presumably helped the women with children. The only men in the civilian group were past middle age, but some of them seemed sturdy. The Japanese troops were in fine shape, looking well dressed and well fed; their officers looked just as arrogant as ever and still stood apart from their men. All groups were silent, and the vacant expressions on most faces were probably not attributable so much to Japanese impassiveness as to the shock of the sudden reversal of fortune.

The shouting, dirty Russian troops in charge of the proceedings seemed to have the Japanese well cowed. Occasionally a shot would ring out as a trigger-happy Russian lent emphasis to his orders. The Japanese under his surveillance milled about like sheep. I figured that the Japanese falling into Russian hands were worse off than we had been as prisoners of the Japanese. Of course, if we had lost the war we would probably have remained slaves of the Japanese until they were ready to send us home. *Vae victis.*

We did not stay in the vicinity of the prisoners any longer than necessary for the droshky to pass. We headed south along a road paralleling the railroad and turned right at the first underpass. A block beyond the railroad we came upon a crowd of ex-POWs with droshkies and wagons gathered before the gates of a compound.

We were told that this was the brewery but that the gates had been closed and we might not be able to get any beer. A drunken Russian soldier was shouting and waving his arms at the gates. Then he pounded on a door and shouted to a Japanese within to open up the gates. When the gates opened the Russian waved us all in.

From the gatehouse it was a short drive through a landscaped compound to the storehouse, where other ex-POWs were bringing out cases of beer. Naylor and I went into the storehouse and brought out one case of beer each, thinking that would be sufficient. An American soldier from our camp shook his head and said, "That Russian won't let you out of here unless the axles are about to break."

We went back in and got three more cases, which our driver and his helper cheerfully loaded into the droshky. We climbed into our seats and sat with our legs stretched out over the beer. The fifth case was between us, readily accessible for the long journey back to camp. Our carriage was top-heavy with the load, and we had to hang on precariously at each turn. We must have taken sufficient beer, for we were not turned back at the gate.

Our "footman" leaned back and opened the case for us. He deftly removed the caps of a couple of bottles on the whip holder and passed the bottles back to us. We did not mind the beer being warm, and we finished off the quarts in a surprisingly short time. While the "footman" opened two more bottles, we passed a couple of bottles to him and the driver. They drank their beer slowly, and whenever we passed a group of Chinese, our men made a great show with their bottles. Naylor, who had spent a lot of time in Hong Kong before the war, explained that they were doing this to make "face" in front of their countrymen.

Twice along the way back to camp, we passed Russian soldiers working on trucks at the side of the road. We handed out a few bottles of beer to them to prevent being stopped and possibly losing all the beer. It wasn't long before Naylor and I had pleasant glows, and though it might not have been apparent to anyone else, we "owned Mukden."

It was dusk when we reached the camp gates, and we had the problem of paying off the driver and getting our beer to the barracks. I rushed inside the gates and gathered up an armful of old clothes from a nearby pile to solve the first problem; willing friends solved the second one. In the barracks I kept one case of beer for myself and distributed the other case among my friends in the section. Naylor did the same in the British section.

That night I invited the officers from our Nagasaki camp to finish off my case of beer. It went very fast, even though there were other parties going on that night. Some of the officers had gotten hold of Chinese whiskey and "brandy"—vile but potent stuff. There were headaches the next morning, but no one had gone blind. I don't know whether the credit for that goes to the quality of the whiskey or to our rugged constitutions.

The ease with which the beer had been obtained from the brewery that first day inspired other officers in the camp to try their luck. Naylor didn't feel like going out again, so I decided to stay in the camp too. That afternoon most of the beer foragers came back empty-handed. One British party had had a harrowing experience. To carry a large load of beer, they had procured a wagon with two horses and driven it to the brewery. As they left the brewery with their load, more than a hundred cases, Russians drove up in a jeep, promptly shot both the horses, and ordered the British to turn around and start marching. At first they thought they would be shot themselves, but after marching for about five minutes they found that the Russians had gone back into the brewery. As if they had not had enough adventure for the day, on the way home they got embroiled in a riot between Chinese factions. It was a miracle that the ex-POWs were not hurt.

Almost from the first day that we had been allowed into Mukden, a steady stream of Japanese souvenirs poured into camp. Rifles, swords, cameras, and binoculars were brought in every day. Booth, in my section, never missed a day in town although his legs ached from "dry" beriberi. One day he came back with half a dozen swords and sabers, a rifle, a pistol, a camera, two pairs of binoculars, and a case of beer. The space at the head of his bunk began to look like an arsenal. Later he cut down his inventory by trading or giving away the less desirable pieces. Another souvenir hunter came back with a coupe (a carriage and a team of horses) but had to return them when the owner complained to the American camp commander.

About a week after our liberation, B-29s were sent over our camp to drop supplies of food, clothing, and cigarettes. During the first drop, parcels with unopened chutes sailed through the roofs of several buildings. No one was hurt, but in order to keep a roof over our heads it was decided that future drops would be made in the field outside the camp.

The B-29s would come in low with the bomb bays open. When the load was released, a series of bright parachutes would open and float to the ground. More often the chutes would fail to open and the cartons of rations would whistle to the ground and land with a loud plop. The cartons of cocoa exploded with a puff of brown "smoke," and the boxes that missed the field sent up geysers of muddy water from the adjacent swamp.

All hands joined in collecting the supplies and in beating off the Chinese who tried to collect some for themselves. All undamaged goods had to be turned over to the quartermasters; damaged goods could be kept by the finders. Despite losses, a sizable number of supplies were collected. There must have been a ton of chewing gum.

One day a Russian USO troupe gave a performance in camp. It was a variety show with acrobats and dancers—an all-male cast. As entertainment it was more suited for a ten year old, but the performers were enthusiastic and reasonably proficient. To show our appreciation, at the end of the performance we threw cigarettes, chewing gum, and candy into blankets that some ex-POWs held out. The Russians made a good haul.

The next day I was to see the same show in town. Horrigan put my name down for a dinner and drinking bout that the Russians had arranged; they had asked for ten officers as guests. The USO show at the auditorium of the Russian barracks was to be followed by a party at the officers' quarters. I figured the party would compensate for having to sit through the show again.

The Russians provided a bus for us, and we set off in a party mood. The barracks were formerly a school, a three-story red brick building. While waiting for the show to start, we went up to the second floor to look around. The rooms were tidy, but most of the Russian men needed baths. All the toilet bowls were stopped up, and there seemed to have been no attempt to clear them. Most of the Russians were friendly and smiled at us, not noticing our annoyance.

When the general arrived, the show began. He was escorting a tall woman wearing an evening gown. From where I sat she seemed attractive. Whether she was the general's wife or just local talent I never found out. I managed to get through the show by concentrating on the terrific party that was going to follow.

When the hall was cleared, we waited to be introduced to the general and to set out for the party. One of our group who was checking on details came over after speaking to a Russian officer and explained that the party was only for officers of the rank of major and above. This left out half of us. Horrigan said that if that was the way they felt about it, he wouldn't go either. Only three from our group went. The rest of us got a ride back in the bus and arrived in camp after dark.

I was taken aback by the attitude of the Russian general. I had thought that the Russians were not class- or rank-conscious, that they were good-natured although hard-drinking and inclined to play rough occasionally. No doubt there had been a misunderstanding, but common courtesy should have prevailed. But I suppose a country that had killed off its ruling class and either forced into exile or liquidated its middle class takes time to learn manners.

There was little in Mukden to attract me after the brewery closed. Occasionally I went outside the gates to buy eggs from the Manchurians. Prices were increasing, but I would take an extra shirt or pair of trousers to trade. One day I brought back a dozen eggs for an eggnog. Allen had another can of condensed milk, but Slone produced the ingredient that made the trip worthwhile—a bottle of cognac (Mukden's best, three weeks old). At first it seemed that the cognac would curdle the mixture, but Manchurian eggs and milk were made of sterner stuff. It was a powerful drink, and we were glad that the eggs and milk diminished the potency.

A loudspeaker had been set up in camp. When "Sentimental Journey" was not being played, we heard the story of Herman and his three little Messerschmidts, or something to that effect. It was a Disney-like story of how the air force shot up the Luftwaffe. At least we had been spared some of the atrocities of the war.

I spent part of each day working out on a horizontal bar that had been set up at one end of the parade ground. I hoped to convert a little of my newly regained weight to muscle. The rest of the time I spent reading or talking over our prospects of an early return home. The rate at which the B-24s were taking exprisoners back seemed slow, although I knew that the army air force was doing an excellent job.

New movies were brought in each day, along with newspapers and service newspaper correspondents. One of the correspondents, a Sergeant Friendly, whose name suited his personality, gave lectures in the camp about the European campaign. His lectures drew large crowds. He told us about the "Patton Incident" and identified "The Voice" as Frank Sinatra.

His story about General Montgomery and General Eisenhower was new to us. As the Allied invasion fleet neared the French coast, Montgomery and Eisenhower, who had embarked on a British destroyer to get a closer view of the operation, urged the skipper to get in closer to the beach. The captain, who had been warned of minefields near the coast, nevertheless obeyed the orders of the supreme commander. The ship hit a mine and sank. Eisenhower floundered about in the water and was going down for the third time when Montgomery grabbed ahold of him and pulled him aboard a raft. When they both regained their breath, Eisenhower turned to Montgomery and said, "I'd consider it a favor, Monty, if you wouldn't mention, when you get ashore, that I can't swim." "Righto, Ike," replied Montgomery, "but will you neglect to tell them that I can't walk on water?"

One day Les Naylor and I took a walk out of camp to get a change of scenery. We followed the road in the opposite direction from Mukden for a while and then walked along the bank of a stream to take us back in the direction of the camp. We came upon the ruins of brick kilns and climbed inside. The floors of the kilns were overgrown with weeds, and grass was sprouting from the round walls.

We crossed the stream at a wooden bridge and started back to camp. On the way we passed a compound where Japanese families were interned. A little farther on we came to a village with a few small shops. A couple of drunken Russians accosted us in the village. We exchanged greetings and explained as best we could that we had been prisoners in the nearby camp. When the Russians began to display an interest in my watch, I was anxious to break off the conversation. They had pistols, and we were not sure that they would not use them to relieve us of valuables. We left without incident and after a short walk reached the camp. Just outside the camp was the wreck of a Japanese biplane. Some Russians had taken the plane for a joyride and had cracked up near our camp. Men from the camp had brought the Russians to our sick bay, where they stayed until they could be safely moved.

After repeated attempts to convince the Russians to evacuate the ex-POWs by rail, at last Major Hennessy received permission. One morning in the middle of September, the first of two groups assembled to be transported to the railroad station in Mukden. The second group was scheduled to leave the next day. Most of the officers were in the first group along with an equal number of enlisted men. Levitt and Captain Hoeffel were in the second group with all the naval enlisted men. We climbed aboard American lend-lease trucks at the camp gate and headed for town. At last we were on our way home.

At the station a special train was waiting, and we were told to get aboard quickly to avoid giving the Russians any excuse for holding up the train. The station was crowded with Russians. Apparently a train had just arrived from the north, for there were a number of Russian women in civilian clothes on the platforms. We watched the women until our train pulled out.

The train did not travel as fast as the one we had taken to Mukden, but we assumed that with the disruptions of the occupation, rail traffic was proceeding more cautiously. Some of the group had brought bottles of sake and whiskey, which were passed around to relieve the tedium of the journey. That evening we found that Russian soldiers were making the trip with us. They got drunk on the liquor they had brought along, and began firing their pistols out the windows; this immediately cleared the car in their vicinity. We were relieved when they decided to go to another car.

With the frequent stops and the slow speed, the train covered about 150 miles in twelve hours. That left another 100 miles to go to Dairen. We had a long stop just after daybreak at a station where we were allowed to leave the cars. The stationmaster was Japanese and so were his assistants; they seemed to be carrying on much as they would have under the Japanese regime.

We washed up at a water spigot on the platform and went back aboard the train. For breakfast we had army field rations that had been dropped in Mukden by the B-29s. Natives gathered outside the cars and offered grapes and apples for sale. We threw chewing gum to them as a gift, but we had to instruct them not to swallow it. As the train again began to move, the price of the fruit tumbled.

In the afternoon the train stopped for about an hour, and we wandered about at the sides of the tracks. The sun was hot, and we kept in the shade of the trees near the right-of-way. When the train started this time, we hoped the next stop would be Dairen, but after a few miles we stopped at another station for several hours. At last a northbound train reached the station and the track was clear for us. The other train was moving Russians and their equipment. Flatcars were loaded with tanks, trucks, household effects, cranes, and drunken Russians of both sexes. Some of the Russians wore civilian clothes; I thought that they might have been White Russians who had agreed to go back to Russia with the Reds.

This proved to be our last stop until we reached the vicinity of Dairen. A few miles from Dairen we passed through attractive countryside with rolling hills and prosperous-looking farms. Shortly after passing through a wooded section, we saw a large airfield that extended from the railroad to the hills in the west. About five hundred Japanese planes of all types were parked on the field in neat rows.

As we approached the city of Dairen the train slowed. We passed the usual slums near the tracks, where ragged Chinese children ran to watch the train. We caught a brief view of the harbor and could make out the silhouettes of American cruisers at anchor offshore. The train pulled into the freight yards near the port area and stopped, then it was switched onto another track and crept along to the next switch.

It was dark before the train stopped to allow us to disembark. Off to the left we could see the lights of a ship tied up at a pier. As we approached we could hear American swing music being played over the ship's loudspeaker system. Then we got a clear view of the ship illuminated by cargo lights. It was a U.S. Navy hospital ship, the USS *Relief.* Her gleaming white sides with the broad green stripe and her white stacks with lighted red crosses gave her a holiday look.

On deck were nurses in stiff white uniforms, and seamen in white uniforms lined the rails to watch our homecoming. For the first time on our trip I felt nervous and uncertain. This was what we had awaited for those long years. Somehow I felt that I had suddenly lost something. From the time I had climbed aboard that Japanese destroyer in the Java Sea three and a half years ago, my one thought had been to get back to the States. Now that my desire was in effect fulfilled, I had to find another objective.

We lined up to go aboard the hospital ship. It was hours before everyone was aboard; each ex-POW was registered and given a ward assignment. I was directed to a tidy air-conditioned ward where I received a Red Cross toilet kit, a pair of pajamas, and a pair of slippers. I lined up to take a bath in a real bathtub. Then I climbed between the sheets on my bunk; the innerspring mattress was almost too soft but I managed to get used to it. One of the nurses came into the ward to see Doctor Smith, Fraleigh, and Langdon, with whom she had served in the hospital on Corregidor. She and the other navy nurses on Corregidor had been taken off by submarine before the fall of the island. Smith had a cold, and the nurse rushed off to get him medicine and a shot of brandy. Horrigan remarked from a nearby bunk that he wished he was a navy doctor with a cold. I don't know whether he wanted the attention of the nurse or the brandy, or both.

The next morning we awoke to find that we were well at sea. After dressing we went down into the mess compartment, where we took our meals cafeteria style. I saw some of my British friends at breakfast, and they wanted to know if the U.S. Navy always fed us this way. Even without the comparison of prison camp fare, the food was excellent.

At 11 A.M. ice cream was brought to the ward; we also received a two-dollar book of chits for use in the ship's store, where we could purchase cigarettes, candy, and toilet articles. One day a piano was moved into the ward and a section of the ship's band played music for about an hour.

Two destroyer escorts, a type of ship that was unfamiliar to me, accompanied our ship. One of the seamen explained to me that it was a small destroyer, yet it was larger than the *Pope*. Destroyer escorts were needed because the area through which we were passing had many floating mines that had been dropped by our own aircraft to harass Japanese shipping; the rest were Japanese mines that had become detached from their anchors. As soon as a mine was sighted, the escorts would stop and fire machine guns at the mine until it was sunk.

Everyone on the *Relief* displayed a sympathetic attitude toward us. However, I expected the ship's officers to seek out the naval officers among our group and invite us to the wardroom for a cup of coffee, if not a small meal. This was not done except in the case of the doctors, who had the rank of captain and were known to the ship's doctors.

Dave Nash brought this to the attention of the ship's executive officer, pointing out that Captain Pederson, who was senior to the ship's captain, had not been shown any of the little courtesies that in the prewar navy had always been taken for granted. But then, a hospital ship is a backwash of the navy and the officers are inclined to become apathetic.

Everyone I saw, from the officers on down, was busy counting his "points." We soon learned that a point system had been instituted to determine when personnel would be eligible to go back to the States for separation. This preoccupation with whether it would be one month or the next was incomprehensible to us. One individual said, "You fellows are lucky; you'll go right home."

Just before we reached Okinawa, our destination, we had to stay at sea an extra day or two because of a typhoon. When it hit us, the ship reduced speed to ride out the storm. We were fairly comfortable aboard despite the heavy seas. As Blain said, "She rides this out like a dignified old lady." Our escorts rolled heavily in the seas, and one of the ship's doctors told us that several destroyers had been lost in typhoons during the Okinawa campaign. We had to forgo our usual evening movies, but this was no hardship because at this stage of the trip the programs were being repeated.

After the storm we anchored in a bay off Okinawa. There were more naval vessels than I had ever seen in one place, more than there had been at Long Beach before the fleet maneuvers in 1939. Here was just a part of the war production that had made the victory possible. Despite their modernization we were able to recognize some of the old battleships; nearly everything else was of wartime vintage.

The next morning was bright and clear, and just before noon landing craft came out to the ship to take us ashore. The waves in the harbor were still high from the storm, and we had to jump into the landing craft from the ladder on the ship's side.

We landed at a pier constructed of steel floats and were met by army trucks. On the way to the Repatriated American Military Personnel (RMAP) camp, we passed all kinds of vehicles. Most of us had seen jeeps and the other usual military vehicles before, but we were not prepared for boats that ran on wheels when ashore or for the amphibious tanks.

The camp consisted of tents for sleeping quarters and semipermanent buildings for mess halls and supply buildings. There was an open-air theater ("The Coconut Bowl"), and the Red Cross had set up a stand to distribute soda and candy bars. Clothing and field boots from army supplies were issued to ex-POWs of all nationalities.

Trucks arrived in a steady stream, and reunions took place throughout the entire camp. I saw Syred, Farley, Rinaman, Budding, and the other officers we had left in Nagasaki. We asked them about the atomic bomb explosion and were relieved to learn that no one in our camp had been injured. They had seen the flash of the explosion and thought that a bomber had scored a direct hit on an ammunition factory; they had laughed when the Japanese claimed that only one bomb had been dropped to cause such damage. The prison camp in Nagasaki proper, which had been near the center of the blast, had had some casualties.

Levitt and his party arrived in camp shortly after we did. Their transport had hit a mine en route. Several men in the ship's crew were killed by the explosion, but the ship was not too seriously damaged to proceed.

Later I saw many of the British and Dutch enlisted men who had been in our camp. One of the Indonesians from my party in the foundry came over to greet me. "Remember the fellow who was sent away for striking his honcho?" he asked. "We all thought he would never come back. Come over and say hello to him."

The man was looking fit. I told him how glad I was that he was all right and how we had all felt so bad when Budding made the trip to bring back what were supposed to be his ashes. He was all smiles to be back with his friends again and said that the treatment in the punishment camp had not been too bad.

I hardly recognized the British sailors from our camp. They had been brought back in an American aircraft carrier and were all wearing U.S. Navy dungarees. Several of the men wanted to know how they could sign up in our navy. I asked them about my men, and they said that if they were not here already they would arrive soon. Some of my men had taken off from the camp as soon as they had heard that American ships had reached Japan, hoping to start homeward as quickly as possible.

The army started moving ex-POWs by air to Manila almost immediately. Groups of forty to fifty left camp every hour. Navy personnel were not included in these groups; we were to be taken to Guam for "processing" (physical examinations and intelligence interrogations).

Because we were to leave by naval transport, and there was no possibility of our leaving on short notice, Levitt and I decided to see Okinawa. We thumbed a ride to the opposite side of the island, where we hoped to visit one of the new cruisers or carriers. The ships were anchored so far offshore, however, that we decided it would be too long a trip out and back.

Instead we went to an officers' club, where the bar was scheduled to open shortly. Most of the officers we met were discussing their prospects of an early return home. The officers who had invited us were from LSTs (landing ship, tank) that had brought the army outfits to Okinawa. They had worked out a good arrangement: the navy supplied fresh provisions from the ships, and the army the liquor.

One group asked us to join them in a trip to an army camp where they had been invited to a party. Six of us piled into a jeep and tore along the dark highway. When we reached the camp the party was in full swing; all the gathering lacked was women.

It was the early hours of the morning before the drinking bout ended. We were surprised at our capacity after the long layoff in prison camp, but the few weeks in Mukden after the surrender must have put us back in condition. We turned in at the headquarters tent for a few hours of sleep.

Music from the camp's public address system woke us the next morning. On the way back to camp, our friends pointed out a spot where soldiers had been killed after the island had been reported "secured" (enemy resistance ended); some Japanese who had holed up in a cave had made a suicide attack on an encampment, killing about twenty men before being killed themselves. We passed through the shambles of the town of Naha. On the shoals off the beach was the wreckage of amphibious tanks that had been caught in Japanese gunfire.

We reached camp, thanked our friends for the entertainment, and learned that the naval group had already left for the transport. While we were waiting for a truck to take us to the pier, I met Hoot Horrigan's brother, who had flown from a nearby island to see Hoot. Meanwhile Hoot was on the other side of the island trying to visit another brother aboard a destroyer escort.

The truck got us to the pier in plenty of time. We walked over to a group at the end of the pier and found that my men from Nagasaki were among them. Everyone had come through all right except Rasmussen, who had died in Japan a few weeks after the surrender.

A landing craft took us out to the transport, the *Rixey*, a former Alcoa Line ship. Our quarters were shared with aviators on their way back to the States for discharge on points. Some of them had been awarded a couple of Navy Crosses but were loath to admit that they had done anything outstanding. A Seabee officer, also returning home, told us about the Normandy invasion preparations and the actual invasion. His chief occupation after the invasion had been to fix up a French château for the commander of our naval forces in Europe.

I did not recognize the harbor at Guam. Wharves and warehouses had replaced the beaches and palms around the bay. The last time I had seen the harbor, there had been three ships in the bay; now there were dozens, as well as a large floating dry dock. Where there had been only an anchorage, now there were piers for deep-draft vessels to go alongside. I wondered what Governor McMillin would think of the island now.

We disembarked soon after the ship tied up and were taken to Fleet Hospital 103 for processing. The hospital, which looked permanent, was a collection of specially laid-out Quonset huts with comfortable, clean wards. This was reportedly one of several hospitals built for the casualties expected in the invasion of Japan. We were given a thorough physical checkup. One of the officers in our group was diagnosed with tuberculosis after his chest X-rays were developed. The rest of us had nothing wrong that good food wouldn't cure.

There were movies every night. The enlisted ex-POWs were given free beer at the canteen, and all our drinks were on the house at the officers' club. We even danced with the nurses, all of whom seemed beautiful. A USO troupe presented a mediocre play, but it was a change from the movies. We felt right at home in the ward, even to the extent of raiding the icebox when we came back from the club.

The Seabee officer who had been with us in the transport came to the hospital one night to take us to the Seabee encampment. The club there consisted of two Quonsets that had been built together to form a T. A dining room and porch occupied the leg of the T, and the galley and the bar occupied the arms. Tropical flowers and a banana tree were planted to one side of the barroom. Leatherette seats lined the walls, and over the bar was a mermaid in a fishbowl. Our host explained that since the Seabees had to build all the camps, they always saw to it that theirs was the best.

We got back to the hospital in time to see the nurses being returned to their quarters by their swains. The nurses lived in a stockade that was guarded by marine sentries. Floodlights at the entrance to the quarters and around the sides prevented any guests uninvited or otherwise. There were a few torrid farewells being made in the glare of the lights. I wondered why that could not have been taken care of before reaching the quarters. The sentries may have gotten a few vicarious pleasures, however.

While looking through the hospital newspaper I noticed that a Captain Carter was executive officer of the hospital. I telephoned to find out if this was my old shipmate, Doctor Carter, from the *Salt Lake City*. It was, and I was invited to his quarters for a drink and dinner. His first remark was, "I thought you were dead." We discussed our friends from our old ship, and I learned that most of them were still alive.

Our former skipper, Captain Allen, was also on Guam. I called him, and he invited me to dinner for the following evening. I was disappointed that he had not been promoted to rear admiral, for he had been an excellent skipper and an outstanding officer. On our trip to Guam in 1940, he had had the ship made ready for action in case the Japanese attempted to create an "incident." I felt somehow that with more officers of his mind-set, the debacle at Pearl Harbor would instead have been a crushing Japanese defeat.

Captain Allen was living at what had been Commander in Chief, Pacific Fleet (CINCPAC) headquarters before the war moved closer to Japan. The quarters consisted of three prefabricated bungalows with adjoining gardens. We had dinner with the senior naval officer of the Marianas (the archipelago of which Guam and Saipan were part) and his staff.

The meal was delicious and well served by the Chamorro mess boys. We had drinks before and after the meal and pleasant conversation throughout. The chief of staff had been commanding officer of the *Augusta,* which had been relieved by the *Houston* as flagship of the Asiatic Fleet, and he wanted to know all about the sinking of the *Houston.* Captain Allen had once commanded a division of destroyers in the same fleet; he sadly counted off the ships that had been sunk. At the end of the evening Captain Allen sent me back to the hospital in his car.

A few days later I received orders to proceed to the States and was given a class three priority to travel by plane. Most of the other officers were scheduled to go back by transport, which would take about two weeks. I was lucky to run into a couple of shipmates from the old "Swayback Maru."

I left for the airfield early in the morning. A cold rain was falling, and I was afraid that the flight would be cancelled. We took off only a few minutes late; I guess the pilots were used to flying in worse weather.

The plane was a C-47 that had been used as an ambulance plane. An attractive hostess (seaman first class—what was the navy coming to?) checked to see that safety belts were fastened and, after the plane was in the air, brought us hot coffee. She told us about a crash landing she had made: all the passengers formed a huddle on the floor of the cabin and held tight (someone suggested that she was the reason they all held tight) while the plane landed without serious injury to anyone.

We landed at one of the Pacific atolls, Eniwetok, I think, where we had our evening meal. We waited at a Red Cross hut, where we read magazines until it was time to board another plane. Most of us slept on the next leg of the journey and awoke to find that we were still over the ocean. We landed at an airfield near Pearl Harbor and were met by station wagons from the Aiea Heights Naval Hospital.

I hardly recognized the road to Pearl Harbor. What had once been a three-lane road was now a six-lane highway; where sugarcane had once lined the road were now rows of Quonset-style warehouses. On the way to the hospital we got a view of the harbor, which was crowded with ships. Before the war, Aiea Heights had been a wilderness; now, a huge, modern hospital dominated the area as though it had always been there.

As soon as I got settled, I put through a call to New York. Mother and Dad had received my letters from Mukden, and Fred Feilzer, who had left Mukden by plane before me, had arrived in New York and seen my parents. My brother, Frank, was in the army and married; my parents hadn't told me in their letters because they thought it would make me feel bad in prison camp. All the girls I had known before the war were married and raising families. I felt like Rip van Winkle, but not as old.

That evening I went to the officers' club of the hospital. I felt strange being back in civilization. I didn't dance at the club; it and the music seemed futile and meaningless. The drinks made sense, but the bar closed before we had a chance to prove otherwise. Some of the other ex-POWs went into Honolulu, but I preferred to get to bed early in case a plane was leaving in the morning.

The next day we were told that we would leave by plane that evening. Some men from the *Pope* who had stayed in Makassar when I left for Japan arrived in the hospital and sought me out to give me the names of the men who had died in Makassar. About thirty had died after I left, mainly from malaria. The Japanese had made the prisoners fill in a swamp a mile or so from the camp and build a new camp on the filled ground. Dysentery was another cause of death; the new camp did not have a proper sewage system.

A month or so before the war ended, a group of prisoners was shipped from Makassar to Java, including Jack Fisher. The men told me that to the best of their knowledge the group had not reached Java. Sadly I marked their names on my list as missing. There was no word on the other officers who had been transferred to Java a year or so earlier.

The men were all very thin but in excellent spirits. They wanted to know about our group that had gone to Japan, and were saddened to hear about the deaths of Kirk, McCreary, and Rasmussen. After comparing lots, I decided that my trip to Japan had not been a bad move after all.

I left the hospital late in the afternoon with some Canadian ex-POWs. At the airfield we had to wait several hours for our plane, a navy flying boat. In the waiting room I met Captain Pederson from Mukden. He had gone to Manila from Okinawa and was now awaiting an army plane to take him to the States. While I wandered around killing time, I noticed a car in the parking lot that looked familiar. It was the same model and had the same list to port as the "Flying Wombat," a car I had owned in partnership with three other officers from the *Salt Lake City* in 1940. I felt certain that it was the same car, and I had the strange feeling of being carried back five years to many happy days.

We boarded just before sunset and took our places in the tiers of seats in the after part of the plane. About an hour after takeoff, a seaman crew member called us to dinner in the "dining room," a compartment with tables and seats for eight. The dinner, which had been cooked on the plane, was fricasseed chicken; it was delicious. After dinner we made ourselves as comfortable as we could in the seats and slept. The trip back would have been more pleasant by ship, but I felt that saving time made the discomfort worthwhile.

The mountains of California were in sight when we awoke in the morning. Soon we were landing on San Francisco Bay. A boat met us at the moorings and took us to the naval air station at Oakland. Station wagons picked us up at the landing and took us to a hangar, where we had breakfast at a Red Cross canteen. The women serving us looked as if they might have had sons in the service. I thought they were wonderful to be up at that hour to serve us hot coffee and sandwiches.

Transportation arrived in a little while to take us to Oak Knolls Naval Hospital. It was well named—there wasn't a flat piece of ground anywhere. I was assigned a bed in a cheerful ward where I met other officers who were ex-POWs. After a medical examination by the ward doctor, we were told that we could leave the next day as soon as we got checked out at the administration building. That night I called my mother and father again to let them know I would soon be home. Later I went to the officers' club, an elaborate place that had once been a country club. There I learned of the abomination called "scotch type" whiskey. Fortunately there was real scotch available, and the bartender took pity on me as an ex-POW.

Late the next afternoon, after filling out a number of forms and after an interview by a naval intelligence officer, I was given my orders. While waiting for the station wagon to take me to the airfield, I met Dr. Eppley, who had been in the Nagasaki camp with me. He was waiting to see his wife, who had been sent home from Guam early in 1941. It was not surprising that he was a little nervous.

It was dark when the plane took off. A few hours later we landed to refuel. A bus took us to an all-night restaurant on the other side of the field, where we had ham and eggs. When we returned the plane was ready to take off.

We landed in Kansas early the next morning to await a plane that would take us to Washington. An attractive WAVE checked us in at the desk, and I realized that I had been missing more than the navy's good food in prison camp. Soldiers and sailors slept on the benches in the waiting room; some of them had been waiting for more than twenty-four hours to catch a ride home. I was lucky to have a priority; I boarded a plane after less than an hour's wait.

The plane was equipped with chair seats instead of the usual bucket seats, and a WAVE brought us coffee. During the afternoon the pilots turned on the World Series game and rigged an extra set of earphones so that we could take turns listening to it. I must have been somewhat apathetic, for I didn't know who was playing and didn't care who won.

We landed at National Airport in Washington about 4 P.M. A station wagon was waiting to take me to Bethesda Naval Hospital. There was a chill in the air, and the leaves were beginning to turn. Washington was beautiful on this autumn afternoon.

At the hospital, which looked like a misplaced skyscraper, I was assigned a comfortable room on the eighth floor. My checkup, which was to take more than a week, would begin the next morning. As an ex-POW, I had all meals served in my room; other ambulant patients had to take their meals in the cafeteria.

I was allowed to go into Washington during the afternoon, and I bought winter uniforms and a raincoat. Bassett from the *Pope* and Fulton from the *Houston* were also at Bethesda, but because they had arrived a week before me, they were just leaving. I met Bassett's wife; she had left the Philippines in 1941 before my arrival there. In spite of what we may have gone through in prison camp, I think it was much harder for the wives and parents who had to wait at home and wonder whether their husbands and sons would return. And I think it was more difficult for the married men in prison camp than it was for us single men.

One day I went over to the Navy Department to make my report on the *Pope* and *Perch* personnel. I found that the Department of Navigation was now the Bureau of Naval Personnel, a more appropriate title. At the bureau I ran into Captain Blinn and Antrim, who had returned before me and who were writing a report of the POWs' last action.

Both Blinn and Antrim were still showing the effects of beriberi. We exchanged experiences, and I learned that the people I had put down as missing while I was in Hawaii were all safe. Some of the *Houston* survivors were also at the bureau writing reports. I told them about meeting Levitt, Connor, and Rafalovich. Later Spears and Wilson from the *Pope* joined us. Both of them were badly swollen from beriberi. The propaganda camp at Zentsuji had not been so good toward the end of the war; they had been moved to the Japanese "Alps," where they were literally eating the grass off the ground and the bark from the trees. I began to realize that on the whole I had been fortunate in my prison camp assignments.

A few days later Bill Spears invited us all to a cocktail party at his home in Washington. Bill's mother had corresponded with the families of all the men on the *Pope* and had exchanged information from the prison camps. It must have been especially hard on her with one son in prison camp, another lost on the *Vincennes,* a third son a naval aviator, and her husband, an admiral, away most of the time. Now her husband and two of her sons were back, but I could see that she still grieved her lost son.

At last the hospital finished all its tests on me, and I was permitted to go home. My orders allowed me ninety days' leave before I returned to active duty. In my rush to get away from the hospital, I did not send a telegram home. I caught the train seconds before it pulled out, and by that time I felt I would get home before a telegram arrived.

I settled back for the trip but couldn't rest. Now that I was on the last leg of my journey, my mind kept jumping back to the past. I thought of Manila and the fun I'd had there. Events of the war and incidents in prison camp came back to me, but they seemed distant. It was hard to realize that three and a half years had passed by—wasted. It seemed that the year 1945 followed 1941 and that the time between was an unrelated memory.

It was late in the evening when I reached New York. Rather than spend time calling home, I rushed for a cab, which I shared with a chief petty officer of the Coast Guard. He was on his way home for a few days' leave before reporting to a separation center. He dropped me off at my street and continued uptown.

There had been no changes in the block where we lived, or at least none that I could see. I pushed the button in the vestibule and the door release buzzed. As I climbed the stairs I heard my mother call down, "Who is it?"

I answered, "It's me, Jack. I'm home, Mother."

Postscript

JOHN J. A. MICHEL, Lieutenant (jg) USN (First Lieutenant, USS *Pope*). After my three-month rehabilitation leave I began my refresher training course to learn about all the improved armaments and electronic systems (that would have been dandy to have had in early 1942). Upon completion of the course I received my orders to the U.S. Naval Academy for a two-year assignment as instructor (Navigation and Marine Engineering.) The detail officer at the bureau of personnel was a bit put out when I requested a delay in reporting so that I could marry Kathryn E. Schlesinger on June 1, 1946, and honeymoon in Bermuda for two weeks. Our daughter Marjorie was born in March 1947. In July 1948, I was ordered to the USS *Haynsworth* as Executive Officer, based near New Orleans. I resigned my regular commission in 1949, and accepted a commission in the Naval Reserve. Returning to New York, I joined National Broadcasting Company and settled in Manhasset, New York. By 1951, the Korean "Police Action" had escalated to a war and I was recalled to active duty as executive officer of a destroyer (plus ça change, plus c'est la même chose). By November 1952, I was released to inactive duty with a promotion to full commander, as well as the addition of a second daughter, Susan, to the family. At about this time I decided that my talents could be put to better use in the defense industry. I continued in the Naval Reserve where my assignments included command of the NR Surface Battalion at Ft. Schuyler, New York, and Director of NR Officers School, New York City. We moved to Washington, D.C., in 1965. I retired from the Naval Reserve in 1970, with the rank of captain. At about the same period I left the defense industry to begin a third career in residential real estate in which at this writing I am still actively engaged.

WELFORD CHARLES BLINN, Lieutenant Commander, USN (Commanding Officer, USS *Pope*). I do not remember seeing much of our captain after the war. I may have seen him briefly at the survivors section or during the refresher training course. He retired as a rear admiral June 30, 1948. He died February 10, 1990. He was awarded three Navy Crosses, a Bronze Star Medal, and a Purple Heart for his service during the war. The *Pope* received the Presidential Unit Citation. I recall him as a thoughtful, considerate person. He was an excellent ship handler and steady in difficult circumstances. I believe the loss of the *Pope* touched him deeply. His last action aboard ship was to urge the crew to get clear of the sinking ship before the Japanese cruisers came within range again.

RICHARD NOTT ANTRIM, Lieutenant, USN (Executive Officer, USS *Pope*). I met up again with Dick Antrim after the war in the survivors section and during our refresher training course. He had stayed in Makassar until almost the end of the war when he was transferred to a camp in Java.

Antrim was awarded the Medal of Honor for his intervention in Jack Fisher's beating by Yoshida. Presentation was made by President Truman on January 30, 1947.

Antrim retired as a rear admiral in April 1954. He died in March 1969, and was buried with full military honors at Arlington Cemetery.

DAVID A. HURT Lieutenant Commander, USN (Commanding Officer, USS *Perch*) Makassar Camp, Celebes. Transferred in April 1942 to Japanese interrogation camp at Ofuna. Returned to home in Annapolis after the war and was promoted to rank of captain. Died November 11, 1942 from wounds received in a hunting accident. I did not meet up with Captain Hurt again after his departure from Makassar. I did however meet his son who was a midshipman when I was an instructor at the U.S. Naval Academy.

GERRY JENKINS went on to complete his education at Cambridge University, earning a "blue" in rugby along the way. In 1948, he and Marian (whose brother he met aboard the *Queen Mary*) were married, and Gerry started a successful career with a subsidiary of ICI (Imperial Chemical Industries). His frequent travels brought him to New York and Washington fairly regularly. My wife and I in turn were able to visit with Gerry and Marian in England on several occasions. When I decided to acquire the Montague Dawson painting of HMS *Exeter*, Gerry kindly undertook the negotiations for its purchase. After retiring from ICI, Gerry settled permanently in Cornwall.

HOOT HORRIGAN continued his career in the air force until a physical disability disqualified him as a pilot and forced him into early retirement in 1959. He had a successful second career in the defense industry in California. I visited Hoot and his wife Elinor in Panama City, Florida, in 1949 when I was still on active duty, but our paths did not cross much after that. Hoot retired as a full colonel. He died in 1996.

GEOFFREY BLAIN realizing that the post-war royal navy would be facing drastic retrenchments, decided to put his engineering education and experience to practical use in the international oil industry. We did not see much of Geoffrey for quite a while, but we did receive letters and snapshots from a number of exotic-sounding places. It wasn't until he became affiliated with Mobil that we saw him again in person. When he retired from Mobil in 1982, he settled in Stamford, Connecticut, which made it easy for us to keep in touch.

MAURICE BENNETT went on to a rewarding career in the paper industry. In 1950 he married Esther Pirie. I had the honor of becoming godfather to Sally, the second of their three daughters. Maurice's work at Wiggins Teape brought him to America frequently and we saw him often. In 1959 we visited the Bennetts in Surrey with our two daughters and had a reunion with some of our *Exeter* friends. In 1973 we went to London for Sally's wedding and finished our trip with a visit to the Jenkinses and the Bennetts in Cornwall. Maurice retired to Cornwall about 1983 to spend more time traveling and yachting.